THE LIFE AND WORK OF JOHN EDGAR WIDEMAN

THE LIFE AND WORK OF JOHN EDGAR WIDEMAN

KEITH E. BYERMAN

 PRAEGER

AN IMPRINT OF ABC-CLIO, LLC
Santa Barbara, California • Denver, Colorado • Oxford, England

Library of Congress Cataloging-in-Publication Data

Byerman, Keith Eldon, 1948–
    The life and work of John Edgar Wideman / Keith E. Byerman.
        pages cm
    Includes index.
    ISBN 978-0-313-36633-8 (hardback) — ISBN 978-0-313-36634-5 (ebook)
1. Wideman, John Edgar.   2. Wideman, John Edgar—Criticism and interpretation.   3. African Americans in literature.   4. Authors, American—20th century—Biography.   5. African American authors—Biography.   I. Title.
    PS3573.I26Z584   2013
    813'.54—dc23
    [B]   2013018989

ISBN: 978-0-313-36633-8
EISBN: 978-0-313-36634-5

17 16 15 14 13   1 2 3 4 5

This book is also available on the World Wide Web as an eBook.
Visit www.abc-clio.com for details.

Praeger
An Imprint of ABC-CLIO, LLC

ABC-CLIO, LLC
130 Cremona Drive, P.O. Box 1911
Santa Barbara, California 93116-1911

This book is printed on acid-free paper ∞

Manufactured in the United States of America

Contents

Introduction: Telling the Story of John Edgar Wideman   vii

1   Gathering the Family   1

2   "The Astonishing John Wideman": The Years of Education   5

3   Establishing a Career   9

4   Family Tragedies   17

5   Success as a Storyteller   25

6   Philadelphia Stories   59

7   The Writer as Social Critic   93

8   Wideman's Mash-Ups   129

Conclusion: The Achievement of John Edgar Wideman   173

Notes   175

Selected Bibliography   187

Index   191

INTRODUCTION

Telling the Story of John Edgar Wideman

John Edgar Wideman is a very successful contemporary American writer. He is the author of 10 novels, five collections of short stories, and four works of nonfiction. He was valedictorian of his high school class, an All-Star basketball player at the University of Pennsylvania, and only the second African American to become a Rhodes Scholar. He is the only author to receive two PEN/Faulkner awards for his fiction, and, among his other honors, he was given a MacArthur "genius" grant in 1993. He has taught literature and creative writing at several major public and Ivy League universities. His daughter, Jamila, has been a star basketball player at Stanford and in the WNBA. His son Daniel and his cousin Albert French are both successful writers. From this quick portrait, he could be said to have achieved the literary version of the American Dream.

But cutting across this Horatio Alger story is tragedy. His parents lived largely separate lives during his late childhood, which meant that John had little emotional connection with his father. Later, his younger brother Robert got involved in drugs and petty crime. When a man died during one of these crimes, Robby was sentenced to life in prison without parole. Ten years later, in 1986, Wideman's youngest son, Jake, apparently suffered a psychotic break and stabbed to death a fellow camper. He too is in prison for life; in 2011, his first appeal for parole was denied. In 2000, Wideman's 35-year marriage to Judy Goldman ended in divorce.

These personal experiences are key to John Wideman's career as a writer. He constantly uses members of his family as characters and places associated with his life as settings for his stories. It is often difficult to distinguish between autobiography and fiction in his work. He has talked repeatedly about how he includes ancestors as well as more recent relatives in his novels and short fiction. Sometimes, he seems to be revealing secrets, "airing dirty laundry in public." However, he claims that he has never deliberately embarrassed any member of the family; he will combine traits from different people or he will tell about an incident that actually occurred to someone else.

A key question for this book is why he takes such risks, even if he believes he has control of the situation. One answer I will be exploring is the importance of storytelling in his family. The neighborhood in which he grew up included a large number of relatives from both sides of his family; many of them were excellent storytellers. The neighborhood, Homewood, a black community in Pittsburgh, was said to have been started by some of his ancestors. His aunt May and his mother were among those who kept that history alive by talking about it in their kitchens, in beauty shops, and in barbershops. From the beginning, for him, stories as ways to entertain and instruct people were closely associated with family. They also taught him how to keep secrets while talking. If for example there were things the children should not hear, the women had codes they could use to conceal awkward information. Wideman has often discussed the ways he appears to be revealing a great deal when, in fact, he is carefully controlling the information.

A second answer to the question of connecting life and fiction has to do with his belief that the most important truths about human experience are to be found by delving into the experiences of individuals and small communities, such as extended families. A phrase that he uses over and over is the African saying that "All stories are true." In his view, we need to value the life of every individual and take seriously his or her understanding of the world. For Wideman, such social realities as race, gender, and social class can only be fully grasped if we see how each person lives them. By themselves, such categories tell us nothing about people; it is the personal experience of them that reveals what kind of impact they have. John Wideman can use his long and complicated family history to tell us a great deal about human life.

A third answer is that Wideman as a writer is concerned with many of the big questions about America. He thinks about history, about morality, about race and racism, about sports in American culture, and about the place of art in society. One reason that he writes both fiction and nonfiction is that they are different ways of tackling these issues. He has, for example, written essays, stories, and an autobiography (*Brothers and Keepers*) about the prison system. He is interested not only in the social problem of incarceration and race, but also in the impact of imprisonment on individuals and their families. Having two close relatives in that system enables him to explore it from many angles. History becomes personal when both the yellow fever epidemic of 1792 and the MOVE bombing of 1985 took place in the city, Philadelphia, where he went to college and taught for several years.

Finally, it is important to understand that his life is a writer's life. He has taken virtually every aspect of his experience and made it material for his art. What makes his story worth telling is that he has found the dramatic and storytelling possibilities in the things that most of us either merely accept, or dismiss, or try to conceal. He extends the conventional idea that artists should write what they know by insisting that he will write and rewrite what he and those around him have lived. He finds moral, political, and social significance in what others would pass over or find only interesting or perhaps too disturbing to record. For an intellectual, he has led an intense and intriguing life; what makes him important is his ability to turn that experience into great literature.

This book undertakes to narrate his experience and the ways he has turned that experience into writing. It begins with the several generations who lived in the South and eventually moved to the Pittsburgh community of Homewood. It then takes up his early life and the process by which he became something of a celebrity by the time he finished college, despite being from a working-class black family. Attention is then turned to how he built his reputation as a writer and academic, with jobs at major universities and with novels that earned him respect as an author. His rising star is then crossed by deep family problems that ended with both his brother and son in prison. He undertakes to reconnect himself to the Homewood he had left behind in pursuit of a career. Out of that renewed relationship comes several of his major works of fiction and nonfiction.

Like the great Southern writer William Faulkner, Wideman has found his own special place. As Faulkner said, "I discovered that my own little postage stamp of native soil was worth writing about and that I would never live long enough to exhaust it, and by sublimating the actual into apocryphal I would have complete liberty to use whatever talent I might have to its absolute top. It opened up a gold mine of other peoples, so I created a cosmos of my own."[1] While Wideman has written about far more than Homewood, his work remains grounded in that place, in a spiritual if not physical sense. In talking about this writer and his life, we are going to be talking about that world, about the ways he has used his imagination to reveal and conceal it. We are also going to be sorting out, as much as possible, the fact from the fiction. This effort will help not only to get at the truth of his life, but also to show how he goes about creating his stories, how he takes family and history and turns it into fiction. He has made family the center of his work: "All my books are about family, family relationships, and reordering and transformation of family."[2] In addition, we will see what values and ideas are most important to him and how he has not only talked about them, but also lived them. This is the story of the life he created for himself.

CHAPTER 1

Gathering the Family

The story of John Wideman's family, which is key to understanding both the man and his art, begins during the period of slavery. He remembers his aunt May telling stories about Sybela (also spelled Sivela) Owens, his great-great-great grandmother. According to the family, Sybela, who was a slave in Maryland, was brought to the Pittsburgh area by her master's son, Charles, with whom she had had two children. They established a home on Bruston Hill, and that was the beginning of Homewood, the neighborhood where John grew up. Interestingly, the 1880 federal census lists Civilla and Charles Owens, both African American, both born in Maryland in the 1830s, and with children when they arrived in Pittsburgh during, or shortly after, the Civil War. In an interview, Wideman recalls a story told by his mother's aunt about the origins of Homewood:

> Aunt May claims that the first tree was chopped down by her great grandfather, Charlie Owens. When May was going to public school, there was a day set aside, a holiday, for celebrating the beginning of Homewood. May and her sisters would get mad because, in the story she was told in school, a man she'd never heard of was credited with the founding the community by chopping down a tree. May knew better. She knew that it was Charlie Owens who cut down the first tree.[1]

The 1900 census indicates that Civilla, now widowed, had had 13 children, seven of whom survived. Her daughter, Margaret (known as Maggie), born around 1860, married Frederick Hollinger. The youngest of her nine children was Freeda, born April 11, 1901. She married

John French, originally from Culpepper, Virginia, in 1918. He was about 15 years older than she was, and apparently her family did not approve of him: "As May talked about the old days I saw my grandmother as a little girl and courting and I saw John French coming to steal her away from Aunt and Aida (Addie) and Uncle Bill. And I saw Uncle Bill sitting there with a shotgun waiting for John French."[2]

French had a reputation for being easygoing. As one example, he liked Chinese food but was not allowed to eat inside the restaurant he preferred because of segregation. But he understood that this was not the decision of the owner, Mr. Wong, but of white citizens. So, he would eat out on the back steps with the owner.[3] This laissez-faire attitude did not extend to his daughters; the French girls were kept away from the neighborhood boys, went to the Homewood African Methodist Episcopal Zion Church regularly, and were chaperoned whenever they went out. Once, one of his neighbors had drunk too much while cleaning his shotgun in his backyard. The gun discharged, and a pellet grazed one of the French daughters who was out playing. The man became so frightened of what John would do that he left the state for a few months, until he got word that the girl's father was no longer mad at him. French was known for his wine drinking and gambling. Once, a man cheated him by using loaded dice. All French had to do was say the man's name in a certain tone of voice, and the man left Homewood permanently, despite the fact that John was never known for violence or angry threats.[4] Wideman at one point labels Freeda French as "color-struck," meaning that she believed lighter-skinned African Americans to be better than others.[5] This would help explain the intensity with which she and John protected their daughters.

John and Freeda's daughter, Bette, born May 14, 1921, eventually married Edgar Wideman. This might well have caused some tension in the French family, since Edgar was dark-skinned and only one generation removed from the Deep South. John Wideman notes in *Brothers and Keepers* that his white wife, tanned in the summer, was actually darker than his mother.[6] Their oldest child, John Edgar, was born on June 14, 1941. They had four other children—Letitia, David, Otis Eugene, and Robert.

The Wideman side of the family can be traced back to South Carolina, to the area around Greenwood, in the largely rural western part of the state, near the Georgia border. There were both African American and white Widemans living in Greenwood County for several generations. For example, Sarah Wideman is listed in the 1850 census as having around 20 slaves. In *Fatheralong*, which recounts a trip in 1992 with his father, John tells us that they were able to push back the family line one more generation when they learned of Jordan Wideman, John's great-great grandfather. Records from 1880 reveal three Jordan Widemans living in Cedar Springs, an antebellum community not far from Promised Land, the black village outside Greenwood. The oldest of these men, and the one most likely to be the ancestor, was born in 1812 in Virginia.

The next generation included Tatum Wideman, born in 1841—a farmer who also served as a minister in Promised Land. His wife, Mary, born in May 1867, was probably a second wife, since he was 25 years older and had children before they were married in 1886. James Harris, also known as Littleman (a nickname John uses in his novel *The Lynchers*) and a cousin of John's father, told a story of the death of Reverend Tatum. According to Harris, this patriarch of the family died with his mouth wide open. Though he was only five or six at the time, Harris claims to have seen this for himself. At first, the family did not know what to do, but then someone came up with the idea of tying a string around the head so that the jaw would close, and this, according to the tale, is how the reverend was buried.[7]

One of Tatum's several sons was Hannibal, also known as Harry, who was born on September 10, 1888 in South Carolina. Harry was the first of the black Widemans to move to the North. Among other jobs after he arrived in Pittsburgh, he worked as a janitor for a real estate firm. He was reportedly one of the people who traveled up Bruston Hill and met Civilla Owens. He married Martha Wright, from Wrightsville, Pennsylvania, born in 1896. Their household in 1920 included her mother, stepfather, and sister, as well as his brother and sister-in-law. This would have been a typical arrangement for African Americans during the period of the Great Migration, when tens of thousands of people moved to the North to escape the racial oppression and economic exploitation of the South. Frequently, one member of a family would move, find employment in industry or business, and then bring family up to join them. Because of the large numbers and housing discrimination in cities such as Pittsburgh, it was not uncommon for different related families to live together for an extended period. The couple had three children, Edgar, Catherine, and Otis. Harry died on December 28, 1971, and Martha lived until March 1991.

Edgar, the first child of Harry and Martha, was born on September 2, 1918. He attended school in Pittsburgh and graduated from Westinghouse High School. He played basketball on the courts of Homewood with several men who later became professionals, including Maurice

Stokes and Ed Fleming, whose stories will be told in *Hoop Roots*. Edgar remembers being taken to South Carolina by his father when he was five or six and meeting a large number of Widemans in the Greenwood area. His next trip south occurred while he served in the military in World War II, primarily in South Carolina. He was a private in the army assigned to Charleston. He recalls in *Fatheralong* his work with African Americans from the area. Part of his job was working in a unit whose task was to move cargo. He was trained in the use of equipment to move large crates and other items but he had a difficult time getting his squad to use the labor-saving devices. They preferred to figure how to move the loads by physical effort because that was what they had always done. He even had to fight some of them to get them to change their ways. Eventually, they would do things his way in his presence, but revert to their own methods as soon as he was out of sight.[8] He also spent time guarding prisoners of war on Saipan.

Before his war experience, he and his new wife, Bette, had moved from Pittsburgh to Washington, D.C., where he had a job in the Government Printing Office. It was here that John Edgar was born in mid-1941. The family then moved back to Homewood. His army enlistment record indicates that he was classified as a skilled welder; despite this training, he had a difficult time finding such work after the war as a result of the discriminatory practices of labor unions and industry. Instead, he generally had to piece together several jobs in order to support his family—he worked as a waiter in Kaufmann's department store, as a garbage man, and as a paperhanger, possibly with John French, his father-in-law. He and Bette had five children—John, Gene, David, Letitia, and Robert. Under the circumstances, he had little connection with his family, especially his sons. Eventually, he moved out of the house entirely; much later, John learned that his father had several children out of wedlock, including a son about John's age. Before this happened, however, he and Bette managed to move the family to the Shadyside neighborhood near Homewood. It was a predominately white area, with much better schools. This happened in time for John to be able to attend Peabody High School. Eventually, the family was forced to move back to Homewood for financial reasons.

CHAPTER 2

"The Astonishing John Wideman": The Years of Education

The title of this chapter comes from a story about Wideman that was published in *Look* magazine in 1963 by Gene Shalit, who later became a film and book critic for the *Today Show*. By the time the story brought him national attention during his senior year at the University of Pennsylvania (commonly referred to as Penn or UPenn), Wideman had already established a reputation for himself in both Pittsburgh and Philadelphia. Even in elementary school, the teachers and principal could quiet the other students by having John tell stories. These were often based on comic books or boys' novels or popular movies such as *Tarzan*.[1] By the time he reached Peabody High School, a predominately white school in the largely white neighborhood of Shadyside, he was known as a serious student and good athlete. Though he was popular, he tended to avoid contact with white students either between classes or after school. He was especially careful not to be seen with white girls on the street.[2] Nonetheless, he was a star basketball player, class president, and valedictorian of the senior class.

These achievements earned him a Benjamin Franklin Scholarship to UPenn; in interviews, he very precisely explains that this was an academic grant, since Ivy League schools such as UPenn did not give athletic scholarships. He was one of only 10 African Americans in the 1959 freshman class of 1,700. He felt very isolated and briefly considered returning to Pittsburgh but was talked out of it by his freshman coach, Dick Harter, who encouraged him to stick around until basketball practice started. The strategy worked, since Wideman felt most at home on the court.[3]

One example of his experience at UPenn was a confrontation he had with a white student who wanted to know John's favorites among blues performers: "Who do you like? Got everybody, man. Leadbelly and Big Bill Broonzy. Lightning and Lemon and Sonny Boy."[4] Part of the problem was that John had virtually no knowledge of this musical tradition, having grown up in the urban North in a family that had left the South generations earlier. His musical connections were to rhythm and blues and early rock and roll—genres that the white student labels "junk" and "crap." A second part of the problem was that John's sense of social rules was being violated:

> He stared at me, waiting for an answer. At home we didn't get in other people's faces like that. You talked toward a space and the other person had a choice of entering or not entering, but this guy's blue eyes bored directly into mine. Waiting, challenging, prepared to send a message to that sneering mouth. I wanted no part of him, his records, or his questions.[5]

A third part of the problem was the presence of another black student in the room. Since the space was that student's room, John expected some assistance in this confrontation, but he did not get it: "Darryl had his own ghosts to battle." One reason had to do with social class—Darryl had gone to Putney Prep School and "spoke with an accent I considered phony." Like Wideman, he had been popular in school, but he longed for "his blonde, blue-eyed Putney girlfriend whose parents had rushed her off to Europe when they learned of her romance with the colored boy who was Putney class president." Thus, Darryl had his own reasons to want to fit in and not risk isolation based on race.[6] Without allies and with a sense of his own ignorance, John felt he could do nothing, though he would have liked nothing better than to punch the smug white face in front of him. But the frustration and anger remained: "I can feel it now as I write."[7]

Despite such experiences (and perhaps, as a result of them) Wideman made his peace with the world of the university and became very successful there. He began as a psychology major but changed when he realized that the field had much more to do with conducting experiments than with exploring human nature. Instead, he became an English major. He was also a star basketball player; at six feet, two inches, he played small forward. He began playing varsity in his sophomore year and was made co-captain in his junior year, and captain in his senior year. That same year, he received first-team All-Ivy League and All Big-Five honors. His success on the court led to him eventually being named to the Big Five Hall of Fame. But that achievement also had cultural implications since he had learned his basketball skills on playgrounds, where the game is much more improvisational and individualistic. At Peabody and even more at UPenn, he had to become much more disciplined and team-oriented. This difference in the game and its cultural implications has been a subject of his writing throughout his career.

He took a number of creative writing classes; one of the advantages of being at such a prestigious school was that a number of well-known writers, such as the poets Archibald MacLeish and Richard Eberhart, visited classes and commented on his work. What he gained from this was not only specific comment and encouragement about his work, but also a sense of what it meant to be a professional writer. This became crucial when he realized that he would never be successful as a professional athlete, and so turned to literature as an alternative career. He graduated Phi Beta Kappa in 1963.

Wideman's social life was somewhat limited despite his popularity on the UPenn campus. He and Darryl Dawson managed to find some black social life in areas of Philadelphia not far from the campus. For the *Look* magazine article, he is pictured with a black woman, with the implication that she was his girlfriend. In fact, he was then dating the white and Jewish Judith Goldman who, two years later, became his wife.

In 1963, he was named a Rhodes Scholar, the first African American so recognized since Alain Locke in 1907. The scholarship was named for Cecil Rhodes, a British imperialist who made his fortune in the diamond mines of South Africa. Having attended the University of Oxford, Rhodes left an endowment to enable young men with high achievements in academics and athletics to pursue advanced work at the university. The awards have been offered since 1902 to students from the United States and British Commonwealth nations. Wideman used his opportunity to pursue a BPhil (a graduate research degree) in English literature.

Luckily for him, he did not have the same difficulties as Locke a half-century earlier. Because of his race, Locke was rejected by several of the Oxford colleges before he was finally accepted at Hertford College. One of the benefits Wideman had was that another African American—Stan Sanders from the University of Southern California—received the award the same year. Wideman took a very focused course of study in 18th-century British fiction, with emphasis on Daniel Defoe, Samuel Richardson, Henry Fielding, and Lawrence Sterne. The archives of his materials at Harvard University include a large number of notebooks from his classes and tutorials and detailed correspondence with his thesis committee about his research project.[8]

But life was not limited to academics. The archive also contains numerous stories about travel with friends around England and over to the continent. They are usually about smoking and drinking and finding dates. Perhaps more important to him was participation on a basketball team that included fellow Rhodes Scholar and future NBA star and United States senator, Bill Bradley. Bradley had attended Princeton and so had competed against Wideman in the Ivy League. Their team won the British league championship.

On March 16, 1965, Wideman married Judith Ann Goldman in Oxford, and they took their honeymoon in Greece. They had dated while students at UPenn, and they continued to live in Oxford while Wideman completed his thesis. Judith grew up in a Jewish family in Great Neck, New York, on Long Island near New York City. Her father, Morton Goldman, owned a camp for boys on Long Lake, near Naples, Maine. This camp will later be part of one of the tragedies of the Wideman family.

Upon completion of his BPhil in 1966, Wideman and his new wife moved to Iowa City, Iowa, where he attended the Iowa Writers Workshop, one of the most distinguished writing programs in the country. He was able to work with writers such as Kurt Vonnegut and the Chilean novelist Jose Donoso, and some of the classes were useful in showing him how to teach creative writing. It was here that he completed his first novel, *A Glance Away* (1967). However, he found that the school itself was largely a distraction. It was often much more about conflicting egos, sexual gamesmanship, drinking, and partying than about the serious work of writing.[9] But even this aspect had its uses; it taught him the risks of buying into the myths of being a writer:

> I guess the main myth is that there is such a thing as "a writer," and that that activity can basically change who you are and what you are . . . Being a writer does not solve the problem of living. I think that's an important thing to learn, and you only learn it by actually experiencing it . . . Some other myths are fame, fortune. You don't automatically get rich and you don't automatically get famous if you write books.[10]

At the moment he finished with this part of his schooling, Wideman was on his way, if not to fame and fortune, certainly to a long and distinguished career as a writer.

CHAPTER 3

Establishing a Career

In the fall of 1967, Wideman accepted a position as assistant professor of English at his alma mater, UPenn. He was responsible for courses in creative writing and literature. He also worked with UPenn assistant basketball coach Digger Phelps, who later went on to great success as the head coach at the University of Notre Dame. In 1968, Wideman was asked by African American students to offer courses in black literature and culture. He initially declined, since his training had not at all been in that field and he had actually done very little reading in it. He changed his mind as the demand, like that at campuses around the country, became more vehement. He spent an intense period of reading and research and began offering classes in black literature. He also was instrumental in setting up the program in Afro-American Studies and served as its first director during 1971–1973. In 1974, he attained the rank of professor of English.

The next year, John, Judy, and their two sons, Daniel Jerome, born on November 26, 1968, and Jacob Edgar, born on February 13, 1970, moved to Laramie, where John became professor of English at the University of Wyoming. The decision to move was a desire to escape the pressures of the Ivy League world, which involved many distractions from his writing, "so much busyness, and so much pressure—somebody always wanting something, wanting you to do something, and something always needing to be done." It appeared to be a place where he would be left alone to do his writing. He had given a talk at the university earlier and liked the environment. It also seemed a good place to raise a family.[1] They remained in Laramie until 1986.

It was during his time at UPenn that Wideman published his first three novels—*A Glance Away* (1967), *Hurry Home* (1970), and *The Lynchers*

(1973). These works generally received very positive reviews, though some critics complained that they were too influenced by Western values and too little concerned with African American experience.[2] The process by which he got published did not follow the usual pattern of sending material to a number of editors before one finally accepts it. As Wideman tells the story in *Paris Review*, Hiram Haydn, an editor with Knopf at the time, saw a version of the story that had appeared in *Look*; he was persuaded by his son to contact Wideman. They met before the move to Oxford, and Haydn asked him to send him any fiction that he produced. Sometime later, when Wideman was about halfway through *A Glance Away*, he submitted the manuscript. Haydn, who was then at Harcourt, Brace, accepted it, and eventually published the first three novels.[3]

In these books, the author takes a despairing view of the world, consistent with the modernist perspective of some of his influences at the time, such as T. S. Eliot and Ezra Pound. Those writers held the view that civilization had lost its way and that there were few institutions or belief systems that could be relied upon. The emphasis was on the emptiness and frustration of modern life. Wideman applies this way of thinking to the world of African Americans. In *A Glance Away*, he tells the story of Eddie Lawson, a resident of Homewood who returns from drug rehabilitation. He finds his mother, Martha, who is embittered by the conditions of her life and by what she considers the ingratitude of her children. She never recovered from the death of her son Eugene, who was killed in World War II. She is constantly attacking her daughter and accusing her of immoral behavior, especially with Eddie's friend, Brother, who is an albino. Bette, the daughter, is forced to suffer her mother's insults even though she has devoted her life to the older woman's care. The story is set at Easter, but it is much more about death-in-life than resurrection. Its tone is akin to T. S. Eliot's comment that "April is the cruelest month."[4]

Eddie's return triggers a series of hostile encounters, with his mother, with Brother's sister Alice, who was Eddie's girlfriend until he had an affair with one of her white college girlfriends, and with his old friends in the neighborhood. The latter occurs because his efforts to get clean cause resentment among those who are still addicted. They feel that his efforts to change are an attack on their inability to do so; they prefer to believe that addiction is a permanent condition that they can take a perverse pride in.

Failed relationships also haunt Robert Thurley, a white intellectual, apparently bisexual, who has established a connection with Brother, though it is considered to be exploitative by people in the African American community. Thurley's life has failed because he took as a wife a woman who is much more sexually driven than he is. On their wedding night, he stays down with guests while she falls asleep in the bedroom. Later, they form a threesome with their friend Al, and Thurley always seems to be the observer. The marriage comes to nothing because Eleanor can never be satisfied by him.

It is unclear why he seeks out Brother, though it seems to be related to his desire for someone who is neither threatening nor demanding. Eddie initially tries to steer clear of him, though his friendship with Brother seems to regularly involve Thurley. When Martha, after overhearing Eddie comment about her treatment of his sister, falls down the stairs and dies, he seeks out his friend and his companion. It is not clear in the story whether Martha's fall is suicide or accident, but her son feels responsible for it. His only comfort lies in his connection with other men. Thus, the novel describes the failure of all relationships between men and women, whether familial or intimate. Moreover, nothing within the community—whether church, family, or values—can save anyone.

At the end of the novel, Wideman constructs a remarkable telepathic connection among Eddie, Brother, and Thurley as they sit around a fire in the Bum's Forest. Each seems to be engaged in a stream of consciousness that involves both the present moment and their personal obsessions. For example, Eddie begins by thinking that he and Brother can rob Thurley so that they can buy more drugs—drugs that will allow him to desensitize himself to his mother's death. He then switches to concern about his sister having to deal with the body of their mother. Thurley focuses on keeping the two of them with him at the fire, fearing that he will be abandoned once again. Brother, whose character appears influenced by such figures as Benjy in William Faulkner's *The Sound and the Fury,* lives in the present moment, thinking about the fire and their closeness to it, and what would happen if they got too close. But even in these closing pages, when so much is being thought about by the characters, there is silence; they are not communicating with each other.

This novel reveals some of the ways in which Wideman uses family and stories in his writing. Virtually all the characters, by either name or personality, are connected to family or community. "Eddie" is one version of Edgar, Wideman's father, while the sister Bette is his mother's name, even with the unusual spelling. Martha is the name of his paternal grandmother. DaddyGene, the grandfather in the novel, is clearly based on John French, including the fact of his wife being named Freeda.

Even the family name, Lawson, was the real Martha's name before her mother remarried; she also had a son named Eugene who was killed in World War II. There was a Brother Hall in Homewood when Wideman was growing up, so he changed the last name when he decided to use the character. What he has done, as he will do in all the books based in Homewood and some of the others as well, is to mix up generations and revise names and some personality traits in order to obscure the autobiographical elements. Thus, his grandmother becomes the mother in the story, while his parents become the children. At the same time, the drug problems of Eddie and his friends suggest those of John's younger brother Robby. Martha's husband Clarence, who comes and goes in her life, behaves the way Edgar did when John and his siblings were growing up. These various shifts allow Wideman to tell a very harsh tale of suffering, anger, and frustration without insulting members of the family. By mixing up names and relationships, he can present an embittered Martha because everyone who matters to him would know that she was not actually Bette's mother. He can create a promiscuous Clarence because there was no Clarence in the family and thus he is not revealing dirty secrets about his father. The narrative can be very grounded, since it is based on his life experiences, but he has carefully blurred the lines between fiction and reality. This pattern holds true through most of his writing, even when the stories are not set in Homewood.

Wideman's second novel, *Hurry Home* (1970), differs from the first in that the characters cannot be directly connected to family members. Instead, the protagonist is an intellectual alienated from his community by his advanced education, much like Wideman himself. Cecil Braithwaite is based on someone the author knew when he was growing up, a man who graduated from law school but never, in fact, practiced law.[5] Cecil returns to the old community, but takes care of an apartment building in exchange for living space in the basement for himself and his wife. In this sense, he is similar to the characters in *A Glance Away* in that he does not know what to do with his life. When their newborn baby dies, he abandons his wife, eventually ending up in Europe. Here, he finds himself in the company of a white man who is estranged from his mixed-race son and who takes Cecil on as a kind of surrogate. They visit various museums. In an episode that may be actual or may be a dream, the protagonist travels to Africa to try to get a sense of his own identity. In the end, he returns home to his wife, though it is not clear why.

While Cecil may be seen as an anti-hero in that he lacks strong character and seems to wander through the story, it is also true that the community has little use for him. He is regularly ridiculed when he walks the streets, and he has no friends in the neighborhood. His manner of speaking and walking make him suspect in his own world. In this sense, the character may be thought of as Wideman's effort to work through some of his own issues as a young black intellectual. He went off to the "white" high school and succeeded, then to the Ivy League university, and then to Europe, where he did additional study and learned the language of academics and of upper-class speakers of English. The white man Charles Webb can then be interpreted as a white American culture that, for its own reasons, wants to patronize those young blacks that fit a certain model of what blacks should be—well-spoken, admiring of Western culture, and not concerned with questioning too closely ideas about race. Webb symbolizes those who give Wideman a scholarship, an Ivy League education, and an opportunity to study 18th-century literature in England. He becomes the proof that racism is not a real problem. When he comes to visit Homewood, he is obviously someone different from the boy who grew up there and the relatives and neighbors who stayed behind. He can no longer identify with the issues and concerns of the community because he is on his way out. Like Cecil, he tries to leave it behind, but his first two books suggest that he really cannot. It is this place and these people that he needs to give his writing substance.

In both of these books, Wideman shows how the community can be a trap, how it can limit the potential of Eddie and Cecil, how it can use their weaknesses to tie them down. The third novel, *The Lynchers* (1973), tells of characters trying to break out of this prison through an act of violence. Frustrated by the racism, humiliation, and exploitation they face every day, they decide to take matters into their own hands by staging a lynching, the ritual of torture and death most often associated with the racial violence of the South. After the Civil War, Southern whites worked to keep blacks from gaining political or economic power, even though the Thirteenth, Fourteenth, and Fifteenth amendments to the U.S. Constitution gave them full rights as American citizens. Whether led by terrorist groups such as the Ku Klux Klan or the Order of White Magnolias or by groups of local residents, white citizens saw violence and intimidation as the best means to restore something close to the society that had existed before the war. Black men (and sometimes women) could be accused of almost any crime, but the real charge was that they had in some way "bothered" white women. In most cases, there was no evidence of any such offense, but it was that kind of allegation that would arouse white anger and that was rarely challenged. What then happened was that the target person was taken by a mob, often but not always at night. The violence typically involved hanging, shooting, burning at the stake, or any combination of these. It often included castration or dismemberment, sometimes for the purpose of taking souvenirs. Conservative estimates put the number of African Americans killed in this way as around 3,500 between the 1880s and the 1950s, though small numbers occurred before and after these decades. These crimes were seldom prosecuted (often because law enforcement officials participated) and virtually no one was ever convicted. To make this point, Wideman begins his book with "Matter Prefatory"—20 pages of incidents and facts related to slavery and lynching that are taken from history. Instead of general statements about racial violence, such as those at the beginning of this paragraph, he provides concrete information, including names, dates, and descriptions of actual experiences.

The point of this detail is to suggest how powerful the idea of lynching would be in black communities and among black men. The main characters can assume the shock value of committing such an act in their neighborhood. Their idea is to reverse the process. They plan to capture a white police officer while he is with a black prostitute; they decide to kill the woman, accuse the man of the murder, and then hang him in the street. They hope that such a radical action will inspire the community to rise up against racial oppression.

The scheme is clearly morally irresponsible, since it requires them to imitate the violent behavior that helped to create racial oppression in the first place. And regardless of what one thinks should happen to a racist policeman, the black woman they would kill has done nothing to deserve such a fate. The moral questions, as well as the personalities of the plotters become the central concerns of the story. Are these men morally and emotionally prepared to take such an action? In other words, the novel is much more about psychology than about action; the drama is internal rather than external.

The four men involved come from different backgrounds and have different personalities, though all have been negatively affected by what has happened to their community. Willie Hall (Littleman) is a failed poet who believes he has a sense of racial history. Because he is also handicapped, he feels that he is not a true man; he conceives the lynching in part as a way to demonstrate his masculinity. Thomas Wilkerson is a middle-school history teacher who does, in fact, have a sense of the past and a desire to make a difference in his community. It is his sense of frustration with both society in general and the black community specifically that leads him to initially go along with Littleman's scheme. Leonard Saunders is a man of the streets, who came from a broken home. He is cold and mean as a result. He is willing to sacrifice his own sister-in-law for the lynching. He is the one member of the group most capable of carrying out the violence. Graham Rice is essentially a thug, not as cold as Saunders, but capable of action; he kills Wilkerson out of hostility and jealousy of the other man's abilities.

One point of this novel is to raise questions about the nature of black activism around the time of the publication of the book. By the early 1970s, the civil rights movement had run out of steam. African American frustration with continued racism expressed itself in widespread urban violence (sometimes called "riots") in the late 1960s, especially after the assassination of Martin Luther King, Jr. in 1968. What replaced non-violent resistance was a much more militant perspective, represented by the Black Panthers and the slogan "Black Power." Other groups, such as Darryl Dawson's Army of Liberation, proposed even more radical action, including in some cases, acts of violence. In literature, Amiri Baraka (LeRoi Jones) led what came to be called the Black Arts Movement, which insisted that writing by African Americans should focus on immediate black issues, be aimed at black audiences, and be judged by black people. It argued that artists who tried to examine larger human concerns, speak to a variety of audiences, or create work that had permanent literary value were not really a part of African American society. A significant group of authors, mainly novelists, challenged this view. Wideman, along with Toni Morrison, Alice Walker, Ernest Gaines, Charles Johnson, and Clarence Major, not only felt that the Black Arts Movement restricted their artistic freedom, but that the Black Power philosophy behind it was socially dangerous. Some of them did what Wideman does in *The Lynchers*—offered a critique of the violence and futility of black nationalist ideology. It is worth noting that this group of writers, whose careers began around 1970, have won many of the prizes for literary achievement, including a Nobel Prize, Pulitzer Prizes, National Book Awards, Pushcart Prizes, and PEN awards; they are also the ones who continue to be taught in schools and universities and written about by journalists and scholars.

This initial set of books tended to reflect Wideman's training in the great tradition of Western literature, with its emphasis on sophisticated techniques in writing and a pessimistic view of life. They located that negativity in the African American community and can therefore indicate why he spent the early part of his career away from places such as Homewood. While he was using the community as the source material for his writing, he saw very little that was positive in it. It was, as much as possible, a place to be *from,* not *in.* In a sense, he had to work through the troubling aspects before he could begin to see the positive ones.

CHAPTER 4

Family Tragedies

As indicated in Chapter 1, Wideman managed to escape the world of Homewood, especially during its period of significant decline in the 1960s and early 1970s. His youngest sibling Robby, however, did not. The family was forced to move back from Shadyside, which meant that Robby attended Westinghouse High School, which was not nearly as good as Peabody, where all his older brothers and sisters went. Moreover, he had to deal with the pressures of having a brother 10 years older, who had already received national and even international attention both for his athletic and academic skills. In the Wideman household, where there was high expectation of achievement, it was difficult to be the youngest child. However, matters are not so clear-cut. John hints at various times of his own problems with the law, and his brother David was also incarcerated at Western Penitentiary, apparently for drug use.[1] Nonetheless, the older children, especially John, were always presented as role models.

Robby's response was to become, as much as possible, a part of the young black culture of Homewood. He formed a singing group that performed rhythm and blues standards, and he began smoking marijuana. He adopted the views of the Black Power Movement and led a protest in his high school demanding more African American faculty, more courses on black history and culture, and more opportunities for black students to congregate away from white students and faculty. While these issues were not resolved to the students' satisfaction, the pursuit of them gave Robby prominence in the school and the community. However, they did little to improve his relationship with his parents and siblings, who were much more concerned with his education than his politics. In his memoir *Brothers and Keepers* (1984), John recalls visits home, where Robby and his friends were hanging out in the living room, playing music very loudly and bothering his mother. By this point, John himself was married, had a professional job, and was beginning to publish. He had very little influence on Robby because he was seldom around and lived in a very different world.

The decision to stay in Homewood with his friends, given the small opportunities for meaningful employment, meant that it was easy for Robby to become involved in heavy drug use and petty crime. His heroin addiction required more money than he could get from occasionally stealing from his mother's purse. Eventually, he and two friends got involved in a scheme involving stolen property. They arranged with a local fence to provide him with stolen televisions. But it was a scam; there were no televisions, only an empty truck. The idea was to rob the fence when he showed up, knowing that he could not go to the police, given the circumstances. When the fence, Nicola Morena, decided to take off, Michael Dukes, one of Robby's friends, pulled a gun and shot him in the shoulder. Morena later died in the hospital.

Robby, Dukes, and Cecil Rice decided to run. They headed west, occasionally stealing cars along the way. Meanwhile, John, who was living in Laramie, Wyoming, with Judy and their children, Daniel, Jake, and the infant Jamila, was professor of English at the University of Wyoming. He had found out about the incident and decided to write a letter to his brother, with whom he had not had contact for a long time. He did so, even though he had no idea where to send it. The next day, Robby called him from a pay phone in Laramie. John invited his brother to come to their nice house in the suburbs. By this time, Cecil Rice had returned east to turn himself in. Robby and Dukes visited for a short time and then went to Fort Collins, Colorado, where they were arrested. For a short time, John was investigated for aiding and abetting fugitives, but he was not arrested. The two men were extradited to Pennsylvania, where they were indicted for felony murder. The indictment against Robby was the same as that against Dukes even though he did not even have a gun; anyone involved in the commission of a felony in which a killing takes place is considered as responsible as the actual killer. Moreover, that death becomes first-degree murder, even if there was no intent to kill.

The end result was that Robby went to prison for life without parole and continues to be incarcerated in Western Penitentiary, near Pittsburgh. Initially, he was a problem prisoner, but eventually chose to take advantage of the education program available at the prison. He studied mathematics and became a teacher's assistant in classes such as algebra.

The family made repeated efforts to get new trials and to challenge the sentencing, all without success. One outcome was Wideman's involvement with prison reform and, as letters in the Wideman archive indicate, he gained a reputation as an activist, based on the writing of *Brothers and Keepers*.

Almost exactly 10 years after Robby's incarceration, John's younger son, Jake, apparently experienced a psychotic break and murdered his roommate Eric Kane. The two were visiting Arizona on a trip to the Grand Canyon arranged by Camp Takajo, the summer camp in Maine owned and operated by Jake's maternal grandfather, Morton Goldman. The boys had known each other for seven years and had been bunkmates at the camp. They had arrived in Flagstaff to stay at a local motel before going on to the Canyon. Sometime during the night of August 13, 1986, for reasons that have never been made clear, Jake used a hunting knife he had purchased the day before to stab Eric twice. He then took the group car and traveler's checks and fled. His journey by car, bus, and plane took him to Phoenix, Los Angeles, Las Vegas, New York, Minneapolis, Duluth, and back to Minneapolis, where he contacted his family. A few days later, he surrendered to local police in Flagstaff. He was accompanied by his parents and a lawyer. He was charged with first-degree murder and released into the custody of his parents, who took him back to Amherst, Massachusetts, where John had taken a position at the University of Massachusetts. They placed Jake in a mental health facility. From there, he called an Arizona detective and confessed to the killing, though not offering any motive. He did express remorse.

At this point, he was returned to Flagstaff, where he attempted suicide while in the Coconino County Jail. He also confessed to the killing of Shelli Wiley, a student at the University of Wyoming. He later recanted this confession and charges were dropped. On September 9, 1988, more than two years after the Kane killing, he entered a plea of guilty to first-degree murder as part of a plea bargain that he not be given the death penalty. He was sentenced to 25 years to life, with no opportunity for parole until the 25 years had passed. On May 16, 2011, he had his first parole hearing, which included statements from his parents, those of Eric Kane, and those of Shelli Wiley, whose mother remains convinced that he is responsible for the death of her daughter. His application was denied, but he is permitted new requests every year.

The Wideman family has been very reluctant to comment on Jake's case, in part because they feel the press both sensationalized and distorted the situation. Three pieces of writing stand out as indicative of what they consider to be the problem. The first, by Sally Kalson, appeared in the Pittsburgh *Post-Gazette* about a year after the killing. The author presents elements of the psychological profiles that suggest problems within the family, especially with Jake's feelings of inadequacy in a high-achieving family; he was, according to the reports and friends, always in the shadow of his older brother and often compared to his uncle Robby.[2] Kalson also talks about problems with shoplifting and with encompresis, the involuntary soiling of the pants. While the article seems carefully researched, it is easy to see how a family that was generally considered very private would take offense about so much of their lives being revealed. An unsigned handwritten evaluation in the Wideman Papers tends to confirm her comments.[3]

The second piece appeared in *Vanity Fair* in March 1989, shortly after Jake had been sentenced. Wideman has special dislike for this one, since the author, Leslie Bennetts, had been a student of his at UPenn and he had written for the magazine on various topics. The author works from the perspective of Laramie, by interviewing several people who knew the Widemans when they lived there, and specifically about what they knew and thought about Jake. She talks to neighbors, school officials and students, and the local police.

She is especially interested in the unsolved 1985 murder of Shelli Wiley, a part-time student at the University of Wyoming, who worked in a truck stop and lived in an apartment nearby, in what was considered one of the worst parts of town. After her death, the building was set on fire in an apparent attempt to destroy evidence. The crime is relevant to Jake's case because he later confessed to it, though there is not strong evidence to link him to it. Bennetts sees his confession as part of his troubled history, including minor theft and running away, which suggests a pattern of psychological difficulties. He once saw a school counselor and a psychiatrist for a few sessions, but in both cases, there was little follow-up.

She rather clearly assigns that trouble to the parents, whom she sees as neglectful of their middle child. One of Jake's best friends reports that he was seldom invited to the Widemans' home; he felt the reason was that Jake did not want him to visit:

I never really knew them, because Jake didn't want me to go over to his house and see how his parents treated him. He was really uptight around them. I saw him as a parent-destructed person. His parents put all this pressure on him, and they caused most of his problems. Everything he did was wrong. They told him that if he didn't try harder he wasn't going to amount to anything and he was going to be a nobody.[4]

In an incident that reinforces her claim, she reports on a conflict between John, Judy, and the high school basketball coach, Dale Parker. During the year when Danny was a senior and Jake a sophomore, they both made the varsity squad. During a period when the older brother was not playing well, the coach benched him in favor of Jake. John complained to the coach about his decision and, when it was not reversed, John and Judy tried to organize a parents' group to get the coach fired. While this effort failed, Parker remembers getting calls about Danny (but never Jake) from their parents and also hearing them shout instructions from the stands that were contrary to his game plan. In contrast, Jake would always do exactly what the coach asked of him. He was expected to be a star player the following year. The final blow to him was the decision of the family to move back east when Danny was accepted at Brown University. John took a position at the University of Massachusetts at Amherst. Jake asked to remain in Laramie, and the coach tried to make arrangements for him to stay, but the parents were insistent. Bennetts also reports that, ironically, Jake did not want to take the Camp Takajo trip that summer, but was told that he had to.[5]

Bennetts's charges against the Widemans include their defensiveness and insensitivity. She notes that Rogene Peak, the family's neighbor, commented to Sally Kalson that Judy always seemed unfriendly. After the quote appeared, Bennetts reports that Peak received a four-page letter from Judy, attacking her. More significantly, the $50 million lawsuit filed by the parents of Eric Kane against the Widemans and Camp Takajo seems motivated in part by their sense of the Widemans' callousness. Sander Kane tells her that Jake's parents did not contact them at the time of Eric's death or for many months afterward. They did not attend Eric's funeral, though Judy's father did. A year after the death, Kane says he received a letter from John, criticizing him and his wife for expressing their view that Jake should receive the death penalty. He notes that John ends the letter by saying that he forgives the Kanes for their attitude. He does not express remorse or sorrow for their loss.[6] Bennetts then goes on to describe the devastation to the Kane family caused by Eric's death. She concludes by pointing out that Jake should have received treatment in a mental health care facility and that the legal system, the media, the Kanes, and the community of Flagstaff have treated them and their son unfairly.

The third article was written by Chip Brown and appeared in *Esquire,* another outlet for Wideman's nonfiction. Brown contacted a number of the family's friends and colleagues, both to get information from them and to encourage the family to cooperate. He largely failed in both these efforts, though, according to letters in the Wideman archives at Harvard, some did make an attempt to try to get him to see the Widemans' point of view. He emphasizes the theme of the "bad seed," not because he believes that Jake was born bad, but because as a child he came to believe it about himself. He was sometimes compared to Robby when he got into trouble. He also had developmental problems, such as thumb sucking into his later childhood and the encompresis mentioned by Bennetts. He also claims that Jake was verbally abused by other campers at Camp Takajo. He talks to the same friends in Laramie that Bennetts had interviewed, and they blame John and Judy for Jake's troubles. Brown asserts that the psychological reports after the killing reinforce this view.[7] He also talks about the "Kane Game," the harassment of Eric by boys at the camp, including—sometimes—Jake, who would other times defend his bunkmate. He then presents the details of the investigation, the confession, and the court proceedings. He concludes by describing this as a tragedy for two families, both of whom need answers, but are unlikely to get them.

These two incidents have had a role in several of Wideman's writings. Two stories in *Damballah,* "Tommy" and "Solitary," involve a young man in trouble. The first of these has him wandering through the streets of Homewood and noting how the neighborhood has deteriorated over the years. In effect, it suggests how it is that someone who stayed there would end up in a world of drugs and crime. The second tells of an older woman returning from a visit to her incarcerated son. It describes the humiliations she goes through at the prison and also her sense of feeling lost and embittered in the community she has lived in all her life. Wideman has commented that it was intended to be a study of lost faith, but that somehow the resilience of the character overcame her doubts. He uses it as an example of how a character can take a story in directions the author did not originally intend.[8] A more lengthy story about "Tommy" comes in *Hiding Place* (1981), a novel that is part of what is often referred to as the Homewood Trilogy and includes *Damballah* and *Sent for You Yesterday* (1983). Tommy, like Robby, has become involved in petty crime and has to hide out when a man is killed during a robbery. He goes to Bruston Hill, where Mother Bess, a relative, lives in isolation while she waits to die. This encounter transforms both of them in ways they did not expect.

Out of Robby's experience came one of John Wideman's best-known books, *Brothers and Keepers* (1984). He undertakes to explain not only how it is that two brothers from the same family could end up in such different situations, but also the nature of his relationship with Robby. Part of the work, as is often the case with his writing, concerns the larger social issues of race, poverty, and imprisonment in American society. The book emerges out of conversations between the brothers, with John trying to capture Robby's perspective rather than assume that he can speak for him. We are told in great detail about family dynamics, about the differences between living in white and black neighborhoods in Pittsburgh, about generational differences even with siblings. In the process, we get a sense of John's sense of guilt that his commitment to his own escape from the restrictions of that world meant that he ignored what it was doing to his younger brother. At the same time, he suggests that Robby was the one who was truer to the community and to his racial identity.

Each brother is depicted as a man on the run, Robby from the consequences of the life he has entered until he is caught and can no longer run anywhere, and John from the kind of world that eventually trapped his brother. John uses college, writing, and a professional life to put as much distance as he can between himself and Homewood. He goes as far as Laramie, Wyoming, to stay out of that life. But he cannot escape; connection in the form of Robby, the fugitive, brings him back to his roots. Having been drawn back in, he must now figure out what it means. He has to come to terms with both his choices and with the world as it is seen through his brother's eyes.

To do this, he writes in alternating passages, with Robby's language of the streets alternating with his own more educated style. In fact, one of Robby's teachers from the prison sends Wideman a letter complaining that *Brothers and Keepers* presents Robby's speech as much more "ghetto" than it really was; in this sense, the younger brother is more like the rest of his family than the book indicates.[9] The method of alternating voices does not give special privilege to either brother. The result can sometimes be uncomfortable, as when Robby comments that he has little respect for the lives chosen by his older brothers and sisters, who worked hard at their educations and made themselves respectable members of the community. John, with his white wife, high-achieving children, and Volvo station wagon, are implicit, if not explicit, targets of such statements. By including this material, Wideman is, in effect,

doing penance for his feelings of guilt that he had done so little to prevent what happened to Robby. Interestingly and perhaps significantly,
material about Jake tends to be much more scattered, in *Fatheralong,
Hoop Roots, Briefs,* and magazine pieces. This would suggest that,
even after 25 years, Wideman cannot quite absorb the meaning of that
tragedy.

CHAPTER 5

Success as a Storyteller

From 1973, when *The Lynchers* appeared, until 1981, Wideman published no long fiction. Nonetheless, this was a period of great activity for both him and the family. He was promoted to professor at UPenn, the family moved to Wyoming, Jamila was born, Wideman received a National Endowment for the Humanities Fellowship; also, of course, it is the period of Robby's troubles.

The birth of Jamila was especially difficult. It came shortly after the family had moved from Philadelphia to Laramie and she was nine weeks early. Judy had to be taken from Laramie to Denver by ambulance, and both mother and daughter nearly died. The newborn weighed two pounds, 14 ounces and had a malfunctioning heart valve and necrotizing enterocolitis (death of intestinal tissue that occurs in premature infants). She soon also developed salmonella poisoning. She was so tiny that her father's finger was larger than her arm. The hospital gave her little chance of survival, but she somehow managed to thrive.[1]

Part of her growing up involved annual trips back east so that the family could stay at Camp Takajo and visit Robby in prison. Even though she was young and small, she was a success in both environments. Playing basketball at home with her talented father and brothers, both of whom played high school varsity ball, she was able to challenge the boys at the camp, despite the fact that many of them were athletes. At the prison, she was the one who would talk to Robby about his life in jail without feeling awkward.

A significant event in the development of Wideman's career was the funeral of his grandmother, Freeda, in 1973. It is worth noting that his editor, Hiram Collins Haydn, died around the same time. According to the story Wideman has told many times, after Freeda's funeral, the family gathered at the house for food and drinks. His aunt May, while sipping bourbon, began telling stories about the history of Homewood and the variety of characters who lived there. While these were tales that Wideman had grown up with, he claims that this was the first time he thought about their potential for his own work. His first three books had made use of local material, but he had always felt the need to overlay that with elements associated with the literary masters of the 19th and 20th centuries. Now, he had a glimmer of how these stories might work on their own terms.

What came of this experience is what he has called years of "wood shedding,"[2] trying out new ways of storytelling that combined the voices and realities of the world of Homewood with his own situation as both an insider and an outsider to that world. He studied African American history, literature, and even speech practices. He had, of course, already been doing this as part of his work with Afro-American Studies at UPenn, but now it became more directly relevant to his own writing. Some observers have suggested that he was doing little else during this period, but the fact is that he was publishing essays on the black experience, including literary criticism and commentaries on jazz. More important, he was producing fiction that was not accepted by publishers. Partly, this failure came from the change in style he was working through. Publishers had created a niche for him as an African American writer who produced pessimistic, even naturalistic novels, but he was not staying in that box. He was a respected writer, but not a popular one; his name was not so prominent that the public would accept anything that he did. Part of what he sought was a way to speak more directly to an African American audience, such as his family in Homewood, without compromising his own sense of what modern literature should be.

The end result was that he decided to release his new books through Avon, a paperback publisher. *Damballah* (1981), *Hiding Place* (1981), and *Sent for You Yesterday* (1983) form what is often called the Homewood Trilogy, though Wideman does not care for the term. A fourth book, *Reuben* (1987), is also set in Homewood, but was published in hardcover by Henry Holt. It is these books that established Wideman's mid-career reputation as one of a group of writers—including Toni Morrison, Ernest Gaines, and Charles Johnson—who immersed their readers in black history and culture without being committed to a particular political or social agenda. They moved away from the Black Arts ideology that emphasized the empowerment of black people in the late 1960s and early 1970s toward works that told complex, sophisticated stories of the black past and the present. The authors made use of folklore, of historical figures and events, and of very modern techniques of narration to connect the African American experience to the larger human experience.

We can see all of these elements being played out in *Damballah,* a collection of related short stories. Wideman opens the book with a dedication to Robby, in which he says that "stories are letters. Letters sent to anybody or everybody. But the best kind are meant to be read by a specific somebody."[3] That somebody, in this case, is Robby. Thus, we can see that Wideman has moved from a broad audience for his earlier works to a personal one for this book and the ones that follow. They should be read in conjunction with *Brothers and Keepers,* which moves from the monologue of the trilogy (John speaking to Robby) to a dialogue between the brothers in the 1984 nonfiction book. In *Damballah,* Wideman also creates a "Begats" page and a family tree, both of which mix actual family names with fictional ones.

While most of the pieces involve characters that are connected to family members already mentioned, the opening story, "Damballah," is a version of a roots story not directly linked to Homewood. In it, a character named Orion, though enslaved, refuses to accept the ways of slavery. He will not learn English, or eat the food supplied by the master, or adopt the Christian faith accepted by most of the slaves. The story is told through the eyes of a young boy who is caught between those, like his relatives, who consider Old Ryan to be crazy and heathen, and his admiration for the African, who has magical powers, such as his ability to catch fish with his bare hands. The boy is threatened with a beating by his aunt for using one of Orion's words, "Damballah," even though he has no idea what the word means. When Ryan strikes the overseer and then sits naked on the porch where the mistress of the plantation sees him, the master has had enough and orders the old man killed. Though he appears not to resist, it takes several men to carry him into the barn. There, terrible things seem to happen, though the boy does not witness them. The next morning, he finds Orion's head and carries it to the river where, in a ritual he invents that mixes African and Western traditions, he starts the dead man on his journey back to Africa:

> Damballah said it be a long way a ghost be going and Jordan chilly and wide and a new ghost take his time getting his wings together. Long way to go so you can sit and listen till the ghost ready to go on home. The boy wiped his wet hands on his knees and drew the cross and said the word and settled down and listened to Orion tell the stories again.[4]

The references connect the religious expression of the spirituals and black preaching to West African perspectives. The cross the boy makes is not only Christian but also the sign of the crossroads made by Orion, and the word he speaks is "Damballah," which an introductory note describes as the name of the African-based father spirit. The crossroads is sacred space in most African cultures, as well as those of the Caribbean, where Damballah originated. It is sacred because it connects the past, present, and future (where you have been, where you are, and where you are going). It is also the space where experiences with God or the gods can occur. It has special significance in blues tradition, as the place where musicians sell their souls to the devil to enhance their talent. In Christian terms, the cross is a vertical crossroad, connecting the two aspects of Jesus as divine and human. In drawing his image of the cross in the dirt, the boy is bringing together these different worlds, with himself at the center. Having done this, the boy throws the old man's head into the river, where it can begin its journey back to Africa.

At the end of the introductory note, Wideman indicates that part of the tradition is that Damballah "gathers up the family." The tale could be said to "claim kin" with all those who were enslaved, regardless of their origins or beliefs. In this sense, the author is creating a mythology for African Americans. Placing it at the beginning of his collection of family stories allows Wideman to claim for himself the role of Damballah, as his stories bring together the threads of the experiences of Widemans and Frenches through history.

The story also suggests Wideman's response to those writers and public figures of the 1970s who believed that it was possible for African Americans to recover their African identity. The most famous work of this period was Alex Haley's *Roots* (1976), which was made into a very popular television miniseries the next year. In Haley's version, it was possible to locate the specific community from which his ancestors came and to return to that place. That reality was questioned when it was learned that Haley had borrowed much of the material from other sources and that the Africans may have merely told him what he wanted to hear. For Wideman, it is not possible to fully regain ties to the long-ago past. In the story, Orion himself is said to have lost the ability to talk to fish. In addition, his name is a reference to the Greek mythological figure who became one of the constellations, and thus is not African. The classical Orion was a great hunter who could walk on water because his father was Poseidon.[5] This name probably was given to the character by the slave owner, following the Southern practice of naming slaves after classical figures or prominent historical people; this was done to make the enslaved appear ridiculous.[6] Rather than being a pure African, Orion attempts to maintain as much as he can of his original culture. The boy cannot understand the man's speech or his rituals; instead, he respects his integrity and courage. Rather than trying to be African, the child ties together the old and new worlds in creating a new being, the African American. If he cannot be African, he also refuses to simply accept the conditions imposed by slavery. This identity is the one that Wideman is claiming for himself in joining the traditions of his family with the literary values of Western civilization.

With this ground established, he then goes on to tell stories of the family and the community that show how people have adapted over the centuries to this new identity. In several instances, he uses individuals or experiences of the family, with some name changes. Thus, "Lizabeth: The Caterpillar Story" recalls the childhood of a character modeled on his mother. In this tale, John French is a boisterous figure whose self-assertion sometimes gets him into trouble, or at least, causes deep worry for his wife. The title refers to an incident in which Lizabeth bites the end off a caterpillar. Her mother Freeda panics, but the father John picks up the rest of the bug and swallows it, claiming that if the big part does not kill him, the little part will not hurt their daughter. Freeda is not calmed by his action, since the end result could be losing both her child and her husband.

This is a story mother and daughter share over the years, as they seek to understand the most important man in both their lives. He always seems to live on the edge and refuses to resign himself to the harsh conditions of black life in early 20th-century Pittsburgh. He gambles, drinks heavily, and will not allow others to take advantage of him. These things put him at risk in his community. Another memory they share is the time Freeda was holding Lizabeth in her lap at the window, waiting for him to return. She sees him coming, but sees behind him, a man with a gun. She jams her fist through the glass to warn him. The point is clear: "Then I hear you talking and think about John French and know there ain't no way he could have lived long as he did unless a whole lotta people working real hard at saving that crazy man. He needed at least as many trying to save him as were trying to kill him."[7]

Even Lizabeth has a story about protecting her father. He once threatened to shoot the person who was dumping ashes in the lot next door, a place where he one day planned to create a garden. Even as a child, she knew that such an incident would lead to her father disappearing, because the police would come after him, meaning that he must disappear or end up in prison. So, she swore a vow that she would not sleep until either John French got drunk and went to bed or the trespasser came so that she could warn him of the danger, not because she cared about the trespasser, but because she did not want to lose her father. Her concern carries weight because she was present when her mother found a gun hidden under the icebox that belonged to John's friend Albert Wilkes, who had killed a policeman with it and had to leave Homewood because law officers intended to execute rather than capture him. This, in fact, happens in *Sent for You Yesterday,* the third book in the trilogy. In "Lizabeth," the very presence of the gun puts the French family in peril, and Freeda forces John to get rid of it.

While the story makes women the tellers of the tales, its theme is the dangerous lives led by black men. Their circumstances of underemployment, racism, and limited opportunities encourage them to create a code of masculinity that values loyalty, risk, and self-assertion above respectability, lawfulness, and passivity. One must live on the edge of the law because those in power assume that blackness is equal to guilt. Personal integrity and self-esteem have to be demonstrated within the community because they are not granted by society at large. John French's risk-taking with the caterpillar, the ashes, and Wilkes's gun are not bravado or irresponsibility—at least, in his eyes. Rather, they are examples of his belief in family, the future, and friendship. That his wife and daughter are more concerned with his survival than he appears to be only suggests Wideman's belief in fundamental gender differences within the family and the community.

As mentioned briefly in the previous chapter, the stories "Tommy" and "Solitary" grow out of Robby's problems with the law. In the first of these, Tommy wanders the streets of Homewood and thinks about how the community has deteriorated. He notes the empty storefronts, the graffiti, and the presence of unemployed and drug-addicted men. He looks for his uncle Carl, but realizes that he is at the clinic, receiving his methadone treatment. In other words, the neighborhood has become a wasteland, with no possibility of recovery. He imagines the only improvement to be an end-of-the-world scenario:

> Somebody should make a deep ditch out of Homewood Avenue and just go on and push the row houses and boarded storefronts into the hole. Bury it all, like in a movie he had seen a dam burst and the flood waters ripping through the dry bed of a river till the roaring water overflowed the banks and swept away trees and houses, uprooting everything in its path like a cleansing wind.[8]

The story then goes on to describe what this environment has led Tommy into. Wideman retells the events of Robby's crime, with different names and changes in the details. For example, in the story, the person killed is not the white man that they are trying to scam, but his black assistant. In addition, Tommy is not at the scene of the shooting, but is waiting inside to get the money from the white man. He fails to get the money, and they manage to escape. The last scene takes place at the home of Tommy's brother John, who lives out west with his wife Judy and their children. He explains to John that he and his partner have to keep moving because they have already been labeled murderers and that he cannot stand the idea of going back to prison.

The story may be considered a first attempt to tell Robby's story from his point of view. By making him aware of how bad life is in Homewood and suggesting that he wants the money in part to escape that life, Wideman is making Robby more sympathetic by suggesting that he is trying to get out of a certain kind of life. By ending the story in John's home, we are invited to see Tommy (and, thus, Robby) as part of a caring family.

In "Solitary," the point of view shifts to the mother, who goes to visit her son in prison. Wideman has said in interviews that his original intention had been to make the story about her crisis of faith, with the possibility that she would lose her religious belief in the face of what she has to go through. In fact, it turns out to be something different after he puts her through a series of difficult and humiliating experiences.

She calls the prison "the Other World," and shows this through the journey she has to make to get there. She has to take a series of buses that do not always follow a strict schedule. This means that the trip takes almost two hours each way on a good day, and all day if the connections are not good. Once she gets there, she has another mile to walk to get to the gate. Then, she must go through a series of corridors and checkpoints, with "buzzing machines that peek under your clothes."[9] The narrator points out that this is part of a design:

One Sunday, walking the mile from the prison gate to the unsheltered concrete island that served as a bus stop and shivering there for over an hour in freezing November rain she had realized the hardships connected with the visits to her son were not accidental. The trips were supposed to speak to her plainly. Somebody had arranged it that way. An evil somebody who didn't miss a trick. They said to reach him you must suffer, you must fight the heat and cold, you must sit alone and be beaten by your thoughts, you must forget who you are and be prepared to surrender your dignity just as you surrender your purse to the guard caged outside the waiting room entrance. In the prison world, the world you must die a little to enter, the man you've come to see is not your son but a number . . . To enter you must be prepared to leave everything behind and be prepared when you begin the journey home to lose everything again.[10]

But the situation is even worse than this because once she has gone through this dehumanizing process, the son she has come to see spends the time verbally attacking her. He blames her for all his troubles. It was her choices as a parent that failed to protect him. It was his needs that she failed to meet. His accusations are contradictory— she paid both too much and too little attention to him; she disciplined him too much and too little. "Her love, her fears are to blame."[11] She understands that he attacks her because, as his mother, she will sit and take his hard words— words that he cannot use against those in the prison and that he is not yet ready to turn toward himself. Despite her knowledge, she is always hurt by the attacks; she has traveled physically and emotionally all this way out of love; yet, the one she came to see feels it necessary to assault her, to make his pain her fault.

The story spends relatively little time on his experience or their meeting. We know that he is kept in the Behavioral Modification Unit, referred to in the prison as the Hole, where he is locked in his cell 23 hours a day and only gets out for exercise if there is a guard available to take him. We know that he receives only two meals a day, at 11:00 A.M. and 2:00 P.M. We know that he has taken a Muslim name, Salim. We know so little because the focus is on her experience, her version of solitary confinement, on the buses, on the empty streets, in her empty house. When she returns to Homewood, she decides she cannot face the house, so she walks up Homewood Avenue; what she sees is what her son saw in "Tommy"—empty lots, burned-out buildings, general decay. But unlike him in that story, she calls on memory to help her get through. She imagines being on the street with her father John French, with her husband window-shopping, with her children. But they are all ghosts to her on this day.

The missing figure for her on this journey is God. Throughout the day, she wonders what has become of Him during her suffering. She arrives at the AME Zion Church, her church for all of her life, but she feels that she cannot go in, that it will be just another empty space. Instead, she walks to Westinghouse Park, where she went on Sundays with her mother and siblings. She gets halfway across the pedestrian bridge to the park, when she suddenly stops. She recalls those Sundays and the odd fact that her mother would always dress them in white and not allow them to play with other children. She also recalls the bitter woman her mother became after John French died and she suffered a stroke. From that point on, Freeda never tolerated talk about God or the church. Lizabeth turns around and goes to find her brother Carl in the Brass Rail Tavern. They walk for a while as she tells him about the visit to the prison and about her inability to go into the park. She believes she has lost her faith, which, as mentioned at the beginning of this discussion, was where Wideman thought the story was headed.

But this time, she stops again in the middle of the bridge and realizes that a train is coming on the track beneath them. She has always feared the trains when she was on the bridge. Carl keeps trying to reassure her, but she tells him that the real issue is that she fears she is becoming like their mother. She then imagines God as a train, coming in "thunder and lightning." But instead of cowering or cursing the divine, she turns to face the train that will pass beneath her: "She'd wait this time, hold her ground this time. She'd watch it grow larger and larger and not look away, not shut her ears or stop her heart. She'd wait there on the shuddering bridge and see."[12] Her decision to stand and wait suggests John Milton's comment on the ways to serve God: "They also serve who only stand and wait."[13] The story ends with the passage about her facing the train, so we do not know how well she has gotten through this crisis of faith or how much strength she will have for the next journey. But we are led to hope that she can now endure.

The last story of the collection is entitled "The Beginning of Homewood." In it, the author circles back to the notion of origins by telling the story of Sybela Owens and Charlie Bell. In constructing his tale, he largely follows the legend as reported by his aunt May, who retold it after Freeda's funeral. In his version, Sybela was a slave and Charlie was her lover and the son of her owner. He runs away with her to Pittsburgh, where, after being rejected by local whites, they establish a home on Bruston Hill, and thus found Homewood.

But the story begins, not with the tale of Sybela, but with a return to the letter to Robby that begins the book. The speaker says that it is a letter that never was sent and that failure has interfered with completing the story. What he really wants to do is connect the story of Sybela with that of Robby, as parables of the quest for freedom. He points out that she was often simply called Belle, both because it was easier to pronounce and because she reminded the old people of an enslaved African woman who, as punishment, had to wear a cage over her head that had a small bell on top. Other slaves started calling her Bell at first to make fun of her, but then continued with the name Belle because she endured her punishment with such dignity.

The name also serves as a pun, since the man who takes Sybela to freedom is the master's son and the father of her two children, Charlie Bell. The narrator reports that Charlie has learned that his father plans to sell her and the children as part of a gang of slaves. In anger, he runs away with them from Cumberland, Maryland, to Pittsburgh; they hide by day and travel by night. If they had been captured, the mother and children would have been returned to the master in chains. It is this image that Wideman uses to connect her story to Robby's. He was, in fact, captured and put on display for the media in "old-time leg irons and wrist shackles and twenty pounds of iron dragged through the marbled corridors of the county courthouse in Fort Collins, the Colorado town where they'd finally caught up with you and your cut buddy Ruchell."[14] Thus, Robby/Tommy becomes a modern-day slave, bringing the family story full circle.

Having made this connection between generations, Wideman turns the story over to his great-aunt May, who actually saw Sybela up on Bruston Hill. In effect, he shares the role of Damballah with her; she tells the stories, and he records them. In this way, he can present them with the qualities of oral history, and yet, retain his own very modern concerns as a family member and a fiction writer. In her telling, the story takes on magical qualities. The fugitives are said to "run a hundred miles a day with little children on her back, her and that white man Charlie Bell and them babies run by night and sleep by day, crisscrossing rivers and forests full of alligators and wolves."[15] She is also said to have "a freeing kind of power," which May herself experienced as a child.[16] Finally, she had the power of the curse. When they first arrived in Pittsburgh, Charlie Bell purchased land on Hamilton Street, but the local white men informed him that they would not tolerate his relationship with a black woman. He took his family up on Bruston Hill, where he and Sybela had 18 additional children. But the racial insult was not forgotten—she put a curse on the Hamilton Street property, and he warned the white men never to set foot on that land. According to May, the curse still holds:

That spiteful piece of property been the downfall of so many I done forgot half the troubles come to people try to live there. You all remember where that crazy woman lived what strangled her babies

and slit her own throat and where they built that fancy Jehovah
Witness church over on Hamilton that burnt to the ground. That's
the land. Lot's still empty cept for ashes and black stones and that's
where Grandmother Owens first lived. What goes round comes
round, yes it does, now.[17]

But such power does not prevent the harsh reality of life in Homewood. May also remembers the younger generations who have produced
children out of wedlock, committed crimes, or gotten involved with
drugs. There is also love and families and success, but there is little evidence that struggles and sacrifice guarantee anything. The story seems to
offer evidence that freedom is a constant effort and that there are many
ways to be enslaved. The story and the book end with a hint of hope in
a world of trouble. The narrator tells his brother that the Supreme Court
has agreed to hear the case of a group of prisoners who claim the right
to try to escape because the conditions of their incarceration amounted
to cruel and unusual punishment. "The court has a chance to say, yes,
a chance to author its version of the Emancipation Proclamation."[18]
Through "Solitary" and "The Beginning of Homewood," Wideman
makes clear his view that the modern prison system is a version of slavery in that it dehumanizes people and treats them like objects that can
be used and abused in any way it wants. The irony here is that his hope
is in the very legal institution that repeatedly justified slavery before the
war and permitted segregation after it.

"The Beginning of Homewood" raises at least two questions when
it is compared to the actual family history. The first is why the founding father has both his name and his race changed. Why does Charlie
Owens, a black man, become Charlie Bell, a white man and the son of
a slave owner? The name change works to reinforce the idea of Bell/
Belle mentioned earlier; it is a sound cue to remind us of the suffering
of black women. It also gives some history in slavery to Sybela; Owens
in this version must come from an earlier master, since slaves would
be given or take the last name of an owner. Changing the man's race
certainly makes the story more dramatic, especially since it is set several
years earlier than the actual migration, which occurred during or right
after the Civil War. A white man stealing his lover and children from his
own father suggests a radical challenge to the social order of the time.
By running away, he is rebelling not only against his father, but also
against his whole society. In this way, Wideman creates an interracial
relationship that is a quest for freedom, not only for Sybela, but also for
Charlie, who wants the right to love whomever he chooses, regardless

of society's rules. The quest theme is reinforced by the exaggeration of the escape. The "five hundred miles" they travel is in fact 113 miles from Cumberland to Pittsburgh, and the border of Pennsylvania is only about 10 miles from the Maryland town. Thus, free territory would only be a night's walk from the plantation. But it is important to keep in mind that the story is, in part, for Robby. Making the journey relatively easy would make it harder to connect his experience to Sybela's. It must be made almost impossible, just as Robby's quest for freedom is full of difficulties.

The second question about Charlie is why his character is a minor one in the story. If we accept the version told by May, he and his wife are the founders of Homewood. Yet, in the fictional version, after the journey and after the move to Bruston Hill, he disappears. It would seem that after having made him a white man to add drama, Wideman no longer wants him to be associated with the family. He needs this to be an African American legend, with the focus on Sybela and her descendents. They become the ones who must survive the racial attitudes of a society that, in Wideman's view, is similar to those Pittsburgh men who did not want an interracial couple in their community. These African Americans have to make it on their own.

An additional reason for making Sybela the center of the story is that Wideman is publishing this work at the time of the increasing popularity of black women writers. Toni Morrison, by this point, had published four novels, and Alice Walker had published two novels, three books of poetry, and a collection of short stories. *The Color Purple* would appear a year after *Damballah*. Many male writers and commentators were showing a strong resistance to this development, especially since they felt that such books were attacks on black men. The alternative, to quote one of the spirituals, was to "git on board." By putting May and Sybela at the center of his story, Wideman could demonstrate his appreciation for the experiences of African American women. In fact, six of the 12 stories in the collection are primarily about women. Thus, a writer who is often viewed as focused on issues of black masculinity could gain credibility with a female reading audience.

The novel *Hiding Place*, published the same year as *Damballah*, returns us to the hill where Charlie and Sybela lived years earlier—only now it is a place of despair rather than hope. Bess, one of the Hollinger sisters and a granddaughter of Sybela, has moved up there to hide away from the loss of her son and husband, and she is joined there by her great-grandnephew, Tommy, who is trying to escape the police after his involvement in the crime depicted in the *Damballah* story

"Tommy" and repeated here. Each is, in a sense, a fugitive from the world of Homewood, which no longer has the vitality represented by John French. Thus, *Hiding Place* can be said to return to the depressing tone of the first novels.

The story is told from the perspective of three characters—Bess, Tommy, and Clement, a mentally-challenged young man who does odd jobs for people in Homewood and who lives in the back of the barbershop. Clement is used to provide the viewpoint of an outsider, one who struggles to understand what is happening with the other main characters. In this way, he serves as the reader's eyes and ears in the novel. He also has something like magical powers; he can hear Bess calling to him, even though he is down in the town. Bess's first chapter tells us about her character and her relationship to the extended family. She remembers playing up on the hill when Sybela would sit in her rocker on the porch of the family house and seem to watch her, even though the old woman was blind. She recalls her courtship and the early days of her marriage. And she reflects on her arguments with the family about her decision to move back to the Hill and into the run-down shack that remains of the house. By returning there, she appears to be rejecting what Homewood has become. We also learn that, unlike the woman in "Solitary," she has lost her religious faith, though she can remember the songs. She is really getting ready to die.

What changes the situation is the appearance of Tommy, her great-grandnephew. When she first finds him hiding on the property, she has trouble figuring out who he is, though she knows immediately that he is family. What he seeks is refuge, a hiding place. The title of the novel comes from a spiritual verse that is the epigraph:

> Went to the Rock to hide my face
> Rock cried out, No hiding place.[19]

She continues to assert that he cannot stay, though he does sleep in the lean-to outside the house, and she eventually gives him drink and food. Once she learns the reason for his appearance, she is especially concerned that he go back down the Hill to Homewood.

In his chapters, we get yet another version of Robby's story. The second Tommy chapter almost exactly duplicates the version in the *Damballah* short story. The difference, of course, is that the earlier version takes the fugitives out west. In this telling, written at nearly the same time, Wideman tries an alternative approach that keeps Tommy within the community and the family. By doing so, he can explore the nature of family and not just brotherly love. In an earlier scene, when the family is debating whether to allow Bess to live up on the Hill, we have this exchange:

> I just don't want this to turn into one of those fussing and crying and somebody stomping around and slamming doors things.
>   That's the way this family does business.
>   And that's what's wrong. We don't take care of business. We fuss and argue and somebody wins out because they got more mouth or tears.[20]

What we see with Bess and Tommy is a variation of this behavior. They bad-mouth each other and make judgments based on their own needs and troubles. And yet, she does not make him leave, and he helps her to plant the seeds that Clement has brought for her.

At this point, each of them reflects on the losses they have suffered in their lives. Bess describes how she waited for years for a message that the telegram was wrong that told her that her only son had been killed by a sniper two days after World War II ended.[21] She later loses her husband, who had been both a father figure and lover. But she makes the decision never to leave the Hill when Shirley's baby Kaleesha dies. Shirley, Tommy's sister, had brought the sick baby up the Hill because she believed that Bess had some kind of special power; the doctors had already told her that there was nothing they could do. Bess desperately wants to help but cannot. This event leaves her in true despair:

> . . . there ain't nothing else to say when babies die and old dried-up just as soon dead as alive things like me left walking the earth. What kind of world is that? What kind of world give that baby beautiful eyes and then put a drop of poison so they roll around like crazy marbles and she can't see nothing and can't hear and can't swallow her food? What kind of world is that? I'ma tell you what kind. It's the very kind run me upon this hill. It's the kind grab you and chew you up and spit you out and grind you into the dirt. . . .[22]

Tommy's sense of loss is initially more personal. He thinks about his failed relationship with Sarah. She refuses to see him as a true father to their son because he prefers life on the streets to taking responsibility for his family. He recalls going with her to the funeral of his grandfather, Mr. Lawson, based on Harry Wideman. Lawson was constantly working at various jobs to support his family, and he felt uncomfortable when he was merely socializing, even if was with his children and grandchildren. Implied in this memory is the contrast with Tommy and his generation, who want to assume the position of the father without putting in the effort. The younger man sees himself as evil, as someone who has destroyed his wife's life because of his choices.

Out of their private sorrows, Tommy and Bess have one last conversation that in many ways is as sharp as any they have had. In it, he asserts that she stays there because she is afraid of the world, not because of her sense of independence. And Bess tells him that he has no true understanding of the blues. At that moment, he decides not to hide any longer; he wants to be the kind of man that his grandfather and Bess's husband were. So, he thanks her and then leaves. Bess, who has been drinking, falls asleep, but is awakened by the police cars climbing Bruston Hill. She hears sirens and gunshots. She goes out onto her porch, where she sees a spotlight focused on the water tower at the very peak of the Hill, a moment which echoes the scene in Richard Wright's *Native Son,* in which Bigger Thomas is captured on just such a tower. At that moment, she decides to leave. She sets her shack on fire and heads down the Hill. She leaves with a mission:

> Because somebody has to go down there and tell the truth. Lizbeth's boy didn't kill nobody. He wasn't scared. All he needed was another chance and somebody needs to go down there and tell them. And she was going to do just that. Burn down that last bit of shack on Bruston Hill and tell them what they needed to know. That he ain't killed nobody. That he needed one more chance. That he staked his life on one more chance. They should know all that down there. She'll tell them. She'll make sure they hear. Yes, indeed.[23]

She has, in effect, claimed him as the son she lost. She chooses to act for him, as so often in her life, she had not been able to act to save family. Though she could not do anything about the loss of Eugene or her husband or Kaleesha, she still believes she has a responsibility to do what she can for Tommy. While readers may doubt her ability to do anything, the important point is having the courage to try.

Wideman's own coming to terms with family can be seen in the way he puts himself into the novel. He is introduced sitting in the bar with Carl, his uncle. Carl introduces him to the bartender, Violet, by saying that he lives in Colorado. John corrects him, and they talk about

Tommy's problems. They fear that he will be killed by the police. They express concern about Lizabeth's health in this new crisis. John then states a view of his brother that he will spend most of *Brothers and Keepers* trying to repudiate:

> Sometimes I get close to hating him. Everything inside me gets cold and I don't care what happens to him. I think about all he's done, all the people he's hurt. The way Mama is now. And that man who got killed in the robbery. I know it's not all Tommy's fault. I know he's a victim in a way too. But on the other hand he's hurt people and done wrong and he can't expect to just walk away. But he does think he can walk away. Like he walked away from his wife and son. He's still like a child.[24]

Later, Bess says something similar directly to Tommy when he is complaining about his life, using John as an example: "Didn't have to be that way. Everybody down there ain't like that. You got a brother done alright for hisself. He's a snotty, dicty-talking nigger but he made something of hisself. Plenty people down there ain't got squat but they ain't stealing and robbing. They ain't outlaws."[25] Even as Wideman makes fun of himself in the comment, he also makes it clear that the family understands that Tommy's choices were not the only ones available.

If the first two books of the trilogy are almost exclusively about Wideman's family, he extends the third one, *Sent for You Yesterday* (1983), to include those who are outsiders, but whom the family takes in. Like the others, it takes on qualities of oral history, primarily about Albert Wilkes and Brother Tate. The novel covers three generations of the French family, from John and Freeda French to "John," who is clearly a version of the author. Each of the three sections, however, is named after one of the outside characters—Albert Wilkes, Lucy Tate, and Brother.

Wilkes is a legendary figure in Homewood and was mentioned in "The Caterpillar Story" as the man who left his gun with John French after killing a policeman. The fear that Freeda experienced in that story is repeated when Wilkes returns in 1934, after seven years away, and comes calling for her husband. An important theme in the novel is male friendship, as John French tries to explain to his wife that loyalty sometimes involves risks, that you cannot abandon a friend even if he is in trouble as a result of his own behavior. Wilkes seems compelled to return to Homewood, even though he knows that the police will kill him if they find him:

If someone had asked him *to* where, Wilkes would have gone blank inside, his eyes would have picked something, anything, and stared at that piece of Homewood, that crack in the pavement, that tree, that brick, that shadow moving across a windowpane, stare as if it was his job to keep it in place and if he faltered, if he lost concentration for one split second, the thing would disappear and all of Homewood with it.[26]

This is his home, and he must return, even if it means his death. He even renews his relationship with a white woman, though he understands the danger of his action. Moreover, he invites attention, returning in a long gray duster and a Stetson hat.

The other part of the Wilkes legend is his musical talent. He plays blues piano in a way that is immediately recognizable. He frequently visits the home of Mr. and Mrs. Tate, who live in the neighborhood and take in children who have no place else to go. In exchange for various jobs he does around the house, Wilkes has access to their piano, on which he practices when he is not performing at the bars in Homewood. It is in the Tates' home that the police find and kill him in cold blood. Lucy, one of the children in the house, witnesses the event and has to clean up afterwards. Out of it, she saves a piece of Wilkes's skull, which she finds near the piano. She notes that years later, the instrument still has bloodstains on the keys. One question that emerges as part of the Wilkes legend is who revealed his whereabouts to the police. Speculation includes the white woman, who might feel desperate and jealous because he may have to leave again, or perhaps a traitor in the neighborhood, who hoped to gain some benefit from whites through the betrayal, or perhaps a child who would not know any better than to say something in the wrong place or to the wrong person. The mystery only adds to the myth and encourages the retelling of the story. In choosing to tell the tale this way, Wideman reinforces the sense of a folk community that passes down its stories from generation to generation.

The next generation includes Lucy, Brother, and Carl, the son of John and Freeda French; all of them are born around 1920. Lucy and Brother are both orphans taken in by Mr. and Mrs. Tate. Brother was abandoned; no one even knows when he was born. Much of their story is told from Carl's point of view. Brother was his best friend as a child, though people in the neighborhood thought of him as strange because he was albino. Lucy saw him as her younger brother, even though he was apparently older; she even pushed him around in a baby carriage for years, until it finally broke down. Brother first made an appearance in *A Glance Away;* Carl is a version of Eddie Lawson from that same novel. Each of these "Three Musketeers," as they call themselves, was a young teenager at the time of the killing of Albert Wilkes in 1934. Their section of the novel, called "The Courtship of Lucy Tate," jumps back and forth in time from their childhood to Lucy's eyewitness account of the killing of Wilkes (1934) to Brother's music (1941) to World War II to the death of Brother's son (1946) to the death of Brother (1962) to the present time of the story (1970), when the narrator/author is talking to Carl and Lucy. It is a kind of saga of their generation, with both the joys and sorrows of long-lasting friendship.

The problem for young Carl was that his mother was very strict about his behavior, but Brother seemed to have no limits. Freeda raised her children to be obedient and tidy, but Carl wanted to run the streets and be messy, like his friend. As an example, on the way home after a rain, Brother pulls down and then releases a tree branch so that it soaks Carl. The target of the trick then faces two bad options—he can go home with wet clothes and be punished by his mother, or he can go to the Tates and wait until they dry, which will also get him into trouble, since his mother considers Lucy a fast girl inappropriate for her son. What is important here is that Carl is aware of his dilemma, but makes the more adventurous choice, just as his father would. At the house, Lucy tells him her version of Wilkes's killing, then shows him the piece of skull, which she has carefully preserved and then has sex with him; they are both 13.

In 1941, at the Elks Club where the three of them go to listen to jazz, Brother suddenly goes to the piano during the band's break and begins playing blues in the style of Albert Wilkes. He had no training and no one had ever seen or heard him practice. Both Freeda and Carl had watched him drum his fingers on a table or in the air (this behavior was maddening to Carl's mother, who liked quiet in her house), but no one thought of this as anything but hyperactivity, simply a part of Brother's strangeness. For five years, he performs almost as the reincarnation of Wilkes.

Just as suddenly, in 1946, he stops playing and stops talking as well. The cause is the death of his son, Junebug. The child was the result of a relationship Brother had with Samantha, a young, dark-skinned woman who takes as her mission to populate the world with as many black children as possible. She feels that the world is out to destroy black people, so she wants to make sure that there are always new generations. The problem for her is that her son with Brother is pale like his father. She sees this development as a betrayal of her mission; so, she shortly after this produces two additional babies with dark-skinned men. Her attitude is communicated to her children, who neglect or abuse Junebug. He is happiest as a child when he is, in effect, invisible, that is, when the other children just ignore him.[27] On July 4, 1946, Samantha decides to have a neighborhood celebration by making barbeque over an open fire in her yard. When she is not looking, Junebug somehow gets covered in kerosene and falls into the fire. Nothing can be done to save him. As a result, Samantha is committed to Mayview, the mental hospital, and her other children are put into foster care. She is haunted by a dream in which she is both herself and Junebug:

> Something icy splashes my back. Like being high and dizzy all the sudden. I can't breathe nothing but kerosene. I'm tasting it, it's rushing up my nose. I see it shining on my bare feet. Then hands pushing. Becky [one of the children] screams and I fight the hands. I wonder why anybody wants to hurt Becky. She stops the others sometimes when they're hurting me, and now she's screaming No no no so I fight the hands and try to turn around and help Becky cause she's in trouble. I'm twisting to find her. The stones are wet and slipping under my feet . . . I'm fighting . . .
>
> He never made a sound. Not a mumbling word from that poor child's lips. So when the scream comes I know it's me. I know I'm not Junebug anymore. Junebug's gone. That's how it [the dream] ends. Me screaming and him burning up.[28]

In this horrifying passage, we can see Wideman making several points, both about the characters and about larger social issues. Because it is a dream, he does not have to break away from his narrative voice to try to give us the perspective of Junebug, who would not be able to tell the story. Samantha can tell the dream to Lucy, who can then report it to Carl and the narrator/author. Second, we learn something of what might have been Junebug's character; his concern is for Becky, the one child who seems to care for him. He assumes that she is the one in trouble and tries to help her. He is no longer just a strange being but instead a good child; he fights "the hands" to save her, not himself. Third, the dousing with kerosene and "the hands" reveal something that Samantha's conscious mind denies—one (or more) of her other children probably deliberately killed Junebug. His death was no accident. But to know this means that she is in some way responsible, since she clearly had difficulty knowing how to treat this not-black child. Her problems with him become known to the children, who want nothing to do with him. In a second dream, she goes to each of them and ask if they did it, and they all say "Yes, Mama." A potentially more damaging part of the story is that, when Lucy visits Samantha in about 1969, she brings along "cards and things" from the children, who have now grown up in various places around the United States. What is communicated is that they all seem to be living normal lives and remember their mother fondly: "They sure love their Mama Sam. They don't forget you."[29] What they seem to have forgotten is the trauma of Junebug's death, the very thing that keeps Samantha in the mental hospital.

The final point to make about this episode is what Wideman seems to be saying about issues of race. In *The Lynchers,* he commented on the Black Power Movement by showing that African American men were willing to use the same methods as white racists to accomplish their political goals. Here, he seems to be suggesting that a similar perspective, one that used skin color to determine the value of people, was also destructive. Samantha's desire to produce dark-skinned babies led her and her children to consider Juneboy to be of less value than them. The end result is the death of a child, the insanity of the mother, and the silencing and eventual suicide of the father. For Wideman, of course, this was personal. He was the son of a light-skinned mother and the father of three light-skinned children.[30] For him, any version of racial essentialism is highly problematic.

What we also learn about the generation of Carl, Lucy, and Brother is that they are less able than the older generations to handle the difficult circumstances of life in Homewood. All three become addicted to heroin. They find it a pleasant alternative to the racial realities of the post–World War II world. For example, Carl, who served in the Pacific during the war, uses money from the GI Bill to take art classes at a local university. While he is good at what he does, one of his instructors pulls him aside one day and explains to him that no company was going to hire a black artist: "Best student we have but you're wasting your time here. Can't earn a living with what you're learning here." Carl understands that this is the end of his career:

And that was my graduation day. No way to go back to class after that. Shaky enough being the only spook at Tech. Wasn't like he was asking me if I wanted to quit. And nevermind it wasn't none his business. Shaggy-lipped motherfucker made it his business. Quituated me on the spot.

What do you think you're doing? [teacher's words] Damn. I really didn't know. Not then, not now. So he made up my mind for me. Let me know I was making him uncomfortable so it was time to go. Put it to me so I'd be calling him a fool or a damned liar if I stayed. And shaky as I was I just quit. Gave it up.[31]

It is easy to see how the teacher would justify his action as simply offering a dose of reality to a naïve student. After all, this happens before the civil rights movement, and even though the government had banned racial discrimination in the defense industry, there was no obligation for fair employment practices in other businesses. Thus, the instructor sees Carl as unemployable in his field even with a degree. He believes he is saving the young man from frustration by aborting his career. But he does so by blaming the victim for seeking a career that would make use of his talents. He takes advantage of Carl's insecurity about his art to eliminate the one black person in the program. By doing so, he returns the program to its lily-white comfort zone. He is willing to sacrifice his best student to his own underlying racism.

Thus, this middle generation suffers from racial attitudes coming at them from both blacks and whites. The result is that none of the "three musketeers" is able to lead a productive life. None of them have careers or even long-term jobs, as far as we know. Unlike John French or Mr. Lawson or Mr. Tate, they are unable to establish a family life; none of them marries and the only child produced by them—Junebug—is considered an undesirable even by his own mother. All of them are talented—Carl has his drawing, Lucy is a dancer, and Brother is both a musician and, as Lucy learns after his death, also a skilled artist. But their abilities cannot be translated into productive work. What they have is each other, and that emotional attachment enables then to survive; because of their weaknesses, however, none of them can really prosper.

Wideman brings himself into the story in order to try to understand this lost generation. His connection to them is through his childhood nickname, Doot. In the final section of the novel, entitled "Brother," much of the focus is on the dead. We learn of John French's heart attack in his own bathroom between the toilet and the tub. We get another version of the burning of Junebug. Brother dreams that he was the one who betrayed Albert Wilkes. We learn that Carl's mother Freeda has died[32] and that Brother was killed while playing the game he and Carl devised as children of running across the tracks in front of an oncoming train. Whether this was an accident or suicide is not clear. The section opens with a dream about being in a boxcar that Brother has for the first but not the last time:

> They were not Brother Tate's hands. In the pitch and shudder of the train nothing belonged to anybody. The woman who had been hurled into his lap did not own the soft breasts that dragged over his thighs as she scrambled away. They weren't her fingers that mauled and grasped as she tried to find him and push him away all at once. A stew of bodies sloshed helter-skelter over the wet floor of the boxcar. Brother couldn't stand. He couldn't disentangle what belonged to him from the mass of bodies struggling in the black pit.[33]

The dream combines images of the Middle Passage of the slave trade with the transportation of Jews and others to death camps during the Holocaust. This part of the "Brother" section is dated 1941, which is approximately when stories of the German death camps began to emerge. The time of the writing of the novel (the early 1980s) coincides with the publication of a number of books arguing that the slave trade and the period of slavery was also a Holocaust. This position was highly controversial at the time.[34] The dream serves to suggest the author's view, apparent through much of the trilogy, that black communities were being devastated in many ways. But while the earlier generations took for granted that the world was prejudiced against them and turned inward to take care of themselves and their community, this younger group seems to believe that they ought to be treated differently, based on their individual experience and abilities. When that does not happen, they have fewer resources to draw on for survival.

Despite this pessimistic view, the novel ends with nostalgia and something like hope. Lucy describes Brother's drawings:

> She began to understand why some faces she couldn't name looked so familiar. Brother had drawn the old people young again. Mr. and Mrs. Tate. John French. Freeda French. Young again. Owning Homewood again. They smiled back at her under the heavy light. In their long dresses and big hats and coveralls and eight-buttoned suits and high collars like an extra set of wings around the men's necks . . . Carl's mother and father, Albert Wilkes, the Tates. All the good old people and good old times. She could see Brother's hand, pale as the paper, moving across each sheet. Like the magic hands of the old-time healers. See him laying on his

white hands and see through them to the old Homewood streets, like the people coming to life at his touch.[35]

Lucy mourns the loss of what she calls the "solid" people who built Homewood; now, she says, they do not even take care of the old people in the community.

The hope comes in her memory of Doot. It is 1941 (the year Wideman was born), and the three musketeers are at John and Freeda's house, listening to music. Baby John stands up and tries to dance to the music; at this moment, Brother names him Doot, a nonsense syllable associated with the scat singing of Louis Armstrong and Ella Fitzgerald. The narrator has a vision of the moment:

> Brother Tate appears in the doorway. He's grinning his colorless grin and pointing at the piano and Albert Wilkes starts unsnapping the duster and aiming his behind for the piano bench. I know how good it's going to sound so I start moving to the music coming from the radio, I know Albert Wilkes will blow me away so I start loosening up, getting ready. I'm on my feet and Lucy says, *go boy* and Carl says, *Get it on, Doot.* Everybody joining in now. All the voices. I'm reaching for them and letting them go. Lucy waves. I'm on my own feet. Learning to stand, to walk, learning to dance.[36]

This passage that ends the trilogy is Wideman's desire to connect with the past generations, to make their lives and stories available for those who come after. Gathering their experiences is a way to stand on his own feet as a writer and perhaps even to make his language dance.

But even with this hopefulness, he has a caution; the song that he danced to was Jimmy Rushing's *Sent for You Yesterday,* which was first performed with Count Basie's band. The song is a simple blues:

> Sent for you yesterday, here you come today
> If you can't do better, might as well just stay away.[37]

Like classical blues, it is a song of love and trouble. The narrator of the song tells the listeners that the help he is seeking comes too late. Whether that help is the lover or a friend, coming after the needed time is useless.

This idea can be applied to the message of the novel. Lucy tells Carl that she could never marry him because he lacked the strength of character that the older generation had, and that even Brother seemed to demonstrate. They should have been able, given their families, to have done something for Homewood, but they were too focused on their personal problems rather than on the bigger picture and the bigger problems. And for the author-narrator, the question is even more significant. He went away to escape the limitations of life in a deteriorating black community. Now, he comes back, to gather the stories and reconnect with his past. The question is what good his efforts do for Homewood. He has shown throughout the trilogy what has happened to the neighborhood and to people like his brother; meanwhile, he has moved into a completely different world. He has returned, but only for a visit. He was needed yesterday, when it might have been possible to make a difference, but he comes today, knowing that it is too late. He can tell the stories of the past, of the legends and the tragedies, but can he really make a difference? The novel does not answer the question.

The trilogy focuses almost entirely on the maternal side of the family. While the father sometimes appears, he does not have a significant role, except in one piece from *Damballah*. That story, "Across the Wide Missouri," suggests the reasons for his absence. The story is told from the point of view of the adult John, living in Wyoming, but remembering an incident from his childhood. At the beginning, he recalls, not his father, but Clark Gable in the movie the story takes its title from. In the scene, Gable is brushing his teeth with scotch and looking at himself in the mirror, smiling and confident. The narrator says: "The white man at the mirror is my father."[38] We then step back to view the day leading up to the movie. John's mother takes him to Kaufman's department store, where his father works as a waiter in the dining room. Her idea is that father and son will spend the afternoon together.

John is very nervous in the dining room, since it is obviously a place for white people. As he waits for Edgar, he recalls his father's place in their apartment, which is in a tiny closet actually on the landing. We get a strong sense of Edgar's isolation from his family, a situation that makes the son anxious; he wants to be close to his father, but does not know how. When the older man shows up with a newspaper and wants John to choose a movie, the boy can only sit silent. He says to himself that nothing matters except that he is with his father. The tension here indicates why he makes the remark about wanting Clark Gable as his father. He wants someone he can look up to, who can be the center of attention and not be serving other people, hoping for good tips; he wants a father who can move through the world with confidence. He loves the father he has, but wishes he could be different.

What is significant about this notion of fatherhood is that we also get, in the present time of the story, John as father. It turns out that his son, probably Jake, knows the words to the theme song from the movie and, in fact, is going to be singing it for a school event. But John wants to be center stage rather than watch his son perform. On the night of the event, he chooses to go out to dinner and drinks with a visiting writer who has won a Pulitzer Prize. Like his own father, who mostly lived away from his family, John prefers his work and his own life over that of his child.

The second story involving the Wideman side of the family, "Backseat," was written after the publication of the trilogy and appears in *The Stories of John Edgar Wideman* (1992); nonetheless, it is very much a Homewood tale. It is primarily about his grandmother Martha, whose first husband was Harry Wideman; she was married a total of four times. Her story is framed by episodes of adolescent sexuality involving John. One connection is that these experiences occur on Martha's property; another theme is the connection between gender and race. The real tale begins with her on her deathbed and John trying to decide when exactly he will fly to Pittsburgh. We can date the present time precisely: "Yesterday, Thursday, March 26, 1991, around eight-thirty in the evening my grandmother died."[39] He remembers learning about her life when he had a brief conversation with her 10 years earlier. She tells him that she was born in Wrightsville, Pennsylvania, in 1892 and, though her family name was Lawson, she was really a Rutledge. This meant that she was the illegitimate daughter of a local white man—a fact she is willing to acknowledge, though not talk about. She is later married to Harry Wideman, the father of her three children, Mackinley Overton, Reverend J. R. Morehead, and Otis Fallen.

While she was not emotionally expressive—unlike the women of the French family—John recalls two incidents from his childhood that indicate her view of him. In the first, she takes him on the incline up to the top of Mount Washington in the evening so he can see the lights of Pittsburgh. In his memory, she takes special delight in his excitement. The second is more complicated. She works as a cook for a wealthy white family. She apparently talks so much about her five-year-old grandson that the Ricks invite him over for breakfast. Overton, their chauffeur and her new husband, drives John and Martha in the Ricks' Lincoln Continental. While the child is impressed with the car, he is anxious about the purpose of the trip. When he joins the family at the table in the breakfast room, the tension just keeps building. He even imagines a lion sitting in the middle of the table, ready to pounce on him. The scene is similar to the one in the department store dining room. Being in the space of whites is emotionally very disturbing for him; recording those moments seems to be his way of showing how far he has come from that childhood, though they may also explain the lifelong attention to race matters in his writing.

The story also concerns the passing of a generation. She was the last of his grandparents. He describes in some detail the death of John French, who died in the tiny family bathroom in the house on Finance Street, when he collapsed and was stuck between the toilet and the bathtub. We then learn how difficult it was to get his body out. Compared to this awkward end, Martha goes quietly in a hospital room. The two deaths reflect in a sense the two sides of the family—one very expressive and even, at times, embarrassing; the other, quiet, almost to the point of coldness. We learn, for example, that Martha was a respected member of the same A.M.E. Zion Church as the Frenches. But unlike them, she never talked about religion. The narrator implies that, having been the wife of ministers, she had a very practical view of the church rather than a deep personal commitment to it. He suggests that this emotional calm came from the traumatic experience of losing her son in World War II. Though all three of her children saw military service, Eugene was the only one who went into battle. Martha's ritual was to get the mail each day to see if there was a letter from him. After the war ended, she continued the practice, since he had not come home. Finally, she received a message from the War Department saying that he had been killed after the war was officially over, either by a mine or a Japanese combatant who did not know of the surrender. In John's view, the absurdity and trauma of his death is what made her so quiet. From that moment, she never expressed openly any deep emotion.

Through her story and that of his father, Wideman attempts to understand his own life. For example, their secretiveness and independence could be the reason he tended to compartmentalize his life, separating himself from Homewood by becoming as much as possible the opposite of what was expected of a young man from the inner city. Like them, he placed himself in the world of whites, though none of them ever in any sense seems to have thought of whites as racially superior. They also were very private people; even in writing about them, Wideman is reserved, keeping their secrets if he knows them and not trying too hard to reveal the full extent of their characters. In part, doing this for them justifies the games of hide and seek he plays with readers in telling about his own life.

The question left hanging at the end of *Sent for You Yesterday*, about the ability of the writer-intellectual to make a difference, is addressed again in *Reuben* (1987). Wideman's sixth novel takes place in

Homewood, though it only indirectly involves the family. The book tells the stories of Kwansa, Wally, and the title character. Reuben is a trickster figure; he helps people with their legal problems though he has no formal training as a lawyer. He operates out of a trailer on Hamilton Street, where, according to family legend, Charlie Bell and Sybela Owens first settled when they moved to Pittsburgh. The people of Homewood come to him with their difficulties involving City Hall or the court system, and he goes downtown to negotiate assistance for them. At one point late in the story, he is arrested for impersonating a lawyer, but by the end, he is back at work again. Physically, he is very distinctive:

> Reuben was a small man. His face was long and his hands long, but Reuben never grew taller than the average twelve-year-old boy. That long head atop a puny body, the way he carried one shoulder higher than the other, reminded people how close Reuben came to being a hunchbacked dwarf. He wasn't built funny enough to be pitiable, but he wasn't put together quite right either . . .
>
> Reuben's long bony face tapered to a point. From the splotched gray hair on his head to the splotched gray of his Vandyke beard, the face narrowed drastically, coming to a sharp point at his chin, a point, some said, sharp enough to bust balloons or prick your finger and that's why he wore a beard.[40]

We also know that he always dresses in three-piece suits and speaks very formally.

He is something of a mystery in the community; when Kwansa comes to talk to him, she does not know if Reuben is his first or last name (and readers never find out either). Moreover, though we get into his mind, learning about his past life, his doubts about his work, and even his nightmares, we know virtually nothing about his everyday life in Homewood. We do not know if he makes money from his clients, or whether he has relationships with people outside of his office, and where or how he lives. He seems to be a variation of Cecil Braithwaite of *Hurry Home* and is perhaps based on the same figure:

> My best friend in Pittsburgh lived with an aunt and uncle and I noticed that the uncle had a lot of framed documents on the wall. I never payed [sic] much attention to the uncle. Then one day I was waiting for my friend and I looked at these things and they were really quite prestigious credentials. One of them was a law degree. Who he was and what he was stuck in my mind. Why would a

black man who went through law school and made all the sacrifices one must make to do that, then just disappear, just decide to
go down a different path altogether?[41]

Reuben can be considered a reverse character from Cecil and the real-
life model. He does not go to law school, but learns about and practices
the law. How he gains that education is a version of the slave means of
gaining literacy, as reported by Frederick Douglass and others. In his
Narrative, Douglass describes how he began to learn the basics of reading from the plantation mistress, who was unaware of the laws against
such education. When the training was discovered and stopped by her
husband, the young slave then turned to the spellers and primary readers discarded by their son. Later, he would bribe white street urchins
to show him more of the alphabet.[42] Reuben's technique is to work in
a white fraternity house at UPenn and borrow the law books from the
students and read them whenever he has free time.

This phase of his life ends tragically when the fraternity boys, who
consider him a kind of pet, decide to take him to a brothel run by a very
distinguished black woman, Flora. They pay specifically for Flora's services. After a short time, they break into the room and start beating up
the couple. They had never intended to allow a black man to be with a
woman who catered to white men like themselves. As this is happening,
the piano player, who sees himself as Flora's protector, comes upstairs,
setting the staircase on fire. Reuben is thrown out the window, and the
frat boys jump out after him. Flora, who had been tied to the bed by the
boys, and the piano player die in the flames. After this, Reuben returns
to Homewood and eventually sets up his practice.

We actually see very little of that practice during the novel. Instead,
we get a great deal about the interior lives of the three main characters.
For example, Kwansa comes to him because her ex-husband has decided
to take their son to live with him and his new wife. We never see Reuben
either investigating the situation or going to officials to try to return the
child. Instead, we watch Kwansa running around in the rain hysteri-
cally trying to figure out where he may have been taken. She thinks and
later in a bar talks a lot about her failures as a mother. Her part of the
story is about this emotional crisis rather than about the recovery of the
child. At the end, the situation is resolved when the husband appears at
the bar and attacks her. A friend of hers, who is a lesbian, defends her.
That woman cuts his throat. In a final scene in the novel, Reuben is at
the courthouse, where he is scheduled to meet the son. We do not know

how this was arranged or what happened to either Kwansa or her friend as a result of the father's death.

Similarly, Wally initially comes to Reuben for advice about an emerging scandal involving basketball recruiting. We never learn the outcome of that situation. In place of that, we find out about Wally's experience as a college basketball player, which seems to be very much like Wideman's own. The school is UPenn, and Wally, like the author, is isolated on both the team and the campus. Many of the incidents recorded happened to Wideman in real life. Wally feels comfortable only on the basketball court, and he occasionally sets out to find local black life as a way of being at home. While the author was not a recruiter for the team, he did serve as a volunteer assistant coach working with Digger Phelps, who later became famous as the coach of the University of Notre Dame. This connection between author and character may have some psychological significance for one of the two stories about Wally related in the novel.

Wally is careful to set up the scene:

A public bathroom, but large and clean, immaculate even, the kind that the public seldom uses, in a public place away from the beaten track, an art gallery, the stacks of a library. A cavernous, deserted, regularly cleaned oasis with no graffiti on the walls and toilet paper on the rolls, paper towels in the dispensers, mirrors clean and black as holes.

Into this setting, this almost antiseptic, almost oppressive as a hospital corridor's quiet and chemical chill, this setting that surprises Wally and momentarily confuses, disorients him . . . into this setting walks another human being. Male. Caucasian. Middle-aged. Unlucky.[43]

We then learn what may be the motive for what happens next:

He is dressed more appropriately for this bathroom than Wally. The man's subtle double take lets Wally know. Wally feels for a second like a roach. He wants to scurry away, return to his proper element. The man either decides against pissing in Wally's presence or knows better than to soil this kind of public bathroom with human waste because he proceeds directly to the bank of marble-topped sinks and begins washing his hands . . . Rights and privileges and priorities. Even in a bog this large the two of them competed for space when there was space for fifty. Fifty of him or fifty of Wally but no space for one of each.[44]

While there has been no insult expressed or maybe even intended, Wally clearly feels that he is being attacked, in part because he senses the man's assumption of superiority and, in addition, experiences that assumption so strongly that, for a moment, he feels like an insect. Having known this feeling throughout his life, he chooses this time to respond violently to it:

[H]e swiftly brought the knife-edge of his right hand down on the man's neck. An ugly whoomp knocked flesh senseless as a sack of flour. Sharp clicks of bone or teeth cracking on marble edges as the suit crumbles and the body caves to the clean, hard floor.

Wally drags him by the scruff of the neck to a stall. There is very little struggle. Perhaps he snapped the neck. Karate was a passing fancy but he remembered some useful concepts. And his body was basketball hard and willing in spite of the extra pounds he carried.

A splash getting the head in the water. Not very much, actually. The place was neat as a pin. Even the water in the toilet bowl. No sense making a mess. Some people, you just couldn't take them anywhere. But Wally wasn't like that. He remembered how delicately the man had washed his hands. Wally patterned himself on that example. Gingerly, slopping very little water out of the bowl, he lowered the face into the spick-and-span fluid. Stepping back he raised his leg and brought his foot down slowly, scrupulously on the white-collared neck. He braced himself for a struggle. Weight back, arms stretched so he was tautly poised between the walls of the stall. Then he pushed down. More water splashed the clean floor. But it was clean water. Didn't even stain his shoe, although one foot was soaked by the end.[45]

The passage is quoted at length to show the level of detail and precision in telling the event. We are invited as readers to notice everything, yet not get emotionally involved. Everything about it is quiet and calm; even the narration creates a distance—though it is Wally's perspective, it is told in the third person. It is a cold scene, with hard marble edges, precision of movement, and constant repetition of the word "clean."

The level of care with the language and style suggests a scene that Wideman worked hard to get just right. It may well be a kind of fantasy that his own frustration and anger with his life experiences and those of his family led him to play out through his fiction. His sensitivity to racial insult or even innuendo is well-established in his writing and in the comments of others about him. His responses to attitudes of superiority and condescension from whites that are evident in the treatment of his grandfather John French, his brother and his mother and his family at the prison, and himself at college demonstrate a deep level of hostility. The random murder of a white man in a novel could well serve as a safety valve for those feelings. But he deflects that possibility by making it impossible for us to know if the crime really happened. Reuben wonders if the story is true. Wally only answers that it is a dumb question, but his mental response is more complicated:

> Wally doesn't think he ever really saw the man's face. What entered was a pinkish blur expressing its disapproval of Wally before Wally could register its features. Then a glimpse of a face in the mirror. Wally'd given no warning so it was unlikely that the man's eyes had bloated with panic when he saw in the mirror a dark shape suddenly looming behind him. It all happened too quickly, but for some reason an image of the man's startled face was becoming part of Wally's memory of the scene in the bathroom. A fish face. Popeyed, wide gasping mouth, the raw obscene white of a fish belly yanked from sunless depths of a mirror. The truth was he didn't know what he'd seen in the glass. His own dark face? The man's white one? An image of dying or guilt or just a flash of light billowing in from the streets as walls collapsed around them and the building disappeared, and the city disappeared and he was here on his bed dreaming the death clash of two puppets on a bare stage. Open to the sky, the wind.[46]

While some parts of this version indicate the reality of the event, they also show the problems with memory. Did he see the face at all? For some reason, he needs to attach a face, a personal identity to his victim. But the ending raises questions about whether this was all simply a dream, an unconscious acting out of his anger toward those who might sacrifice him to save themselves in the recruiting scandal that initiated the visit to Reuben or, perhaps, more generally, toward whites who assume that the world is theirs

The second Wally story involves his childhood friend Bimbo. They grew up together on the streets of Homewood. They got along well because Bimbo's easygoing attitude complemented Wally's nervous intensity. One incident seems to have defined their adolescence. While they are wandering the streets one day, Wally suddenly decides to climb to the top of a bridge that goes over a railroad track, much like those mentioned in the Homewood trilogy. The top of the bridge rises 30 feet above the street and 100 feet above the rail tracks. The difficulty, Wally points out, is getting up to the top and down the other side, because those parts require attention and skill. Once on the top, the span is wide and easy to walk. So, he goes scrambling up and then challenges Bimbo to follow him. Once he crosses and gets back down, Wally sees his friend is stuck at the top, afraid to move either direction. He begs Wally to help him, but the immediate response is to call up insults and urge him to just jump. When nothing happens, and Wally realizes the seriousness of the situation, he helps Bimbo down.

This story becomes relevant because, years later, Bimbo has become a rhythm and blues star, with a career that seems to be modeled on that of Barry White. Wally comments that the songs are so sensual that he is surprised that they are played on the radio. Unfortunately, Bimbo is in a car accident that leaves him paralyzed from the waist down. While he is able to continue his career, making songs that are more sexual and more popular than ever, he feel imprisoned by his disability. Although he has a luxurious house and all the material possessions, drugs, and women that he wants, he feels lost and hopeless. On one of Wally's visits, after they have talked about the bridge incident, Bimbo asks if he can help him now, by giving him one of his legs (Wally goes running each morning when at Bimbo's) or perhaps he would "rent" him his sexual organs. They both know that this is senseless talk, but it brings them to the real point. Because Wally is the only person he can really trust, Bimbo requests that he send him pills that he can use to kill himself. He is unable to get what he needs alone, so he begs his friend to assist his suicide. All he has to do is send the pills though the mail with a certain code printed on the envelope. Mail marked that way is opened only by Bimbo. No one will know of Wally's involvement. In the present time of the story, we learn that Wally carries the address with him and has arranged to get the pills, but cannot bring himself to send them.

This episode can be understood through aspects of Wideman's life. Bimbo represents the music of his youth—the music that the white student at UPenn mentioned in Chapter 2 referred to as "crap." Here, it is something that Wally holds onto despite all the changes in his life. We also know that Robby belonged to an R&B group called the *Commodores* when he was in high school and that he often used his music to seduce girls. In a sense, Bimbo is what Robby might have become if the group had gotten the recording contract they were promised. In addition, both Wally and Wideman struggle to figure out what they can do to help the men in their lives whom they most care for. Robby and Bimbo are both, in some way, imprisoned for life and find it hard to carry on under their circumstances. Both the author and his character, who have been more fortunate and who feel that, at some point, they betrayed their responsibilities, deeply need to find a way to be truly helpful.

Reuben, then, might be said to be a novel about how the main characters struggle to do some good, while being well aware of their imperfections. They have plenty of reason to feel deep resentment of those who use their status and power to cause problems and often suffering. They doubt their ability to make any real difference to those in need. Yet, they keep trying. In this sense, they carry on the pattern of the Homewood trilogy in trying to find some reason to continue in a troubled world—one that seems, in fact, to become worse for African Americans, despite apparent improvements. To quote W.E.B. Du Bois, his characters and the author himself seek a "hope not hopeless but unhopeful."[47]

In addition, Reuben himself can be seen as a version of Wideman. He is a private man who reveals only so much about himself. He talks about a brother that is only real when Reuben talks about him; we never know for certain whether he does or ever did exist. What we know is that Reuben carries around a small image that is a constant reminder of this sibling. Finally, the title character's role seems primarily to be to be the intellectual insider-outsider who collects the stories of others, just as Wideman does. He is educated, but he uses that achievement to aid others, primarily by listening. As mentioned earlier, it is unclear whether he ever actually helps anyone in practical terms. Instead, he gives them the chance to express themselves, to try to make sense of their experience. He provides an opportunity for those who have been silenced or abused to find their voice. In this way, he is a variation of the author.

CHAPTER 6

Philadelphia Stories

The city of Philadelphia has been almost as important to John Wideman's life and art as his hometown of Pittsburgh. Not only was it the place where he earned his early reputation as a student and athlete, but it was also where he began his teaching career and made his commitment to African American culture. But Philadelphia, even more than Pittsburgh, has a larger symbolic significance. It is the place most associated with the founding of the United States and was the first national capital. Its name, which means "city of brotherly love," reflects its establishment as a Quaker community. For African Americans, there has always been some irony in the name. In the 1790s, African Americans were so badly treated in predominately white churches that they left to establish their own congregations. The African Methodist Episcopal Church was created as a separate denomination in the city by Richard Allen in 1816 because the Methodist churches discriminated against blacks in a variety of ways. The Wideman and French families in Pittsburgh belonged to the African Methodist Episcopal Zion Church, which was established in New York City about the same time for the same reasons. Thus, there is a spiritual as well as racial link between Richard Allen and John Wideman.

Moreover, during the same time period, a yellow fever epidemic that struck the city was publicly said to have been caused by the black population, even though African Americans were victims and were heroic in their efforts to aid the white citizens. The rumors and claims were so bad that Allen had to write a pamphlet defending his people against the slander. Almost 200 years later, the city decided to drop a bomb on the headquarters and home of the radical black group MOVE. That assault led to the destruction of an entire block of homes in a black neighborhood, as well as the deaths of 11 men, women, and children.

As in the case of Homewood, Wideman seemed to need to get some time and space between himself and Philadelphia before he could write about it. He had left his position at UPenn in1975, then remained in Laramie until 1986, when he took a professorship at the University of Massachusetts at Amherst. There, he was part of the English Department, the program in creative writing, and the W.E.B. Du Bois Department of Afro-American Studies. His friend and fellow novelist Michael Thelwell started the program, and James Baldwin had been a visiting professor the semester before Wideman arrived. Given the fact that the Homewood trilogy and *Brothers and Keepers* drew significant media attention, including the PEN/Faulkner Award for *Sent for You Yesterday,* it made sense to be closer to major urban centers, bookstores, media outlets. Documents in the Wideman Archives at Harvard University show a steadily expanding demand for readings, lectures, and interviews during this time. In practical terms, this meant a substantial increase in money earned through speaking fees, and as a result, increased royalties from book sales. Since these events tended to occur on the coasts, travel was much more convenient from the Boston area than from Laramie. Going to Amherst was a way of being back in the east without being affiliated with either the Ivy League or the cities associated with his childhood and young adulthood. It was only at this point, when he had completed four books on Homewood and the story of his brother's troubles, that he took up the story of the second city in his life.

For Wideman, Philadelphia, more than any other city, demonstrates the complex relationship between American history and the African American experience. In *Fever, Philadelphia Fire, Two Cities,* and *Cattle Killing,* he explores both historical and contemporary issues and seeks to identify patterns in what he finds. The books are also very much about family; in these cases, the families are more often made up of unrelated individuals who come together for various reasons. They are also about fathers and sons, though here again, the relationships are seldom biological. What interests Wideman, then, is how black people, in the past and in the present, come together to figure out ways to deal with their suffering. In the process, he tries out new ways to let ordinary people tell their own stories—much as he did with his brother Robby in *Brothers and Keepers.*

The title story of *Fever* (1989) is concerned with Richard Allen and the yellow-fever epidemic of 1793. Wideman takes the point of view of the minister, who is both doing what he can to aid citizens and responding to the accusations made against his people. Because it was falsely believed that people of African descent were immune from the fever, they were asked by the mayor and Dr. Benjamin Rush to serve as nurses. Richard Allen and Absalom Jones, another minister, responded by organizing a nursing corps that Rush helped to train. The work of this group was generally seen as heroic. However, after the epidemic ended, the publisher Matthew Carey, who had left the city for several months to save himself, published an attack on the African American community, accusing them of exploiting the situation for profit and plunder by robbing the sick. His statement proved very popular, and had to be answered by Allen and Jones in their own pamphlet. Carey, who was editor of the influential magazine *American Museum,* was quite generous in his praise of whites who organized assistance during the crisis. He named the physicians, the public officials, and the ordinary citizens who risked their lives to aid the sick and dying. Any flaws in white behavior—such as family members abandoning ill relatives—he mostly blamed on panic. When it came to African Americans, however, he was much more limited in his praise and severe in his condemnation. After pointing out that "hardly any white nurses could be procured; and, had the negroes been equally terrified, the sufferings of the sick, great as they actually were, would have been exceedingly aggravated," he goes on to point out that Allen and Jones organized a team of nurses. But then he immediately attacks this group:

> The great demand for nurses, afforded an opportunity for imposition, which was eagerly seized by some of the vilest of the blacks. They extorted two, three, four, and even five dollars a night for such attendance, as would have been well paid by a single dollar. Some of them were even detected in plundering the houses of the sick.[1]

He goes on to somewhat qualify the remark: "But it is unjust to cast censure on the whole, for this sort of conduct, as many have done." He adds a short footnote saying that some white nurses were equally bad.

But a more significant attack was one that would not be noticed by outsiders, though residents of the city would understand it. Earlier in his reporting, Carey discusses the hospital that was set up on the edge of the city at an estate known as Bush Hill. It was organized quickly, with little supervision. Two prominent citizens agreed to take charge, and a quick review of the conditions was undertaken. The report was distressing:

A profligate, abandoned set of nurses and attendants (hardly any of good character could at that time be procured,) rioted on the provisions and comforts prepared for the sick, who (unless at the hours when the doctors attended) were left almost entirely destitute of every assistance. The sick, the dying, and the dead were indiscriminately mingled together. The ordure and other evacuations of the sick, were allowed to remaining the most offensive state imaginable.[2]

While the race of these attendants is not stated, everyone familiar with the situation would assume that they were African American, given Carey's earlier statements. Jones and Allen had recruited them. Thus, the two men feel obligated to respond to what they considered Carey's libel against them, even though he praises them briefly by name. Their answer to the charges is very straightforward. They point out that they immediately reacted to the mayor's call for help by going directly to the homes of sick people. They quickly discovered that the task was overwhelming, so they called on the mayor and were authorized to hire other African Americans to nurse the sick, carry them to the hospital if needed, and bury the dead. Carey had observed that some of the volunteers were prisoners in city jails; what Allen and Jones point out is that almost all of these men were African American. The two of them are specifically trained by Benjamin Rush to bleed patients; the practice of drawing blood was believed to relieve some of the symptoms of the fever. They and their recruits, in effect, become the front line in the battle against the epidemic.

They are especially offended by the charges of financial exploitation of the sick. In a direct hit on Carey, they say, "We feel ourselves sensibly aggrieved by the censorious epithets of many, who did not render the least assistance in the time of necessity, yet are liberal of their censure of us, for the prices paid for our services, when no one knew how to make a proposal to anyone they wanted to assist them."[3]

They then attach an accounting for the money they received and expended specifically for burying the dead. They paid for coffins for which they were not reimbursed and took care of "the poor and strangers," which they paid for out of their own pockets. They note that, on just this one part of their work, they lost considerable money. They go on to argue that Carey is not wrong in saying that some people made exorbitant wages, but that the question is who is responsible for the situation. The two of them would offer volunteers six dollars a week, but would be rejected because someone else offered two to four dollars per day. Given the difficult nature of the work, they were not surprised that poor people would take advantage of the situation. They asked what Carey would have charged if he had been in their position. But then, they note that Carey, despite having an official assignment in the emergency, chose instead to leave the city.[4] They also note that, while the conditions at Bush Hill were deplorable, only two African Americans were employed at that time and that they were both retained when others were dismissed.

Wideman uses this situation to discuss the nature of racism in American history, showing how even black suffering and contributions to society can be turned against them. He does this by carefully delving into the records of the events and then imaginatively reconstructing them. He primarily takes the point of view of Allen, but sometimes uses a third person voice when, for example, he provides scientific definitions and descriptions related to the epidemic. He also tells us of a black man in the hold of a ship who is stung by the mosquito that causes the fever.

The story mostly follows Allen as he wanders the city, trying to help those in need. We see him visiting the area around Water Street, where the poorest residents live in squalor. He had come here repeatedly to preach to those who have recently arrived from the slave South, but they reject his efforts:

> But were these lost people really his people? The doors of his church were open to them, yet these were the ones who stayed away, wasting their lives in vicious pastimes of the idle, the unsaved, the ignorant. His benighted brethren who struggled to reach this city of refuge and then, once inside the gates, had fallen prisoners again, trapped by chains of dissolute living as they'd formerly been snared in the bonds of slavery.[5]

Here, Allen seems to reflect Wideman's own complex relationship to African Americans such as his brother. The author and his character have found ways to move beyond the places where they began (Allen had been born a slave) and into respectable lives, even if they were occasionally confronted by racial difficulties. They are both troubled by those who remained behind, especially when they see how the mistakes of the others just add to their misery. Wideman and Allen can neither walk away nor simply accept the choices others make.

Allen returns to this area of the city during the fever to do what he can for those who live there, the poorest of whom live in the caves and cellars because they cannot even afford the miserable shacks in the alleys. We learn that the first settlers created these underground residences until they were able to construct houses. Each new wave of immigrants begins here; only the blacks are not granted the chance to move up in society. He finds the effect of this neglect in one of the caves:

> At the rear of the cave, so deep in shadow he stumbles against it before he sees it, is a mound of rags. When he leans over it, speaking down into the darkness, he knows instantly this is the source of the terrible smell, that something once alive is rotting under the rags . . .
>
> Two Santo Domingan refugees, slave or free, no one knew for sure, inhabited this cellar. They had moved in less than a week before, the mother huge with child, man and woman both wracked by fever. No one knows how long the couple's been unattended. There was shame in the eyes and voices of the few from whom he gleaned bits and pieces of the Santo Domingans' history. Since no one really knew them and few nearby spoke their language, no one was willing to risk, et cetera. Except for screams one night, no one had seen or heard signs of life.[6]

Allen has come after a day of working with Doctor Rush at Bush Hill and elsewhere around the city, tending mostly to the whites. What he discovers in the cellars and caves helps to explain why commentators such as Matthew Carey assumed that the fever had little effect on the black population. Such men would never come to such places and see what Allen saw.

Through his protagonist, Wideman explores the symbolic meaning of the fever. The key comes in the epigraph to the story: "Consider Philadelphia from its centrical situation, the extent of its commerce, the number of its artificers, manufacturers and other circumstances, to be to the United States what the heart is to the human body in circulating the blood."[7] The statement was made by Robert Morris, who was a key figure in the American Revolution and in the state of Pennsylvania. As a businessman and a representative to the Continental Congress, which wrote the Constitution, he was well aware of the importance of the city to the new country. Wideman takes Morris's metaphor of the heart and body and extends it to the idea of race in the new country. Racial attitudes circulate through the United States, with Philadelphia at the center, since it is the site of both commerce, which depends so much on slave labor, and the political documents and institutions that validate and support the system of slavery. Racism is a kind of fever moving through the body politic; Allen sees it as a spiritual condition:

We have bred the affliction within our breasts. Each solitary heart contains all the world's tribes, and its precarious dance echoes the drum's thunder. We are our ancestors and our children, neighbors and strangers to ourselves. Fever descends when the waters that connect us are clogged with filth. When our seas are garbage. The waters cannot come and go when we are shut off one from the other, each in his frock coat, wig, bonnet, apron, shop, shoes, skin, behind locks, doors, sealed faces, our blood grows thick and sluggish. Our bodies void infected fluids. Then we are dry and cracked as a desert country, vital parts wither, all that dust and dry bones inside. Fever is a drought consuming us from within. Discolored skin caves in upon itself, we burn, expire . . .

Fever grows in the secret places of our hearts, planted there when one of us decided to sell one of us to another.[8]

So, the yellow fever, which came to Philadelphia from the West Indies as part of slavery and the slave trade, as the mosquito carrying it is brought in on the bodies and clothes of slaves as well as the produce grown by them, becomes an opportunity to reinforce negative prejudices and actions against darker-skinned people. People such as Richard Allen must battle not only the physical disease, but also the spiritual one. To do so, he must go among the whites, who are either hateful or condescending, and the blacks, who distrust his faith or are beyond his help.

Near the end of the story, Allen talks with a Jewish man dying of the fever at Bush Hill. The man asks the question that is perhaps most relevant to both Allen and Wideman—Why do you stay and do this work? Why not go home to family and even flee the city? The work is unrewarding, miserable, and lonely:

Who forces you to accompany that madman Rush on his murderous tours? He kills a hundred for everyone he saves with his lamebrain, nonsensical, unnatural, Sangrado [bloodletting] cures. Why do you tuck your monkey tail between your legs and skip after this butcher? Are you his shadow, a mindless, spineless black puddle of slime with no will of its own?[9]

The man is, in some ways, racist—he calls Allen a "black son of Ham," a "slack-witted Nubian ape," and the "progeny of Peeping Toms and orangutans." But he also expresses the minister's own doubts; just before this episode, Allen had wondered why he was not taking advantage of the situation. He could exploit the situation in the way Carey accused blacks of doing. There was no government to stop him; the social order had collapsed. If he did not want to do that, he could take the precaution that Carey did and walk away from the city with his family, returning only when it was safe to do so. So, when Abraham questions him, he is hearing his own voice, even if in negative terms.

Moreover, the dying man recognizes the fundamental goodness of Allen, but sees this as a flaw. The very nobility of his actions limit his possible influence. He needs a larger vision than just caring for the needy in this emergency. He could be a Moses of his people, but instead, he places himself in a situation in which his own health is at serious risk and the impact of his efforts are very limited. But then, Abraham tells him of a Jewish legend that may explain his choice. He describes the Lamed-Vov, 30 men "set apart to suffer the reality humankind cannot bear."[10] What is crucial about these men is that they are not like Jesus, both human and divine, and thus able to transcend the suffering. They are ordinary men who take upon themselves the world's grief and misery.

Allen is clearly intended by the author to be such a man. He does not get the fever, though he goes deeper among the sick than anyone else. His faith requires that he bear witness both to the misery caused by nature and that caused by human evil, ignorance, and prejudice. He feels compelled to put aside his own safety and the security of his family to go into a world that mistreats him even as he tries to save it. When the emergency is over, he then must fight a battle for his own reputation and that of those who he asked to sacrifice their own well-being. And as if *that* were not enough, he had to challenge the very faith he so strongly believed in because whites refused to worship with blacks.

If Allen can be seen as a version of the Lamed-Vov, Wideman can be seen as a version of Allen. As a writer, he has taken it upon himself to bear witness to the suffering caused by racism. Like the minister, he has chosen to use his considerable talents to confront the harsh realities of American society. Despite the privilege of education and literary talent, he focuses his attention on trying to do something about matters that seem to be beyond anyone's control. From his first book, he has written about poverty, human frustration and violence, and the damage done to families and communities. With his talent, he could have written works that would gain him wealth and popularity. He could have stayed away from the harsh realities of Homewood and instead have created happy stories of black strength and endurance. Instead, he chose the "path less travelled-by" and spoke the truth as he saw it. And as if this career path were not difficult enough, he had to come to terms with the personal tragedies of his brother and son. Again, he could have walked away from them as a writer, but chose instead to struggle with their meaning to him and to society. By telling us the story of Allen and of a particular moment in American history, he has told us something important about his own calling.

It is probably not accidental that Wideman makes Allen's dying critic Jewish. He had married a Jewish woman and spent each summer at the camp run by her Jewish father. Thus, he would have absorbed, through this side of the family, a sense of the long periods of suffering that human beings inflicted on each other, based on issues other than race. He can pair the long history of anti-Semitism with the history of slavery and racism. Also, during this period, the language of an African holocaust began to emerge; this version of history argues that the attacks on African life and society during the slave trade and slavery is exponentially greater than the genocide practiced by the Germans and their collaborators in World War II.[11] It is a language that Wideman does not use directly, but that can be suggested through the linking of African American and Jewish men in a time of suffering.

Lest we assume that the fever was isolated and long extinguished, he brings into the ending of the story the MOVE incident. Wideman blends the story of Allen's time with his own:

> A new century would soon be dawning. We must forget the horrors. The Mayor proclaims a new day. Says let's put the past behind us. Of the eleven who died in the fire he said extreme measures were necessary as we cleansed ourselves of disruptive influences. The cost could have been much greater, he said he regretted the loss of life, especially the half dozen kids, but I commend all city officials, all volunteers who helped return the city to the arc of glory that is its proper destiny.[12]

The MOVE episode is explained in detail later in this chapter; at this point, what is necessary to know is that it involved the decision of the Philadelphia police, with the approval of the black mayor, to drop a bomb on a house occupied by a radical black group; the fire resulted in the destruction of an entire block of African American homes in addition to the deaths mentioned. What is clear from this passage and Wideman's later work on the subject is that this was an extension of the fever of racism. The reason he can make such a connection is that the language of the official statement places so little value on black lives, just as Carey could largely ignore the effects of the epidemic on poor blacks and focus his criticism on those blacks who aided the sick and dying. In both cases, blackness itself comes close to being labeled the disease. It is this insult that both Allen and Wideman bear witness to in "Fever."

The Cattle Killing (1996) takes up much of the same material from a different perspective. The narrator is a young African man who has become a traveling preacher around the time of the epidemic. As he moves through the countryside, he has experiences that challenge his ideas of Christian love. He comes in contact with a man who would rather die than be treated by someone with black skin. He is run out of one church for daring to try to preach to whites.[13] When ill himself, he is taken in by a mixed-race couple, who survive by pretending that the man is the servant of the white woman. For a short time, the three of them form a family, as the preacher helps the husband, who is in a deep depression about the discrimination they face, to see the value of his wife's love. When he returns after a short time away, the young man discovers that the couple has been murdered by their white neighbors, who learned of their secret. On the road, he finds a young servant carrying a white baby, which had been thrown out by its own parents when they found out it had the fever. Only the black maid is willing to care for it.[14] He also encounters a woman who had been a maid in the home of Doctor Thrush, who is clearly based on Benjamin Rush. She shows him a journal, supposedly dictated to her by Thrush's blind wife, in which the servant has also recorded the sexual assaults she has endured from the doctor. The wife's story in the journal is about her missionary work with black orphan children, whom she encourages to endure their suffering because God will reward them one day. We also learn that they are locked into a cellar each night. It eventually catches fire and this kills all the children. These experiences suggest Wideman's view that racism is destructive of the most basic human relationships and eats away at the heart of the nation.

The novel opens, not in the past, but in the present. The narrator/author is walking to his father's house up the hill in Pittsburgh. He remembers, when he was 15, the dances that used to take place in homes that he was not supposed to visit. He remembers because the night before, two boys—one 15 and one 14—were shot to death by other young black men outside the same kind of party. He also recalls a story from 19th-century South Africa in which a young woman had a vision that the Xhosa people should kill all of their cattle and destroy their crops, and that if they did so, prosperity would come to their land and the white invaders would leave. Most of the people, encouraged by their leaders, follow the prophet's advice. Since the cattle were the source of wealth and food, the result was massive famine and starvation. It was a form of national suicide.[15] Wideman links these two events through a passage about sacrifice:

> Shoot. Chute. Black boys shoot each other. Murder themselves. Shoot. Chute. Panicked cattle funneled down the killing chute, nose pressed in the drippy ass of the one ahead. Shitting and pissing all over themselves because finally, too late, they understand. Understand whose skull is split by the ax at the end of the tunnel.
> The cattle are the people. The people are the cattle.[16]

Wideman makes matters complicated for readers from the beginning of the book. In his version, the victims are also the victimizers. The Xhosa chose to follow the false prophecy, and thus destroyed themselves. The young black men chose to kill each other, and thereby invite their own deaths. Those who benefit from such suicidal practices—whether the British colonizers or the American power structure—do not have to do anything. While the suicidal practices are clear, the narrator wants us to understand that they emerge out of a history of racism and discrimination.

To do this, he wants to make sure that we understand his perspective and purpose:

> He wanted every word of his new book to be a warning, to be saturated with the image of a devastated landscape. To be hurt by it as he had been hurt. Wasn't the stench of that ravaged countryside burning his eyes, his nostrils as he trudged up Wylie Hill. His book beginning and ending here . . . Deadly prophecy in the air again. The people desperate again, listening again.[17]

He wants to write a new kind of book, not just another American story such as those of Sherwood Anderson or William Faulkner. As he is walking up the hill, he thinks of the people in his family and the name they have given him:

> Eye. Why are you called Eye. Eye short for something else someone named you. Who named you Isaiah. What could they have been thinking of. . . . You are Eye because you grew up in this city. And fifty years later you've returned once more as you always do and your mother and father sister brothers aunts uncles cousins nieces nephews still are here and remember you and remember what they

named you and call you by that name. So why not. In a half century you've invented nothing better or more prophetic than Eye.[18]

"Eye" is, in fact, not the nickname that Wideman was given as a child; like Doot (in *Sent for You Yesterday*), it is one he makes up to serve the purpose of his story. The nickname serves double duty in the novel. First, it associates him with vision, with seeing what is really going on in the world; as in "Fever," he is a witness to a troublesome reality. Second, it connects him to the prophet Isaiah and a different tradition of prophecy from that of the Xhosa.

It is important to understand that the role Wideman takes on here is a different kind of prophecy. He sees himself in the tradition of the Old Testament prophets who came down from the hills with warnings to the people of Israel that they needed to change their ways if they wanted to escape the wrath of God. Such warnings, referred to as jeremiads and used frequently in American history since the time of the Puritans, and produced by African Americans before the Civil War,[19] have often served as both religious and secular demands for reform. By claiming Eye as a nickname and calling his book a warning, Wideman is clearly placing himself in this tradition.

It is also important to keep in mind that he is writing his Philadelphia books in the 1990s. This places them three decades after the achievements of the civil rights movement and the establishment of principles of affirmative action and equal opportunity and a quarter-century after the Black Power Movement had emphasized notions of black pride and racial unity. The early 1990s was also the period when the political parties joined in reducing the benefits of the welfare system and social scientists began insisting that we now were living in a post-racial society. It also saw the steady expansion of incarceration of black men as well as their increasing unemployability as the manufacturing sector of the economy eroded. Between the publication of *Fever* (1989) and *Cattle Killing* (1996), two explosive events occurred that demonstrated the continuing importance of race in American society. In 1991, a group of Los Angeles Police Department officers were videotaped beating Rodney King during a traffic stop; their acquittal the following year led to the Los Angeles riots, which resulted in 53 deaths and over $1 billion in damage to property. That same year, in Crown Heights, New York, a traffic accident that resulted in the death of a black child led to violence in which a Lubavitch rabbinical student was killed. All of this would have set the stage for stories about race in American society; for Wideman, Philadelphia is the symbol of that society.

The dating also places the storytelling during the quincentenary of the arrival of Christopher Columbus in the New World. One major outcome of his explorations was the European slave trade, which brought millions of Africans to the American continents and thus transformed both the Old and New Worlds—economically, politically, and culturally. It also created the modern version of racism, which Wideman sees operating down to the present and generating many of the problems he talks about and warns us against ignoring. Since he tends to see contemporary problems in relationship to the past, readers must understand his commitment to providing a historical perspective.

The difficulty for him is that he is a writer of stories, not a historian or social scientist. His jeremiad and his history lesson must come through narrative, not through argument. For this reason, he invents a young African man who travels in rural Pennsylvania and in Philadelphia. His tale and the tales of people he meets along the way are the means by which the author communicates his message. He builds the story in such a way that we get many perspectives—local, national, and international—on the issues that concern Wideman.

The young man, who has managed to buy his own freedom and that of his mother and brother, serves as an itinerant preacher, in the tradition of John Wesley's traveling ministers, who established the principles of Methodism in colonial and revolutionary America. The narrator, who is never given a name, preaches to white congregations, though his race often leads to hostile responses. At one point, he arrives at the home of a very sick man whose wife has died of the fever. Even though he knows there is little food in the house and none to share, he still cuts firewood and tries to nurse the old man. But the man would rather die than be aided by a black man. He even asks the preacher if he is a black devil. This story establishes the basic ground of racism—that death is preferable to contact with someone of African descent.

But, for Wideman, things are not usually this simple. The next meeting comes near a lake, where the narrator encounters a young black woman carrying a dead white baby. She asks him to help her, but he does not know what to do. She begins walking into the water, and he stands observing her until she disappears. He later feels guilty, but not because he apparently allows her and the baby to drown; he tells the person who hears the story that "I lost faith. Deserted her. She trusted me, ask me to help. but I didn't wait long enough."[20] What he is referring to is an African tradition of the spirit returning to the homeland when it dies.[21] Of even more significance for the message of the novel, however, is the presence of the white baby. Later in the story, the narrator learns of a wealthy white Philadelphia family that wanted to literally throw out their baby when it contracted the fever. Only the black nurse was willing to care for it. Forced to leave the house, she walked out of the city while it died. The family then seal themselves inside to defend against the epidemic but contract it anyway. Because they have locked themselves in, no one can come to their aid, and they all die. For Wideman, this is a kind of justice consistent with the jeremiad. Those who neglect others in need will pay for their selfishness and, in this case, cruelty. It is not merely blacks, but all those who suffer, who must be attended to.

The most extensive episode, which takes up the middle third of the book, expands the criticism to Western culture itself, though it would appear to be quite local and specific. As he travels, the narrator becomes ill, though not with the fever. He is taken in by Liam and Mrs. Stubbs, a black man and a white woman. Though they are married, they have adopted the disguise of a widow and her servant. This pretense is necessary because they fear their neighbors' reactions. They have come from England and settled in rural Pennsylvania, in the area known as Radnor, which is an actual place now in the outskirts of Philadelphia.

Though they came to America with the hope of a better life, Liam has become depressed about the reality and largely refuses to talk or interact with his wife. The presence of the narrator enables him to speak, which he does at length. He tells of being taken from his Ebo home, in what is now Nigeria, as a child in order to be trained in Christianity. But to compensate for the expenses of their missionary efforts, the church leaders apprentice out the children to various tradesmen. As a result, Liam is indentured to Mr. Stubbs, who operates a slaughterhouse—a vocation that obviously links this story to the cattle killing at the beginning of the novel. When the senior Mr. Stubbs dies, Liam is assigned to work for his son George, who is an artist. Part of George's training is to observe the dissection of bodies, an activity considered illegal at the time. He and Liam also observe childbirth, which was not an event open to men. They must adopt disguises in order to participate. Those involved are less interested in the welfare of mother or child than they are in the scientific and artistic knowledge that can be gained. This practice extends so far that one of the "resurrectionists" (grave robbers) sells the body of a recently deceased black woman. George participates in this so that he can improve his art; Liam sees such a woman as a relative:

The African woman on the table was my sister, mother, daughter. I slept inside her dark stomach. I was gripping her heart with both my hands and it was the world's heart, hard and cold as ice. She'd been stolen from me and now I was about to lose her again. Knives would slice her open, hack her to bits. They'd find me cowering in the black cave of her womb again, dead and alive, alive and dead. I wished for the fiery breath of a dragon, for tongues of flame to leap from my mouth and consume that terrible cellar where the auctioneer had already begun his obscene chant.[22]

The "tongues of flame" link the character to his author, since the phrase comes from the book of Isaiah. That prophet warns that those who ignore the law of God will become like dust.[23] A second passage is also relevant. Isaiah has stated that he is inadequate to speak the work of God, so a seraph touches his mouth with a "coal of fire" and he is able to preach (Isaiah 6:6). Wideman combines these passages so that it is the word of the witness that would destroy those who violate moral principles. By extension, he would have his book be that flame.

It is important to Wideman's message that it is not only about the way black women are made victims. Mrs. Stubbs has her own story to tell. As a servant in England, she was forced to provide sex to gentlemen who visited her master. Afterward, they would beat her severely, apparently believing that she deserved punished for contaminating them through her condition as a rape victim.

The only hope for escaping what Liam calls the madness is emigration to America, which they do, disguised as widow and servant. After telling their stories to the African narrator, the couple seems renewed. Liam takes up his art again, and his wife becomes visibly younger and more desirable. But their happiness is only momentary. While the narrator is away, they are murdered in their own home. Their neighbors discovered their real relationship and killed them because of it.

The preacher then moves on toward Philadelphia. Along the way, he receives a packet from a young black woman named Kate. He later learns that she is the maid for the wife of Doctor Thrush, the name Wideman uses for Benjamin Rush, the man who plays such an important role in Richard Allen's story. In this telling of the tale, however, the doctor is not a positive figure. The packet contains the journal of his blind wife. It is transcribed by Kate, who incorporates her own marginal comments about how she is regularly raped by the physician after his wife falls asleep. Meantime, he is also supportive of the efforts of Allen in establishing a separate black church, though he is unwilling to criticize the white congregation for its discriminatory behavior. One reason for his silence is that he wants to maintain good connections in the community in order to advance his medical reputation. He even makes use of the false claim that blacks are immune from the fever in order to encourage Allen to recruit nurses and burial crews. At the same time, his wife is performing her notion of Christian service by visiting African American orphans and telling them that their suffering is proof of God's love. What she ignores is the fact that they are locked in a cellar each night in conditions very like the Middle Passage. After the children die in a fire, she can only express a moment of sadness and then moves on to her next charity.

A key part of Wideman's social criticism here is the link between race and Western civilization. Assumptions about art, science, medicine, economics, and Christian charity grow out of racist views. The Enlightenment—the foundation of modern society—takes for granted the inferiority of certain groups of people. George Stubbs's purchase of black bodies to learn more about painting, the scientists and medical men who bid against him for some of those bodies, and the church men who believe their missionary efforts should be reimbursed through the forced labor of their converts, and the charity work interested only in preaching to children rather than meeting their physical and emotional needs—all suggest a basic value that only whites are truly human and that others can be treated in any way that benefits those whites. Once this principle is established, it can be expanded to see certain whites as also outside the category of human. Sick babies can be treated as garbage and lower-class women as sexual slaves. Thus, Wideman's warning is directed at the fundamental beliefs of the modern Western world. Pointing out its importance as part of the beginnings of the United States reveals how deeply embedded such views are.

Brief mention is made in the novel of MOVE, a black radical organization of the 1980s located in Philadelphia. Discussion of it in *Cattle Killing* serves primarily to bring the reality of race up to the present. That story becomes the main focus of *Philadelphia Fire* (1990) and a key to *Two Cities* (1998). MOVE was established by Vincent Leaphart, who renamed himself John Africa. Born in Philadelphia and a veteran of the Korean War, he came to believe that technology was deeply connected to racial oppression and advocated a return to a more natural life, even in urban areas. In the early 1970s, he established MOVE as an African American anti-science, anti-technology organization. Members all changed their last names to Africa, seeing that continent as their true home. They set up a commune in the Powelton Village neighborhood of the city. The location became immediately controversial, as they accumulated stray dogs, made compost of garbage and human waste (which attracted rats and cockroaches), and used bullhorns to speak out against the groups they opposed. The situation created on ongoing struggle with the Philadelphia Police Department. In 1978, the conflict came to a head, and city officials attempted to evict MOVE. Hundreds of police surrounded the property for days. Finally, they brought in bulldozers to gain access. Gunfire broke out, and a policeman was killed. As a result, nine members were charged with third-degree murder and sentenced to 30 years in prison.

MOVE eventually reestablished itself in a row house at 6221 Osage Avenue, where they took an even more radical position by accumulating weapons and explosives. The presence of this illegal material was reported to the police by Donald Glassey, one of the founders of the group who turned informant.[24] Weapons charges were filed and, in 1985, police again surrounded the group. This time, however, law enforcement was not patient. With clear signs of resistance, they opened fire on the house, and had firemen use high-pressure hoses to destroy part of the roof. When there was still no surrender, they called in a helicopter, which dropped a bomb directly on the house. The resulting explosion killed 11 people in the house, including five children and John Africa and destroyed over 60 houses in the neighborhood.[25] Only two people survived, Ramona Africa and a child named Birdie.

A child survivor becomes the key to the story in *Philadelphia Fire*. The central character, Cudjoe (also the name of Kwansa's child in *Reuben*), a successful writer who has escaped the streets of Philadelphia, has been more recently living the good life in Greece. He returns in response to the MOVE catastrophe, with the idea of finding a boy named Simba who is believed to have escaped the conflagration. His efforts take him back to the streets, back to an old friend who has been compromised by his role in corrupt city politics and indifferent to the deaths of so many people. The novel ends with the failure of an attempted memorial for the disaster and of the search for Simba.

The novel not only includes a character named Wideman, who identifies with Cudjoe, but also a long section in which this figure talks about struggling to tell the story of his incarcerated son and of learning about the MOVE fire while watching television with his wife Judy in their home in Laramie. In addition, Wideman had spent his honeymoon in 1965 in Greece and several days there in 1976 as part of a USIS (United States Information Service) speaking tour of central and Eastern Europe. Thus, readers are invited to make the connection between the author and the protagonist, between the search for lost sons and old homes to the author's experiences with Jake, with Robby, and with what happened to Homewood. The novel, though published in 1990, is set around the same time as Jake's killing of Eric Kane and of the publication of *Brothers and Keepers,* in which Robby spends a lot of time talking about how much Homewood had deteriorated. The character Simba is even speculated to be part of a gang of children who no longer believe in the values or authority of adults. If readers make this link, then Wideman seems to be saying that it is society itself that has produced criminal sons and then punishes them for becoming what it turned them into. It becomes the role of the writer and father to bear witness to this situation and not to use his success to avoid this reality.

At the beginning of the book, Cudjoe seems to be very much in a state of avoidance. He is settled on the Greek island of Mykonos, one of the best known of the Mediterranean resort sites. He has separated from his wife and their two boys and appears to have no focus for his life. When he hears of the MOVE bombing, he decides to immediately return to the city where he once lived, though he is not certain why.

The story then shifts to his conversations with Margaret Jones, who is a stand-in for Ramona Africa, the one adult survivor of the bombing. She is suspicious of Cudjoe's motives, believing that he simply wants to make money from the tragedy, but she agrees to a second meeting after she tries to locate Simba, the only child survivor. They reconvene in Clark Park, just a few blocks from Osage Avenue, where she reports that the boy has disappeared from the home of the family who took him in after the fire.

The park is also near UPenn, where, like Wideman, Cudjoe played basketball and is one of the places where both the protagonist and the author would come during their student days to play pick-up games with the local talent. The action switches to one such evening in the present time of the novel, as Cudjoe initially watches, then joins the games. One point of this digression is to suggest the changes that have occurred in the 10 years he has been gone. The courts have deteriorated, as have the abilities of the players. Many of them are now drug addicts. He learns of a former friend who has ended up in prison in part because of his habit. His younger brother remembers him as a father figure in the family who could not handle the burdens of inner-city life. But much of this section seems to be about the sheer joy of the game, of the physical effort that takes him away from the burdens of his life to the pleasures of playing well and winning.[26]

He also uses the time after the game to get a sense of the community response to the MOVE events. What he finds is a profound belief that the actions of the city had everything to do with race and power and little to do with criminal activity:

Commissioners all members of the same club. Thick as thieves. Downtown chumps all eating out the same bowl. They come in where I work. Smiling and grinning all falling over each other to pay when I bring the check. You think they going to hang one their own? Watch. Commission will claim some poor blood lit the match.[27]

Walking home later, Cudjoe rests on a park bench and imagines himself one of the Lamed Vov mentioned in "Fever." One of the elements of that legend mentioned here is that the group of "Thirty-Six Just Men" "must thaw for a thousand years after they've done their turn of suffering on earth."[28] Here, Wideman plays with images, as the inferno of the MOVE assault produces in his character a cold horror.

The protagonist then meets with an old friend from his college days at UPenn who has become an important official in the city government. Cudjoe goes to him to get his perspective on the fire and on his search for the child. Timbo has become very cynical about contemporary society and has decided that, since the power that really controls the city is greedy, he might as well take advantage of the situation. He interprets the mayor, who approved the bombing, as a practical man who was doing considerable good for the city. This good has included redeveloping some central areas by removing poor neighborhoods and replacing them with condominiums and retail structures. The people who have been displaced have been forced to move to crowded areas away from downtown and thus less visible to tourists and businesspeople.

When Cudjoe asked about the bombing and fire and why a black mayor would approve such an assault on black people, Timbo's answer is clear:

They were embarrassing, man. Embarrassing. Trying to turn back the clock. Didn't want no kind of city, no kind of government. Wanted to live like people live in the woods. Now how's that sound? A Garden of Eden up in West Philly. Mayor breaking his butt to haul the city into the twenty-first century and them fools on Osage want their block to the jungle. How the mayor spozed to stand up and talk to white folks when he can't control his own people? The press ate it up. Nonsense in the papers every day. King's people demanding this and demanding that. Letting their kids run around naked, sassing the police and getting their heads busted, cussing out the neighborhood on loudspeakers, dumping shit in their backyard, demanding the release of their so-called brothers and sisters from the slam. Sooner or later those nuts had to go. Mayor got tired of their mocking everything he was promising.[29]

This cold-blooded explanation serves as a counter-point to Margaret Jones's interpretation of the events and motives seen at the beginning of the story. The improvement of the city depends on the mayor's ability to work effectively with those who have the real money and power in the city; he must convince them of the benefits to them of his approach. When he is faced with the embarrassing resistance of MOVE, he uses his own power to eliminate it. And because he is himself black, there can be no accusation of racism in his decision. It is simply a matter of cold calculation.

What adds to this chilling of the soul is Cudjoe's constant recollection of the breakup of his marriage. Like his creator, the character was married to a white woman and had with her two sons. One of the issues for both Cudjoe and Wideman is the question of fidelity to the marriage. The character reflects on the arguments he had with Caroline and his lies and defections. The story goes into great detail about one particular argument that seems to have much more to do with his power over her than about the actual issue at hand. He calls her sarcastic names as she tries to explain how he ignored her efforts to give him good information. Since the conflict includes their two boys, it is worth noting that the archive at Harvard contains notes from Judy Wideman about John's relationships with other women in which she mentions being the mother of his young sons, about the ages of the children in the novel.[30] Such material is relevant because the author makes the story about lost sons. The novel shows the main character walking away from his own sons and then being mysteriously drawn to another that is not his. Since the novel was published four years after Jake's sentencing, it is possible to say that it is, among other things, his attempt to find his own lost child—a child whose actions seemed to make him a stranger.

Most of the middle section of the novel, in fact, reads more like autobiography than fiction. This part opens with the factual details of the bombing:

On May 13, 1985, in West Philadelphia, after bullets, water cannon and high explosives had failed to dislodge the occupants of 6221 Osage Avenue, a bomb was dropped from a state helicopter and exploded atop the besieged row house. In the ensuing fire fifty-three houses were destroyed, 262 people left homeless. The occupants of the row house on Osage were said to be members of an organization called MOVE. Eleven of them, six adults and five children, were killed in the assault that commenced when they refused to obey a police order to leave their home.[31]

The objective language here is designed to set the factual basis for the story. It comes half way through the novel, at a point at which the very different interpretations of those events have been expressed and at which Cudjoe has more or less given up his search for Simba. Cudjoe largely disappears from Part Two, only to return in Part Three. So, this objective passage marks an endpoint to the author's creation of a fictional version of the disaster.

The rest of the novel may be said to be attempts to understand the kind of society that created this event, and specifically, the situation of black men in that society. Wideman has said explicitly that the voice in the second part that is identified as him is just as fictional as all the others in that "they're voices that are made up to create certain effects within the novel, within the drama."[32] Nonetheless, this particular voice reflects on a phone conversation with his imprisoned son, reads the page proofs for *Reuben* while at a summer camp in Maine, and has a wife named Judy. He also watches the Osage Street events on television in their bedroom in Laramie and remembers living on that street while in Philadelphia. He also recalls living on Copeland Street in the Shadyside neighborhood of Pittsburgh when a child and his father always rooting for the Yankees rather than the Dodgers, even when the Dodgers had Jackie Robinson.

What Wideman has done is to create a version of himself that can maintain some distance from the material of the book. One question is why this is necessary. An answer is that the issues and events are so important to him that he must establish some space in order to enable readers to understand what he wants to say. He sees connections between public history and personal life, especially for African American men. He lived on the street where the fire occurred; he probably knew someone like Timbo at UPenn; he has had direct experiences with the American judicial system. He also has a strong sense of national history, especially in matters of race. Given the emotional and psychological weight of all that, he must find a coherent way to present what he often considers to be the madness that Liam describes in *Cattle Killing*.

The emotional intensity that must be controlled is apparent in the passages about his son. A simple call becomes a traumatic event: "He is my lost son on the phone and I must answer before I don't have the power to say a single word." It is difficult to go beyond a simple greeting: "I've learned the hard way that I've always known next to nothing about him. Except I do know the danger of the place where he's incarcerated, the depth of the trouble he's in, the innocence and terror and guilt he must cope with day after day and little on the horizon but more of the same."[33] For a man whose business is language, part of the frustration is the difficulty with speaking:

> I don't know what words mean when he says them. I don't know if he knows what they mean or knows why he says them. So we can't move beyond the ritual of greeting. To ask how he is opens a door into the chaos of our lives. Perhaps he's unable to tell me how he is. Perhaps I wouldn't understand how to take what he'd say, even if he tried to tell me. Words between us have become useless.

The end result is pain: "Nothing is more painful than the phone ringing and finding him at the other end of the line, except finding him not there, the sound of the phone call ending, the click, the silence rushing to fill the void words couldn't."[34] His son is lost, not because he has died or broken from the family, but because his experience of the place he is in and the reasons he is there cannot be expressed in the only form they can use—language. The irony for readers, of course, is that it is Wideman's skill with language that lets us hear the overwhelming silence.

Later, this Wideman-narrator tries to overcome his ignorance by creating a psychological profile of his son, perhaps basing the character on the reports that were done as part of the judicial process for Jake. In effect, he imagines him with multiple-personality disorder:

> How does it feel to be inhabited by more than one self? Clearer and clearer, in my son's case, that he is more and less than one. Perhaps his worst times are those when he's aware, in whatever horrifying form that awareness takes, that he must live many lives at once, yet have no life except the chaos produced by divided, warring selves.[35] The utter frustration, loneliness and fear accompanying such an awareness are incomprehensible.[36]

He goes on to turn this into a story in and of itself. The son must struggle to take control of and make sense of his life. But to do that, he must somehow have a reliable core to build from, and this is what the narrator does not believe is possible. There is the side of himself that is caught up in rage and another side which can only numbly watch what is happening. To avoid madness, the son must create a story about himself:

He must learn in periods of calm to repeat a story endlessly to himself: there is a good boy, someone who loves and is loved, who can fend off the devils, who can survive in spite of shifting, unstable combinations of good and evil, being and nothingness. Can this story he must never stop singing become a substitute for an integrated sense of self, of oneness, the personality he can never achieve? The son's father. Father's son.[37]

The last two phrases—"The son's father. Father's son"—suggest that the narrator wants the son to follow his example as one who produces stories as a way of making sense of the world and of himself. If the son can give shape to his experience, it will give him some control. It may not provide answers, but it will be better than the chaos. And like the father, he can make himself a character in the drama, "the good boy." He then can imagine that character overcoming his demons. Such an approach may not cure anything, but it could give him some time and confidence to do the necessary work to heal himself.

The passage also can be seen to move in the other direction. The father would seem to have his own demons, reflected in the echoes of Friedrich Nietzsche and Jean-Paul Sartre. Nietzsche's *Beyond Good and Evil* questioned traditional Judeo-Christian morality and substituted the concept of "will-to-power." Human beings are not, according to this view, restricted by older values, but can act in ways that meet their needs. At times, Wideman's fiction, because he questions any morality based on racial difference and oppression, seems to wish to wipe the slate clean. The other reference, to Sartre's book *Being and Nothingness,* is one of the foundations of existentialism, which argues that we must create our own identities out of our experience. We make the meaning of our lives through our actions. Such an approach can be seen in Wideman's own life, as he makes choices that take him away from the life that is expected for black men and into a different world. While many of his characters are victims, some, such as the lynchers, Orion, and Albert Wilkes, try to create themselves on their own terms. They usually fail and sometimes are misguided, but the attempt seems important to Wideman. In each case, the need to do this comes out of a threat to identity and a feeling of the world's hostility. So, stories become ways to release frustration and to make selves for the father as well as the son. The two men are not as different as the narrator would have us believe.

Wideman also uses the fine line between fiction and biography to critique the justice system for its handling of mental illness. This was a very contentious issue in both the criminal case against Jake and the civil suit against the Widemans. The question was whether Jake was mentally ill at the time of the killing of Eric Kane. If he was, then he should have been committed to a facility for treatment rather than tried for murder. The judge found him competent to stand trial, as the Kanes wished. The Widemans were insistent that he was a troubled child. But if this were true, then the civil suit created difficulties for both sides. The Kanes wanted to hold the Wideman family responsible for not getting Jake proper treatment, and the Widemans contended that his problems were not obvious enough to warrant extensive treatment. Since the families continue to contend, most recently at Jake's parole hearing in 2011, it is obvious that the issue has not yet been resolved.

The narrator in this section of the novel takes on a more general target, the refusal of the prison system to give his son the kind of attention he needed:

If my son were wounded or diseased, chances are he'd be treated. The inhumanity of allowing sores to fester, infection to rage, that species of cruelty is universally condemned. Mental illness is just as real, cruel and destructive to mind and body as a gunshot wound. Only a colossal failure of will and imagination allows us to pretend otherwise.

The effects on the son are powerfully destructive:

Why is my son left alone to suffer and try to make sense of his imprisonment, the chaos of his personality, his terror and guilt? That's the portion he awakens to each morning and goes to sleep with each night. Is it any wonder that he's giving up, turning out the light in his cell, attempting to blot out the world by sinking into a profound stupor? That's the instinctual behavior of a wounded animal. To crawl into its den and curl up and die.[38]

He basically accuses the state of slowly killing his son, slowly, but just as surely as if they were executing him. Just as surely as if they dropped a bomb on him to set his house on fire. The link between Jake Wideman (or his fictional version in the novel) and MOVE is that those in power feel no obligation to treat those they have named criminals with any kind of human decency.

It is important to understand here that Wideman divides the world between good and evil, between victims and their persecutors. For him, in this work, members of MOVE are the victims, regardless of their behavior. He is not interested in their verbal attacks on their neighbors or their threat to public health or their storage of weapons and flammable materials on a property that included large numbers of children. He does not concern himself with the crime that the son committed, which resulted in his imprisonment or his family's possible neglect of that son's problems prior to that crime. These concerns do not justify the actions of authorities, but they do lead to a more complicated story—one that Wideman seems unwilling to tell.

The later part of this section goes back in time a few years and brings Cudjoe back into the novel. At one point, while he was teaching school in the city, he came up with idea of having black children put on a performance of Shakespeare's *The Tempest* in Clark Park. His friends tell him that it would be impossible for many reasons, including the abilities of the children and the technical problems of such a production. He insists it can be done and believes that it would help them and himself understand what was happening in society. His version would make Caliban the hero and Prospero the villain. He sets about identifying the right children.

This episode includes a talk that he supposedly gives to the children about the play, but which seems much more like literary criticism in vernacular language:[39]

> Amen, boys and girls. Today's lesson is this immortal play about colonialism, imperialism, recidivism, the royal fucking over of weak by strong, colored by white, many by few, or, if you will, the birth of the nation's blues seen through the fish-eye lens of a fie fi foe englishmon. A mister Conrad. Earl the Pearl Shakespeare, you see. The play's all about Eve and Adam and this paradizzical Gillespie Calypso Island where the fruit grows next to the trees but you're not supposed to touch, see. Point is, long before Fanon or Garvey or Marley or any of that, before the spring storm ate the foliage and opened a line of sight from the window of a motel up on a hill down to the balcony of the divine Lorraine long before a bullet booked down that long lonesome highway and ended the life of a man who'd just enjoyed a plate of fried fish . . . your Godfather Caliban was hatched.[40]

The passage is actually much longer and obviously includes references that young children are unlikely to know or understand. The point is not so much to suggest an actual event in which a teacher tries to prepare a class to read a play by Shakespeare. Instead, it is the author providing a stream-of-consciousness passage that suggests to readers why a black teacher in urban schools in 1968 might want to use classical white literature to show his students how racial attitudes that started centuries earlier might affect their lives. It includes references that students might understand, such as Earl the Pearl Monroe, who attended high school in Philadelphia and later went on to a Hall of Fame career in the National Basketball Association; perhaps Bob Marley, who lived in the United States for a short time in the mid-1960s and whose reggae music became popular in the late 1960s; and certainly the Memphis motel where Martin Luther King was assassinated the same year as the episode in the novel. They are unlikely to know Frantz Fanon, the anticolonial psychiatrist and theoretician, who died several years before the time of the story or Marcus Garvey, whose Back-to-Africa movement was important in the 1920s, or even Dizzy Gillespie, who made significant contributions to jazz in the 1940s and 1950s. These references suggest the character's understanding of African American culture rather than anything that his students might connect to. Altogether, they show the author's awareness of the complicated relationship of people of African descent to Western civilization.

The interpretation of the play that Wideman, through his character, offers is that Miranda is the key to the drama. She is the one who has learned from her father the importance of educating one's inferiors—in this case, Caliban, who stands for all the world's non-white people, but especially those of African descent. She wants to teach him language as the way to civilization. But Caliban, who has already been taught how to curse, is less interested in how to use English properly than he is about basic human needs, such as sex. As he pushes this argument (which he realizes, at one point, might be inappropriate for children), Cudjoe insists that it is important to recognize such needs as part of accepting the humanity of others. In this sense, the version of the play that he wants to produce would make the same argument that the novel makes about MOVE and the narrator's son. This message never gets communicated, however, because the play is never produced; it rains on consecutive nights when it was supposed to be performed. So, whatever message was intended, never is passed on.

Philadelphia Fire ends with a section about a character referred to as J.B., a homeless man who attended UPenn. He is Wideman's effort to create another voice of the city: "I try very consciously in the book to get different points of view. To find a character who is interesting who lived at the bottom of society—somebody who actually was a street person and had to live out of garbage cans. . . ."[41] We, in fact, learn from

J.B. about life at the bottom; he discusses the best places to find quality discarded food and how to panhandle. His name, which is actually James Brown, is one he hides because of the jokes other homeless people make. But the name he uses is also a reference to Archibald MacLeish's play *J.B.*, a modern version of the story of Job. But what happens to this Job is consistent with the rest of the novel. There is no divinity to step in and preserve him. Instead, a gang of white children throws kerosene on him as he sleeps and burns him to death. The fever, the fire that has run through this set of stories is repeated yet again.

At the very end, Cudjoe goes to Independence Square for a memorial for the MOVE victims. What he sees is that virtually nobody, black or white, shows up. While there is a ceremony, one that suggests African connections to the city, virtually all the citizens have begun erasing it from their minds. Earlier in the book, the narrator spoke to a colleague at the University who had conducted research on the events and determined that the official commission had ignored or not received a large amount of information about what had happened. But more important was that the university itself was dismantling the department that had conducted the research. While it was argued that this was a practical and not political decision, it also meant that considerable numbers of African American faculty and staff would be displaced by the decision. So, it becomes clear that at both the official and the popular level, there is a desire to forget. But Wideman argues, in this forgetting, there is the suffering of those left behind.

Philadelphia Fire was given the PEN/Faulkner Award, making Wideman the only person to win it twice. The novel also received high praise from reviewers.

Two Cities (1998) links Philadelphia with Pittsburgh and depicts efforts to construct new family groups out of the remains of older ones in the context of the modern urban decay that has been so much a part of Wideman's fiction. Kassima, the main female character, has suffered the loss of her husband from AIDS, acquired through drug use, and her two sons from gang violence. Robert Jones, 50, who left behind a family, has little hope for any end to the violence around him. Mr. Mallory, a photographer, wanders the streets of both cities, taking pictures of that life after his friend John Africa is killed in the MOVE bombing.

The book opens with a dedication to "Omar Wideman 1971–1992." Wideman then adds, "In Memoriam. We didn't try hard enough." Omar was Robby's son; he was in fact murdered in his apartment by two men on November 8, 1993, after a bar fight in Pittsburgh. Two of the three men allegedly involved in the killing were convicted after a long judicial process that ended only in 1998, the year the novel was published. Wideman has made it very clear that the novel in some ways truly a memorial:

> "I want to make it clear that I'm writing *Two Cities* as a kind of way to cope with the grief of losing a nephew, a way to try and make sense of a horrendous situation," Wideman says. "Omar, in fact, was my brother Robby's son, which heightens the pathos of it, because Robby's in prison, and he wanted Omar to do better. He wanted a life for Omar that he, Robby, had missed. He was hoping and praying that Omar wouldn't make the same mistakes, get involved with the drug culture and fast life."[42]

The story opens with Martin Mallory in 1986 remembering his walks and conversations with John Africa, whom he met on one of his times wandering the streets of Philadelphia. Africa made money walking dogs for people and had even acquired the nickname Dogman, which, in the context of the novel, is slang for a man always after sex. Africa denies such a role for himself, saying that all life should be respected. It is this conversation that provides a key theme, since disrespect for the living and the dead runs throughout the novel. For example, we learn of what the city does after the bombing:

> Poor John Africa dead. They say the cops never found his head. Morning after the fire, and cinders still hot, smoke still stinging the air and city workers clearing away the mess of 6221 Osage Avenue with bulldozers and cranes they say scooping up big heaps of burned trash to haul to the dump and the arm of a crane they say swinging through the air with a hand or leg or something dangling out the steel claw and the operator slowed the machine they say cranked down the bucket and found enough body parts mixed up in the ashes to say it was a dead man. Say it was John Africa.[43]

For the city, human beings can be treated like garbage. This site, after all, was where 11 people were killed. Mallory tries to puzzle through the meaning of such inhumanity, but he feels he needs John Africa to explain it to him, as he recalls that Africa always was clear on matters of importance. The missing head recalls the story "Damballah," in which the boy sends the head of Orion into the water on its way back to Africa. Mallory imagines the body of his friend in the Schuylkill River, on its way back to the homeland.

The story then changes radically, as we are told of the meeting between Robert Jones and Kassima at a bar named Edgar's in Homewood. Kassima, who lost all of her family members within a year, decides to go to the bar for what might be a one-night stand. There, she meets Robert; when he takes her home, he discovers that her house is perhaps the same one he lived in when he was growing up. The house is on Cassina Way, where John and Freeda French of Wideman's own family lived for many years. In fact, several of the memories that Robert has reflect those of the author. Like Wideman, Robert remembers it as a house of primarily women, with his grandmother, aunts, and mother always around to take care of him. His mother's name was Elizabeth Alfreeda Jones; Wideman's mother's given name was Alfreda, but she was called Bette. The house, though very small, was remembered as a true home. Thus, Wideman takes from his own life both factual and emotional elements to create the past of his character. Such nostalgia also enables the character to see what has happened to that neighborhood. Walking back with Kassima, he notices all the houses that have disappeared, leaving only empty, trash-strewn lots. And while the street has been paved, it still remains very much simply the alley it had always been. The houses on it were simply the backsides of nicer homes on real streets that had porches. Because Robert's experiences are some 40 years apart, Wideman can show us what decades of neglect have done here and, by extension, to all of Homewood.

After a couple of days together, Kassima and Robert seem on their way to a meaningful relationship. They spend two days together in bed, getting up only to prepare meals. They talk about their lives and cry together. Kassima, whose name is not given until several pages into the story, has suffered the loss of all the important people in her life. When she was a child, she lost her mother in childbirth. She and her sisters were taken in by relatives but separated. She was raised by church people who used their religion to judge their mother and her children. One of her sons died playing Russian roulette. The other was killed much like Omar Wideman. He was involved in a fight with a gang member, who later came to his apartment and shot him in cold blood. Her husband and their father contracted AIDS after being sentenced to prison for life without parole. All of these deaths occurred within 10 months. So, her life is one defined by death over and over. In a chapter entitled "Lamentations," she describes discovering this book of the Bible and finding that it echoes her emotional condition. Though she has no faith in people who use the Bible to feel superior to others, she finds in this particular book a "song of grief" that reflects her life.

After they share each other's pain, Robert decides to show off his athletic skills in a playground basketball game in Westinghouse Park, where Wideman learned to play ball. While he is now over 40, Robert is still seen as a player and is invited to join one of the teams. Though he lacks the physical energy of others, he still has superior skills and helps his team win the first and second games. He decides to sit out the third, realizing his limits, but when his old friend is injured, he has to substitute. They are playing against members of a gang. Robert is now exhausted and repeatedly makes mistakes. When he tries to claim a foul, an opponent objects. The moment turns threatening when a young gang member, who is not playing, approaches Robert with a gun and then shoots the basketball at the older man's feet. Wideman uses this incident to suggest not only how dangerous the neighborhood has become, but also how some of the traditions, such as basketball games, no longer are the safe spaces for black male interaction that they used to be. Everything is now subject to the inhumanity and violence that once was limited to certain areas and situations. As is seen throughout this book and others, drugs and guns have turned young black men into killers and targets of killers.

Because of the threat to Robert, Kassima, feeling that she cannot survive the loss of another man in her life, breaks off the budding romance. For months, he attempts to contact her but cannot. She prefers to hide away from the harsh reality of her community; her only companion for a while is her boarder, Martin Mallory. She contacts Robert only when Mallory dies.

The old man is a World War II veteran who had the traumatic experience of being shot by racist American soldiers while on a picnic with a friend and two Italian women. The episode is told in detail near the end of the novel; after his death, it is found in a letter he wrote but never sent. He and his friend Gus, who was from Pittsburgh, are assigned to dig ditches for the army, because, as Gus says, they do not want black men to get used to the idea of using rifles. Mallory points out that they have locked up their guns and put them on curfew.[44] Gus argues that it is precisely because of their mistreatment that they should take a holiday with the girls. They go off with food, wine, and gifts for the young women, confiscated from the camp, to a cabin in the woods. After a beautiful day of swimming, sex, and relaxation, they start to go to sleep, only to realize that the military police are coming after them. They try to escape, but Gus and the women are killed, and Mallory is wounded, but manages to get back to camp without being captured.

The incident is covered up, but Mallory never really recovers. After his discharge, he returns to Philadelphia and takes up photography He wanders the streets taking pictures of ordinary people. He falls into a routine, which includes eating at the same diner every day. This fact gives Wideman the opportunity to offer another critique of the prison system. The owner, O.D., one day takes Mallory aside because he believes he is a man he can trust. O.D. then tells the story of a young man he took off the streets and fell in love with. He provided him with everything and tried to protect him from the life outside. Despite his best efforts, the boy ends up in prison. O.D. fears that he will not survive because he is young. He sees prison as a system designed to produce a kind of death for those inside and endless pain for those outside. At the same time, he worries that visiting the boy might only make things worse, since others will see his love for the boy and use it to make his punishment worse. His anxieties have made him incapable of any action, including writing letters. He only wants Mallory to listen and is grateful when he does. We later learn that the boy was the getaway driver for an attempt to rob O.D., during which the robber was shot and killed. Thus, the story is intended to be one more example of the risks involved in love.

Mallory befriends John Africa, whom he often sees walking dogs. Wideman uses this fictional encounter as a means to express some of the ideas associated with MOVE. In the process of telling part of O.D.'s story, John Africa describes the judicial system:

No problem proving human beings the worst-acting animals there is. Except in a court of so-called law, you never know, do you. Ain't worth doo-doo. Lawyers, judges, courts, what the system calls law ain't nothing but a humbug to keep a few folks on top, rest of us on the bottom. Hang people and fry people and gas and shoot and poison and feel good about it cause the law says it's all right. Damnedest thing when you think on it. What other animals you ever heard of invented the electric chair. What other animals build zoos to lock up their own damned kind. What animal's strayed so far from nature it's got to look for rules for living in books.[45]

John Africa offers his solution to the problem, and it is one of the oldest solutions in American history—resistance.

Confrontation's the only way things are going to start changing for the better. Our job's about making people see what they don't want to see. What's right in front of their eyes. We got to be such a royal pain in the ass nobody can ignore us. And we will be. Oh, yeah. Cops are coming, all right. And we'll be ready.

How can you be ready for all the manpower and firepower they'll throw at you if they decide to take you down.

Beauty is, we don't have to win. That's why we can't lose. Just got to let people know a war's going on. Gotta let folks in the Village [Powelton], the whole city see for themselves what we're up against. System wants invisible war. System don't want you to know who your real enemies are. It wants you scared and ignorant and confused so it can keep kicking your ass daily. So you don't make no progress, so you stay up in each other's faces fussing and doping and shooting and stealing and crying the blues and letting your children kill each other.[46]

While the language is very different, this identification of institutions and rules of law as an obstruction to human freedom can be traced back to the Pilgrims, to the American Revolution, to slave rebellions, to the Bill of Rights, to Henry David Thoreau's essay on civil disobedience and forward to women's suffrage and the civil rights movement and protests of various kinds in the 1960s. We can even argue that resistance is one of the major patterns in American history. From Wideman's point of view, the difference with MOVE and the reason for a government response that not even John Africa could imagine is the race of the protestors. The city of Philadelphia could use such extreme violence because it felt that blacks engaged in such protest did not deserve human rights, even if they were children. It does not matter that there is a black mayor in office, since by being there, he has, in effect, agreed to play by the rules of what John Africa calls "the system." Wideman keeps coming back to this story in book after book during this period because, in a sense, he takes on the responsibility to continue the mission of not letting the war be invisible. The city not only destroyed MOVE, but it attempted to conceal its actions, as suggested in *Philadelphia Fire*. Wideman takes on the role of witness to human destruction.

After the bombing in 1985, the results of which he photographs, Mallory moves to Pittsburgh. He takes up writing letters to the modernist sculptor Alberto Giacometti, who had died years earlier. In these letters, Mallory tries to describe his own art. One method he uses is to take dozens of exposures of the same negative. He connects this idea of layering images to what Giacometti does with sculpture, Romare Bearden with painting, and Thelonious Monk with music. The goal is to make people see the world differently, as having more dimensions and texture than we usually see. Uncertain about his work, he takes refuge in Kassima's home, becoming a grandfatherly presence. During the day, he takes his pictures, always asking permission of his subjects, including members of gangs, who are not certain how to respond to the old man. He eventually dies in the young woman's home, with the request that she destroy his photos and the negatives. His passing brings Robert and Kassima together again, as she tries to come to terms with yet another death of someone she has learned to care for. Through his tender concern for her, Robert is able to reenter her life.

At the funeral home where Mallory is taken, there is also the body of a recently murdered gang member. A war nearly breaks out as the killers confront the gang of the murdered boy; their purpose is to show as much disrespect for the dead as they did for the living. In the melee, Mallory's coffin is jostled, and his body falls into the street. Having been unable to destroy the pictures, Kassima brings them to the scene and spills them at the dead man's feet as she bends to protect him. She then launches into a sermon about the need for respect for the living and the dead; her preaching is listened to because she is the mother of boys who belonged to the gangs. The fighting stops as everyone picks up the images and sees themselves. They pass them around and then wander off, talking instead of shooting.

Wideman subtitles the book "A Love Story," but it is clearly not a conventional romance. It is about the frailty of human relationships in a world of violence, racism, and self-destruction. Each of the main characters comes out of a personal history of loss and abandonment. Yet, each one reaches out once again. Mallory does it through his art, as he seeks to give value to each person by photographing them. Robert initially goes with Kassima because he senses that she needs the touch of a man. She responds, believing that because he is older, he will be safer. All around them, the world is falling apart; the title of a review by Walter Mosley is "Love Among the Ruins." While the hope in the novel is very slender—after all, Mallory is dead and the world outside Kassima's house has not really changed—Wideman does suggest that there are at least individual reasons for hope.

One irony of the conclusion of this novel is that it is produced as Wideman's own marriage is coming apart. The family had lived under significant stress since Jake's arrest, with all the attendant publicity and the legal issues involved. Judith had finally finished her law degree at age 52 and established a practice focused on death penalty cases. John's career remained successful as he not only produced fiction and commentary on social and political issues, but also won prizes, including a MacArthur Foundation "genius" grant (1993). This celebrity put him in high demand for lectures, conferences, and media tours. One possible element in the dissolving of the relationship, in addition to times when John was unfaithful, is a pattern evident in the Harvard archive. Friends and acquaintances would initially address their letters or notes to both of them, but then spend the body of the message congratulating John for some achievement or talking about one of his works. Judy is virtually never talked to or about in such correspondence. She seems, for many people, to be simply an extension of him rather than a person in her own right. In effect, with the children gone, with a sense of isolation in the marriage, and with their lives taking different professional directions, John and Judy had less and less to keep them together. The final break came in 2000.

CHAPTER 7

The Writer as Social Critic

In addition to his fiction and his autobiographical works, Wideman has become known for his essays on social issues. These have often appeared in wide-circulation magazines such as *Harper's, Esquire, Sports Illustrated, The New Yorker, Progressive,* and even *Vogue.* He takes on prison reform, basketball, terrorism, and the everyday life of black men in America. His observations are often controversial and provocative.

The crisis known as 9/11 led him to make several public comments on the issue. In June 2002, he joined 70 other writers, intellectuals, and artists in signing a statement that appeared in the British newspaper *The Guardian.* This manifesto asserts that it is important for American citizens to let the world know that some of them opposed the policies that emerged from the events of September 11, 2001. They raise four specific objections to the American government. The first is the use of military force in Afghanistan, with threatened action in Iraq. They see these efforts as done in a spirit of revenge rather than national defense and leading to even greater violence around the world. Second, the government has created a category of people, living in the United States, who have no protection under the law. They are jailed in secret locations or deported without opportunities to defend themselves. Third, basic freedoms of speech and associations are attacked if they come from those who disagree with the policies; the Patriot Act extends police powers to allow for secret proceedings. Finally, the executive branch has overridden the traditional separation of powers by creating military tribunals and declaring certain groups terrorist organizations. They insist that the American people must protest such behavior and speak out against violations of American principles. The letter was signed, by among others, actor Edward Asner, novelist Russell Banks, music producer Mos

Def, radio personality Casey Kasem, Martin Luther King III, feminist journalist Gloria Steinem, and novelist and poet Alice Walker. The list suggests Wideman's association with a largely New York-based cultural and intellectual elite known for political activism.

He speaks directly in his own voice, though briefly, in an article in *The New York Times* on September 8, 2002. The newspaper asked 12 people to comment on the effects of 9/11 one year later. The group included several political figures and members of the legal profession as well as literary figures. Almost all have reputations as public intellectuals; that is, those professionals who comment on social, cultural, and political issues. Clearly, Wideman was now being placed in that category, in addition to his status as a fiction writer. In his brief comments, he worries that the nation has not struggled to find ways to truly understand what has happened:

> The most deeply affecting experiences remain mysterious, unspeakable. Even the commonplace partakes of mystery when we admit it uncensored. The mind explains away mystery to liberate us from suffering the disruptive duty of feeling, of bearing witness—especially when an unprecedented catastrophe assaults hard-won, precarious certainties. Explanations become evasions of responsibility.[1]

The language here is similar to that Wideman uses in talking about race. As with the treatment of African Americans and other minorities, he fears the nation will look for easy answers rather than understanding that some things may be unknowable and "unspeakable." His idea of bearing witness is an African American and, more generally, religious notion that we must acknowledge what we have seen, no matter how disturbing. The task is to testify to its reality, even if we cannot explain or understand it. Because it is often troubling, we cannot assume that we have clear answers or obvious solutions. Jumping to conclusions or believing that we can go back to what existed before will only get us into more trouble. This is why he says at the end of the essay, "This world, whether we like it or not, is as much a source of hope as it is a cause of grief."[2]

An essay on this subject that received considerable attention was "Whose War: The Color of Terror," which originally appeared in *Harper's Magazine* in March 2002, and was later selected for *Best American Essays of 2003*. He opens by pointing out that he is writing five months after the September 2001 attacks on the World Trade Center and other sites. He is also living on the Lower East Side of New York City and thus not far from where the attack occurred. He adds to this the fact that he is a black man from a black neighborhood in Pittsburgh, with a long experience with racism. This fact is relevant because people in that community had to have a sense of solidarity in order to survive, and he believes that this is precisely what the nation needs in its moment of crisis. But he worries that he will simply add to the piles of words that have accumulated over 9/11—piles that he considers to be an affront to the dead.

His problem is that his racial experience causes him to question the government's sincerity about conducting a War on Terror. He reads the war in Afghanistan as a phony war that pretends to be about retaliation for the attacks on American citizens, but which is really a continuation of the long-running battles over control of the Middle East and its oil supplies. Moreover, the language about this war, with its emphasis on attacking the forces of darkness, sound to him too much like the language of racism inside the country. Promises have been made and not kept for people of color at least since slavery, and Wideman sees this phony war as a way of pretending that the real internal war does not exist. It is also a phony war because its stated goal—to end terrorism—is impossible and because it serves not so much to defend the nation as to impose "rabid nationalism."[3] This point, he believes, is the true danger to the country:

> The Afghan campaign reflects a global struggle but also reveals a crisis inside America—the attempt to construct on these shores a society willing to sacrifice democracy and individual autonomy for the promise of material security, the exchange of principles for goods and services. A society willing to trade the tumultuous uncertainty generated by a government dedicated to serving the interests of many different, unequal kinds of citizens for the certainty of a government responsive to a privileged few and their self-serving, single-minded, ubiquitous, thus invisible, ideology: profit. Such a government of the few is fabricating new versions of freedom. Freedom to exploit race, class, and gender inequities without guilt or accountability; freedom to drown in ignorance while flooded by information; freedom to be plundered by corporations. Freedom to drug ourselves and our children to the addictive mix of fantasy and propaganda, the nonstop ads that pass for a culture.[4]

Here, we see another version of Wideman's jeremiad. Unlike *Cattle Killing,* however, this one is not so much about race as about the quality of American society. He sees it as a nation sacrificing its principles for questionable and even corrupt benefits. Like many before him, going back to the Puritans, he views materialism as a threat to higher values. Security for him is not only a matter of national defense, but also personal advantage. His list of new freedoms are only ways to turn our backs on the work needed to create a true national community.

For him, as a writer, one of the most important sacrifices being made is language and reason. The words terror and terrorist become ways of dehumanizing those opposed to us. One traditional way of defining them, as Wideman points out, is as governing through intimidation or using particular methods in conflict. Such meanings could then be applied to George Washington in the American Revolution, since he did not use the conventional strategies of the time to fight the British.[5] In the contemporary world, these words have become synonymous with evil. The antagonist then does not have to be treated as a person, but only as a thing to be destroyed. There can be no dialogue or reasonable exchange of views. Those who define themselves as victims of terror can engage in holy war in order to punish the evil-doers.

Wideman wants to be clear on one point—the destruction of the towers, and especially of the people inside, was a nearly unprecedented criminal act. He in no sense tries to justify such behavior. But he sees that attack (an act of terror by any of his definitions) as different from a war on terror. Terror is a part of human life, from the child's fear of the dark to the gang wars of Homewood to horrific events such as the Holocaust. What Wideman hopes for is that 9/11 can become an opportunity to see ourselves as others see us, to question why we are so hated that young men will sacrifice themselves and thousands of others to express that hatred. It does not help to label them as pure evil, because then our reactions most likely will only lead to further violence. In the process, we also do damage to our own values. We need, he says, another way of thinking: "Although trouble may always prevail, being human offers us a chance to experience moments when trouble doesn't rule, when trouble's not totally immune to compassion and reason, when we make choices, and try to better ourselves and make other lives better."[6]

Not surprisingly, Wideman has also written a number of essays on black men and boys. They connect issues of race and gender to American society, culture, and history. "What Black Boys Are Up Against" appeared in *Essence* magazine in 2003 as part of a section entitled "Saving Our Sons." He opens with a startling statement, "In America, Black boys are not supposed to grow up. . . ."[7] By this, he does not mean that they live a Peter Pan life, but rather that the health, education, legal, and economic systems operate against them achieving maturity. He argues that American society has a love/hate relationship with young African American men. He takes as an example an article in *The New York Times* on gangsta rapper 50 Cent. The piece both praises his music and presents him as doomed. One picture is a typical police mug shot. The other shows him as if he were already laid out on a coroner's table. It also uses the language of violence as though to establish his credentials as a black musician.

His point is that the culture defines authentic black manhood as criminal and rewards those who play up this image. But this same point of view allows for the judicial system to incarcerate vast numbers of these boys and for the young men to use violence against each other to prove their manhood. Wideman is not certain why they buy into this self-destructive image of themselves. Perhaps it has to do with a point he made in *Fatheralong,* that black fathers cannot provide strong models for their sons because they have been deprived of sufficient opportunities for achievement in the society.

As he does so often, he is very concerned with language. The word "boy" usually is associated with childhood—a status we like to associate with protection, nurture, dreaming, and play. But certainly for those in environments of poverty, with health issues, drugs, poor schools, and violence, a normal childhood is nearly impossible. Moreover, the word "boy" has historically been used to rob black males of their individuality and sense of personal worth.

More radically, perhaps, Wideman challenges the word "Black" in his title. For him, it can easily be a counterproductive term, even in African American communities: "Why do good grades and an articulate handling of the standard language make a colored kid White? Are gangsta style and a loud, nasty fluency in ghetto vernacular the only way a colored boy can prove he's not White?"[8] These questions are, of course, personal as well as general for the author. Wideman made the first choice, while his brother made the second, and much of his writing has been about the costs of those choices. Throughout his career, he works to break down the difference. His solution here is to say that the choice is a false one because race is a false idea: "Ascribing skin color quickly gets us hopelessly entangled in superstition, stereotyping, prejudice."[9]

Americans, he says, have always had trouble with color. Some claim color blindness when it comes to race, while others are absolutely certain that color is the only thing that really matters. Some see it as only a slight genetic difference, while others believe that it defines everything (either positively or negatively) that is important about a person. Wideman wants us to move beyond these categories:

> Don't think of color or gender as permanent, absolute, either/or categories. Think spectrum or rainbow. Think of colors shading seamlessly one into another, merging, mutating, morphing, alive, emergent. Think amalgamation, flux, evolving possibilities and surprises that should delight and instruct rather than frighten and isolate.[10]

What does this mean for young black men? Wideman closes by telling them that it is important to remember that poverty and race do not have to determine their fate; nor are they measures of their personal worth. Many people in society want them to believe that they are trapped by their situation and deserve what happens to them. The author encourages them to question everyone—"teachers, preachers, parents, military recruiters, employers, writers"—who claim to have easy answers for them. They must create their own stories and then step into them, always alert.

A more specific story of young African American men first appeared in *Essence* in November 1997 under the title "The Killing of Black Boys." It was then reprinted in *The Lynching of Emmett Till: A Documentary Narrative,* edited by Christopher Metress, who called it "one of the most complex meditations on Emmett Till."[11] A somewhat different version, called "Looking at Emmett Till," was included in *In Fact: The Best of Creative Nonfiction* in 2005; the discussion here is based on this version. As in most of Wideman's writing, his own life becomes part of his subject. He opens by remembering a nightmare he had as a child that continues to haunt him. He is being chased by a monster with a face too horrible to picture. He now believes that the face is that of Emmett Till. One reason for this belief is that he and Emmett would have been the same age (14) in 1955 and that he always was afraid to look at the image of the murdered boy. The image was published in *Jet* magazine because Emmett's mother insisted that the casket be open during the funeral in Chicago so all the world could see what Mississippi white men had done to her child. Wideman came across the photo by accident while looking through the magazine and at first did not recognize what it was. As soon as he did, he turned away and tried to read the story without going back to the picture The face continues to trouble him down to the present, apparently even in his dreams. The reason for this is that Emmett is a kind of double for him, with the implication that he could end up the same way. He sees the face of death, and it reminds him of his own face. In "What Black Boys Are Up Against," he had said that they are robbed of the security of childhood; here that happens to

him. The face reminds him of African fetish figures, which are designed
to remind humans of the reality of evil.

He moves away from Till to talk about the role of *Jet* magazine in
his family. His parents could not afford a subscription, but his father's
sister Catherine, who lived just down Copeland Street in Shadyside, always got copies. After she and her husband read them, they would pass
them on to Edgar and Bette. Wideman points out that skin color often
determined attitude toward the magazine, which as he indicates, both
protested and celebrated racial segregation.[12] Lighter-skinned people,
such as his mother and her family, were unlikely to buy it, though they
were just as likely to talk about its contents. In contrast, the Wideman
clan, much darker, both supported and enjoyed it. One thing that kept
his mother from buying it was that the only place in the neighborhood
where magazines were sold was Brackman's Pharmacy, and Brackman
not only did not carry any materials aimed at African Americans, but he
really did not want them in his store. (He believed that young men such
as John would steal if he was not watched, so Wideman often pilfered
comic books, which he then threw away, as a form of revenge.)

However they got it, *Jet* was important to the community. Wideman's
mother would get together at her mother's house and not only talk about
the contents, but also relate them to people they knew in Homewood:
"I'd eavesdrop while they riffed on *Jet's* contents, fascinated by how
they mixed Homewood people and gossip into *Jet's* features, improvising new stories, raps, and sermons I'd never imagined when I'd read it
alone."[13] Here, we see how Wideman cannot resist talking about storytelling techniques, even when apparently concerned with a very different
subject. He has left Emmett Till behind to describe the very methods he
uses and which he has repeatedly said he learned from members of his
family. The very way of writing the essay shows him doing what his
mother did. This material about *Jet,* in fact, is not part of the earlier
version. He adds it precisely because the magazine brought him in touch
with African American life in ways that none of the other media of the
time could, including the awful aspects, such as Till's murder.

He imagines another connection that might help explain the killing.
He tries to remember if he, like Emmett, carried around a picture of a
white girl in his wallet. Such a picture would have been a symbol of
status among black boys, for whom, even in the North, actual cross-
racial romances would be dangerous. Such an image would be powerful
in Homewood, on Chicago's South Side, where Emmett was from, in
Money, Mississippi, or in his paternal grandfather's hometown of Promised Land, South Carolina. So, Wideman imagines himself showing off,

like he thinks Emmett did in Mississippi, which would provoke a challenge from the Southern boys—a challenge that proved deadly, just as it would have if a young John had done the same thing in South Carolina.

In another part not in the original essay, Wideman talks about an earlier encounter with death. In 1953, his grandfather John French died of a stroke, and the effect on the 12-year-old boy was devastating. He slept for days at a time and would not speak to anyone. While the family assumed that this was grief, he could not tell them that he also wanted everything about the old man to disappear from the house where he had lived with his mother and siblings a short time earlier. Love became fear; he would not go into rooms associated with his grandfather. He and all the dead became ghosts haunting the boy.[14] This reaction helps us to understand the dread of the image of Emmett he finds later.

Having established all these personal connections, Wideman then turns to an analysis of the killing of Till. First, he connects the murder to what he calls "the circle of racism." By this, he means that many people believed and continue to believe that black males are born criminal, born to violate the rules of society (rules that those with such racial attitudes created). So, Emmett Till dared to speak to a white woman; therefore, he deserved to die. But his crime was not speaking; it was being black. In Wideman's view, acts of discrimination, insult, and violence have been and continue to be justified by this belief; when black men, of whatever age, react angrily or unlawfully to this treatment, their behavior only provides more evidence for prejudice, thus completing the circle.

Wideman traces the causes of the killing even deeper, to the slave trade that began 500 years ago. That trade was built on the idea that a truly New World could be created for Europeans, with the aid of unpaid African labor. It was a dream of escape from the poverty, class divisions, and religious battles of the Old World, an opportunity for prosperity and liberty for everyone with white skin. But to achieve it, the new residents had to ignore the moral and religious implications of slavery. They did this by dehumanizing the slaves, by labeling them as less than human. This viewpoint, now called racism, continued to develop, even taking on some claims to be scientific. The Civil War and Reconstruction did nothing to change this attitude. Instead, we have segregation, denial of black rights, and racial terrorism into the present. For Wideman, that centuries-old belief still operates, over 50 years after Emmett Till's death. He does not believe that Americans consciously hold racist attitudes; rather, he thinks that the nation is in a state of denial about the conditions of privilege that have traditionally been granted to whites through the social arrangements established by racism.[15]

Wideman then retells the story, using the account provided in several places by Emmett's cousin, Curtis Jones. In this version, he is challenged by the local boys and so says to Mrs. Bryant, as he is leaving the store, "Bye Bye, Baby." Four nights later, Roy Bryant and J. W. Milam come to the home of Emmett's uncle and drag the boy away. They are charged with murder, but found not guilty by an all-white jury. They then sell their story for $4,000 to *Look* magazine. He dreams again, only this time he dreams revenge on Money, Mississippi, with a band of black men going into the town and destroying everything and everyone. But he also has another idea:

> Sometimes I think the only way to end this would be with Andy Warhol-like strips of images, the same face, Emmett Till's face replicated twelve, twenty-four, forty-eight, ninety-six times on a wall-sized canvas. Like giant postage stamps end to end, top to bottom, each version of the face exactly like the other but different names printed below each one. Martin Luther Till. Malcolm Till. Medger Till. Nat Till. Gabriel Till. Michael Till. Huey Till. Bigger Till. Nelson Till. Mumia Till. Colin Till. Jesse Till. Your daddy, your mama, your sister, brother, aunt, cousin, uncle, niece, nephew Till. . . .[16]

The names are those of men who have worked, suffered, and in some cases, died to make changes in the way blacks are or were treated. The ellipses at the end suggests that the list could go on and on.

The end of the essay returns to the initial image of Emmett in *Jet* magazine. But now, it is something that he does not wish gone; instead, he wants it to be seen by all of us, so that we can begin the conversation that he believes is desperately necessary. In an added note to this version of the article, Wideman describes writing it as being like playing basketball, always improvising, and going with what is working, and not worrying too much about failure. He also asserts what has been the guiding principle of this study of him—he does not make strong distinctions between fiction and nonfiction. He even says that "biographers and historians are fiction writers who haven't come out of the closet."[17] Thus, even a piece such as this, based on historical reality, has a variety of points of view and constructs some scenes as though they were fiction. As he does so frequently, Wideman provokes the reader by saying that the work just read, called nonfiction, in a collection with "Nonfiction" in its title and which refers to real people, including himself, may also be fiction. He seems to mean that what we say about history, society, other people, or ourselves is something that we have to at least partially make up, because what we can know for certain is always limited. Even if we know external facts, that does not mean that we fully understand. By fiction, then, he does not mean simply something that is made up, but instead, something that we shape and define from our own perspective. He can never "know" Emmett Till, even though they had so many similarities. Everyone's life and experience is a mystery to others and often even to themselves. And for someone like Wideman, who makes his art out of his experience, it is important to control what others really know. So, he tells us about himself, then draws back to say, "This is not the whole truth, but you don't know what is or is not the truth."

He does precisely this in another piece in which he takes an everyday event for him and turns the speaker into a black Everyman. "The Seat Not Taken" was published as an Op-ed in *The New York Times* in 2010. He describes riding the high-speed train from his home in the city to his work at Brown University in Providence, Rhode Island. He takes on the role of sociologist conducting an experiment. His conclusion is troubling: "Almost invariably, after I have hustled aboard early and occupied one half of a vacant double seat in the usually crowded quiet car, the empty place next to me will remain empty for the entire trip."[18] He is convinced that the explanation is at least partially race, because, unless the car is full, nine times out of ten, the seat will remain empty. He considers, like a good social scientist, a set of variables, such as smell, visible hostility, clothing, and even deformity, and rejects all of them as explanations. Since the cost of the train is relatively high, it also cannot be low economic status that distinguishes him.

He does point to the advantage that he gains through this occurrence—room to spread out, to rest his briefcase or reading materials. And it is more comfortable than traveling by air or car. But he is disturbed that a nation that had recently elected an African American as President and that proclaimed that it was postracial, would not know what to do in the presence of a black man as part of their ordinary lives. He closes with his sense of the problem:

But the very pleasing moment of anticipation casts a shadow, because I can't accept the bounty of an extra seat without remembering why it's empty, without wondering if its emptiness isn't something quite sad. And quite dangerous, also, if left unexamined. Posters in the train, the station, the subway warn: if you see something, say something.[19]

In the phrase "casting a shadow," Wideman is echoing W.E.B. Du Bois, who a century earlier had talked about "the problem of the color line" in *The Souls of Black Folk*, a book which Wideman had written a new introduction for about a year before this article. Du Bois pointed out that even white people of good will seem to have difficulty treating African Americans as simply other members of the society, as true equals and fellow citizens.[20] For both writers, the shadow of race is something "dangerous," and it is their responsibility to call attention to it.

The article drew considerable attention among readers of *The Times*. Some shared common experiences on that train line; one older man recalled that it was, in some sense, an improvement over his early 1940s trips, when the train would stop as soon as it crossed the Potomac River so that he and his mother (as well as others) could move to the Colored cars that had been added for the trip to Mississippi. A white woman agreed that race was a factor, but that it moved in all directions; she rode through black and Hispanic areas of Los Angeles with no one willing to sit beside her on her way to teach at a primarily minority school. A third reader attempted to complicate the issue by pointing to actual earlier studies which showed that people in public transportation tend to sit next to those most like themselves. *The Awl*, a website devoted to current events, discussed the article a day after it appeared. Dave Bry, one of the writers, recalled an incident just after he arrived in New York City when he was asked by a black man in a suit to hail a cab for him because none would stop. Bry initially did not understand the problem, but notes that when he stepped into the street, a taxi immediately stopped. He then goes on to note that it became a ritual for him to hail cabs for the mixed-race staff of *Vibe* magazine, for which he worked. Posts from others confirm his experience and that of Wideman, though some, curiously, indulge in the language of blackface in an attempt to be humorous.[21]

Wideman has, as should be apparent by now, a history with the prison system, going back to Robby's difficulties even before his conviction for murder. Beginning in the mid-1990s, he became more actively involved in publishing material about incarceration. That work took the form of magazine articles and other short essays specifically related to his son Jake and the internationally known case of Mumia Abu-Jamal.

In his commentaries on prisons, Wideman naturally falls into a personal voice, since he has so much experience with the reality of incarceration. So, when he provides an article for the *Washington Post*, he starts by talking about packing for a trip to Arizona, a rather harmless comment on the surface. He explains that he includes things that are unlikely to set off alarms at airport or prison security. But quickly it becomes much more. He thinks about what it will be like to hug his son Jake and imagines which of the clothes he will be wearing when that happens. So the packing becomes exciting as he reminds himself of its purpose.

He then quickly shifts to criticism:

> Prison depends on make-believe—it's a cruel, artful installation designed to deceive inmates into thinking they've disappeared. Visits attempt to dispel one illusion with another. The sign above the prison entrance doesn't read, Abandon Hope; it says, Abandon Yourself. Prisoners are stripped down to the bone. Clothes gone, possessions impounded, name changed to a number, family and friends removed from sight. The basic rules of society don't hold. For all intents and purposes, there are no rules that apply because the inmate is reconstituted as an unperson with no rights the prison must respect. Choice by choice, as the inmate accepts or refuses the conditions of the prison environment, a new identity is formed. Compromises are effected between the ghostly remains of who you once believed you were and who you must be in circumstances cunningly, brutally contrived to destabilize and play you.[22]

Dante posts the sign, "Abandon hope, all who enter here," over the gates of hell, and the Supreme Court in 1857, in the Dred Scott decision, said that slaves had no rights a white man was bound to respect. Thus, for Wideman, the prison system combines qualities of hell and slavery, in robbing the prisoner not only of his freedom, but of his very identity. Every connection with his previous life is broken. Survival within this system requires various kinds of compromise that more or less rob him of his sense of self.

Wideman then, as often happens, changes the perspective. His son Dan has joined him and brought along his daughter Qasima, whom Wideman is reminded he has not seen in two years. The story is switched to her perspective. We learn of a photograph taken when she was a baby, held in Jake's arms, just as Jamila had been taken to visit Robby when she was very young. But Qasima does not understand the picture, since she has no memory of the experience. Instead, she puzzles over why they are here. She shows signs of confusion, wondering why they are visiting someone in prison, why, if he is a nice man, he cannot come home with them.

He then describes the walk the three of them make to the prison, a walk very different from what he recorded much earlier in the story "Solitary." Qasima walks between her father and grandfather, dressed in a navy and white dress, but also wearing a *hijab,* the traditional scarf worn by Muslim women. Dan's wife is a Muslim from Sierra Leone, and the daughter is expected to make this concession to Islamic tradition. Wideman wonders what the people of Phoenix must think, seeing two African American men with a child wearing a garb they associate with terrorists.

Once they get to the prison, then the experience becomes much like that of the earlier story. They must wait outside in the heat until a guard comes to get their information. Then, they follow another guard through levels of lockup to get to the visiting area. At this point, the story stops, as Wideman points out that it is not yet time for strangers to intrude upon his son. Instead, he tells the story of the phoenix, which lives for 500 years before being consumed by flames. Since the city of Phoenix was established in 1867, he imagines that it will be 363 years before the city will be consumed and the desert clean again.

A *New Yorker* article that became part of *Fatheralong* attempts to show us how John and Judy are dealing with their son's imprisonment about eight years after he started serving his sentence.[23] "Father Stories" takes the form of a letter to Jake, in part about the importance of storytelling as a way of making sense of the world. He recounts a time when his son was very young at Camp Takajo. One morning, the keys for all the vehicles—cars, mowers, trucks—were missing. Hours later, they were all found in a pile under the boat dock. Jake's grandfather, Morton Goldman, who owned the camp, suspected that the child had taken them, though he was small and had been told not to touch them. Morton wanted John to talk to the boy, to see if he had any reaction. John refused, believing his son incapable of such behavior. Clearly though, by the time of telling the story—15 years or more after the event—John believes that Jake is responsible. As readers, we should wonder why he tells the story. Knowing all the things that happen later, it could be an early sign of trouble that the family missed. But given the title of the article, it is more likely about John and his devotion to his son, regardless of what others might think.

In another example, the father misreads the son's fear. John takes Jake for a walk one evening in their Laramie neighborhood; at one point, he puts him on his shoulders and behaves like a horse being ridden. Suddenly, the boy is terrified and holds his father's hair as tightly as possible. John, worried that Jake had hit a low-hanging branch, finally manages to get him down. He realizes then that his son has a fear of leaves. John responds to this phobia in the present by telling of his own fear of feathers, based on a horror movie he saw when a child. The fear is specific—it is feathers on living birds he cannot tolerate. For years, he has a hatred of pigeons and tells of wanting to burn one when a student at college. In this case, the point seems to be that everyone has fears, and sometimes they react irrationally to them.

He then explores Judy's response to the loss of her son. He says that her pain was something that he had difficulty handling and that he tried to explain to her the value of storytelling as a way of dealing with it. But again, he misread the situation. She had to find her own way of working through the grief; he could not "fix" it for her. John's own sorrow comes in part from a deep-seated belief that there was nothing he could do to change the situation. He would take Jake's place if he could, but knows that such a thing is impossible. One reason that it is important to speak these things is that Wideman knows that many of the stories of his own fathers, going back generations, have been lost, in part because of the conditions of slavery and racial prejudice. Knowing that, he wants to keep the stories flowing, even with a son who is in a situation much like slavery.

The story that is not offered here, of course, is the story of the death of Eric Kane, the boy that Jake stabbed to death. We do not get Jake's voice trying to make sense of those events. We also do not get a story from John that would help readers understand his own role as father in that tragedy. He provides us with examples of childhood behavior and fears and with parental sorrows, but avoids making connections to the real story that needs to be told. In other words, he does not even begin the equivalent of *Brothers and Keepers*. But it is precisely that father story that needs to be told.

Wideman's comments on Mumia Abu-Jamal combine his long-lasting interests in the prison system, in the MOVE organization, and in the city of Philadelphia. Abu-Jamal, born in 1954, was a political activist from Philadelphia who began his career while still in high school. After being beaten by a group of whites, perhaps including a police officer, at a George Wallace rally, he helped to form the Philadelphia branch of the Black Panther Party. Later that year (1969), he dropped out of school to work full-time for the party. He left the Panthers in late 1970 and returned to school, but was suspended for distributing revolutionary pamphlets. He began working at local radio stations, reporting and conducting interviews with such local and national celebrities as Julius Erving, Bob Marley, and Alex Haley (author of *Roots* and co-author of *The Autobiography of Malcolm X*). At one point, he served as president of the Philadelphia Association of Black Journalists. He became well known for his support of MOVE, the organization Wideman gives fictional accounts of in *Philadelphia Fire* and *Two Cities*. He provided coverage of the trial of MOVE members for the 1978 killing of a policeman in a confrontation at their Powelton Village compound.

On December 9, 1982, police officer Daniel Faulkner made a stop of a vehicle driven by Abu-Jamal's younger brother, William Cook. Abu-Jamal crossed the street from the cab he drove part-time. What happened next is at the heart of the controversy of the case and has never been fully explained. The end result, however, was that Faulkner was killed and Abu-Jamal seriously wounded. He was charged with first-degree murder. He attempted to defend himself, but, according to the judge, he kept disrupting the proceedings and thus was appointed an attorney. The trial ended when he was found guilty and given the death penalty. The case became internationally known and a series of unsuccessful appeals were filed. At the time Wideman became involved, Abu-Jamal was still on death row. In April 2011, the Third Circuit Court upheld the conviction, but said that for technical reasons, the death penalty was not allowed. The prosecutor's office has said it will not seek a rehearing to impose the death penalty. Abu-Jamal is no longer on death row.[24]

Wideman's essays have Abu-Jamal as a secondary subject. Both were published in 1995 and are included in material associated with Abu-Jamal. The first, "Doing Time, Marking Race," initially appeared in *The Nation,* followed by publication in *In Defense of Mumia* (1996) and then *Behind the Razor Wire* (1999). As usual, Wideman first establishes his personal connection to the subject. One of his credentials for writing the essay is family: "From every category of male relative I can name— grandfather, father, son, brother, uncle, nephew, cousin, in-laws—at least one member of my family has been incarcerated."[25] Given what we know of his family history in Pittsburgh, this statement is not surprising, though he has not anywhere in print identified all those he is including. We can assume that John French's drinking and gambling at some point got him arrested and that Uncle Carl's drug addiction and Edgar WIdeman's temper would have had the same result. In other words, for some of them, the jailing would have been very short-lived. The author admits that he too has been arrested. He also claims knowledge based on his heritage of slavery, which he defines as a particular kind of prison.

His criticism is aimed at the media and politicians who believe that more prisons are a solution for social problems. He describes candidates running on a "get tough" platform as the equivalent of school bullies who attack the weaker members of the community; he notes that they and the audiences they address assume that they will never be caught up in the judicial system they want to create. This means that they believe that those who will be the targets are fundamentally different from themselves and not really a part of the same society. He shows this through a brief example: "I recall a sentencing hearing in a courtroom, the angry father (white) of a victim urging a judge (white) to impose upon a young man (black), who'd pleaded guilty, the most severe punishment because 'they're not like us, Your Honor.' "[26] The author's point is that the father identifies with the judge and the legal system, which he views as designed to put away those who "are not like us."

Wideman sees this as a fundamental distortion of principles of equality and justice and a change in the direction of the country. He points out that there is no evidence that more prisons and longer sentences make the society more secure. Instead, we have a prison complex run by technocrats and bureaucrats who are more interested in the designing elaborate structures, such as Pelican Bay, a super-maximum prison in California, than in rehabilitating prisoners and returning them to society. What especially concerns him is the implied return to a more racist society as a result. He points out that while African Americans are 13 percent of the population and 13 percent of regular drug users, they are 35 percent of those arrested for drug use, 55 percent of those convicted, and 74 percent of those imprisoned for this crime. In other words, law enforcement operates, at least in this case, to remove young black men from American life, creating what Wideman considers another form of apartheid. One unintended consequence of this racialized program is to bring gang attitudes and activities into the prison. Older men who had been incarcerated used to serve as models for survival and even rehabilitation. But the movement between the street and the prison means that the same attitudes and activities that have worried Wideman throughout his career about the streets of Homewood appear behind the walls, The effect is more violence, more drugs, more death. The essay is a call to the nation to overcome its "willed ignorance" and to look for solutions in dealing with poverty, poor schools, and unsafe streets.

More directly relevant to the Mumia case is the introduction Wideman wrote for *Live from Death Row*, a collection of Abu-Jamal's writings published in 1995. Selections from this essay appeared in 2003 on the website EMAJ (Educators for Mumia Abu-Jamal). Unlike much of his writing, here Wideman offers very little of his personal or family history. He briefly mentions the writing of *Brothers and Keepers*, but only to point out information he discovered in his research for that book.

Instead, he focuses on problems in American society and in the prison system and then suggests how Abu-Jamal can help us work toward solutions. He points to the history that his subject studies, such as the Dred Scott decision of 1857, in which the Supreme Court determined that not even free blacks had citizenship rights, or that when Nelson Mandela was freed from prison, he still did not have voting rights in the country he was expected to lead. Wideman's own discovery was that the United States leads the world in the percentage of its citizens that are incarcerated. He worries that such a history and current reality will lead people to give up trying to achieve change; he believes that there is a real need for struggle and responsibility, which Abu-Jamal demonstrates.

For Wideman, if anything, the problems in matters of race are becoming worse. In addition to political campaigns in which candidates battle to demonstrate which one is tougher on crime and more willing to build prisons, there is also the so-called IQ controversy. In 1994, Richard Herrnstein and Charles Murray published *The Bell Curve,* arguing that both environmental and genetic factors were responsible for the differences in IQ scores. They specifically pointed out racial differences in the scores. In effect, they argued that African Americans were born less intelligent on average than whites. This book revived claims that began in the beginning of the 20th century, with the earliest uses of IQ testing to determine service in World War I. The debate was revived in the 1960s and early 1970s with the work of Arthur Jensen and William Shockley, who insisted that the evidence of intellectual inferiority meant that enhanced educational programs such as Head Start would have little impact. Herrnstein and Murray's version of the argument aroused controversy both among scientists and leaders of the African American community. Wideman sees this issue as part of an effort to revive racism and to roll back the gains of the civil rights movement. But he also suggests that more than race is involved. He looks also at increasing white poverty and the decline of the middle class as evidence of a more general effort to establish an economic and political elite, with everyone else as second-class citizens. Prisons are one means among many to deal with the social disorder that comes from these divisions in America.

Given this national situation, Wideman wonders why Mumia's words are considered so dangerous. He notes that he has been censored by public radio, for which he was once a local celebrity. Since, at the time, the writings of several African Americans—Oprah Winfrey, O. J. Simpson, Maya Angelou (we could add Wideman himself to the list)—were receiving positive attention, the question is why this particular man was treated differently. This leads to a discussion of the nature of most

African American work, especially autobiography, from the time of the slave narratives. In the early works, it was an individual, through his or her own efforts, who made the move from the world of slavery to the world of freedom, with all that this meant in terms of identity, education, and the ability to tell one's own story. In the modern version, the main character moves from "ghetto to middle class, ignorance to education, unskilled to professional, despised gangster to enlightened spokesperson."[27] Such stories are safe in that they do not really challenge the order of the society; in fact, they demonstrate that individuals from any background can succeed. This claim means that nothing has to be done for those at the bottom, who remain there because they do not have what it takes to improve themselves. It is not the responsibility of the rest of society to help them.

Abu-Jamal's argument is different, according to Wideman. He thinks in terms of the mass of people stuck at the bottom because the policies of the country are designed to keep them there. He seeks to be a voice, not just for himself, but for all of those who are silenced. While he may seek his own freedom, he does not believe it can be meaningful without the freedom of others. Wideman uses the tale of "The Emperor's New Clothes" to communicate his point. Abu-Jamal is the boy who reveals that there are no clothes, that the emperor is naked. His importance, then, is his willingness to expose the illusions of American society.

A somewhat allegorical narrative of prison life, also included in *In Defense of Mumia,* is "Ascent by Balloon from the Yard of Walnut Street Jail." Published the same year (1996) in the African American journal *Callaloo,* the story describes the first hot-air balloon ride in the United States. The actual event took place in Philadelphia in 1793, the same year as the yellow fever epidemic. Wideman imagines that an African American prisoner accompanies Jean Pierre Blanchard on the brief journey from Philadelphia to Woodbury, New Jersey. The prisoner, Charles Williams, opens the story by talking about the celebrity status he had achieved through his experience: "I am the first of my African race in space. For this achievement I received accolades and commendations galore. Numerous offers for the story of my life . . . A petition circulates entreating me to run for public office."[28] He notes that President George Washington himself was present at the event as well as a crowd of 40,000. But what would seem to be a happy occasion very quickly begins to become more ominous. In the midst of patriotic statements about how the new country is willing to give opportunities to even the most despised of its residents, he tells us that he initially knew little of Blanchard's project because he was "one of those unfortunates who must wear a black hood and speak not, nor be spoken to."[29]

Here, Wideman demonstrates his research into the early American prison system. The first American penitentiary was proposed in Philadelphia in 1787, though it did not open until 1829. It was designed on the Quaker principle that incarceration should serve the purpose of making the criminal think about and become penitent for his unlawful behavior. Solitary confinement was the method for doing this, with the prisoner prohibited from speaking or being spoken to by anyone, including the guards. Each cell of Eastern State Penitentiary had outside access that was surrounded by a 10-foot wall, so that the inmate could only see the sky, encouraging him to look to God. Whenever he went to any other outside area, he was required to wear a black hood.[30] Eastern State, called Cherry Hill in the story because of its location outside the city, was designed to replace the Walnut Street Jail, which could not handle the growing prison population as the city expanded.

Charles Williams was Prisoner Number One in the new facility. He tells us that his cell was damp and cold and that it never improved; in addition, the cell had little light or ventilation. He quickly returns from his complaining to talk about the flight itself. We learn that the reason he is there is to serve as a guinea pig. Doctor Benjamin Rush, who appeared in "Fever" and *The Cattle Killing,* here wants to test the effects of thinner air on the human body. A black man was useful, "since who better than one of us, with our excitable blood and tropically lush hearts."[31] Williams reports that he was very careful to carry out his responsibilities. Intruding into this adventure is the story of the yellow fever epidemic, a version of which Wideman has used before.

The narrator then jumps to what appears to be the real business of the story. He describes the various punishments (tortures) used on disobedient prisoners. One particular white man was especially difficult, since he refused to obey the rule of silence. When "ice water ducking, bagging with a hood,[and] flogging" did not work on Matthew Maccumsey, the iron gag was used. This instrument was similar to a horse's bit, and a variation of it was used during slavery. Williams goes into great detail about how it was attached to the head with the specific purpose of causing maximum pain. Williams witnessed this because black prisoners were assigned to punish whites and whites to punish blacks, so as to increase racial hostility within the prison. The end result was that Maccumsey died. Historically, this torture was one of the reasons for the shift to the methods of Eastern Penitentiary, though Wideman presents it as happening in that prison. Williams keeps returning to the events on the balloon as though to erase these unpleasant memories. Near the end of the story, we learn that the ride is only a fantasy, that Williams had been sent out into the yard of the jail to get his shoemaking tools at the moment of the balloon's ascent. But even at the end, he cannot give up the dream: "How carefully I set the pulse glass above a vein. Register the measured ebb and flow, each flicker the heart's smile and amen."[32]

By setting the story in the distant past, Wideman can appear to be removing it from the present day debates about the treatment of prisoners and even cases such as Abu-Jamal's. But by situating it in what was then the national capital around the time of the passage of the Constitution, he clearly makes it very American. It also fits into his other arguments, since Eastern Penitentiary was the most modern facility of its time; people came from around the world to see it and went home to build versions of it. Its new methods, design, and technology fit very well into the author's view that huge investments continue to be made in building prisons, but his deliberate confusion of the practices at Walnut Street and Eastern show that the objective of dehumanizing prisoners remains the same. In addition, the idea of using Williams as a guinea pig reflects the long history of medical experiments on black people, such as the Tuskegee syphilis research in which the United States Public Health Department allowed poor black men to suffer from the venereal disease for 40 years without treatment in order to trace the development of the disease.[33] The torture and killing of Maccumsey seems a direct reflection of the situation of Abu-Jamal, since part of the controversy around him has to do with his insistence on speaking up both before and after his imprisonment. It is his voice that in some ways has been most threatening to those in power. So, with this story, Wideman finds a way to suggest that our American attitude toward prisons and prisoners has always involved a sense of moral superiority and a desire to rob the incarcerated of their rights and their humanity. Whether we do this in the name of vengeance or rehabilitation, the effect, he insists repeatedly, is that we deny the basic humanity of other people.

John Wideman is often seen by those who comment on him as a writer primarily concerned with issues affecting African American men. We have seen this often in this book and in this chapter, even though he frequently writes about black women, especially those in his family. The same is mostly true about the third subject of this chapter—basketball. He has written articles on Michael Jordan and Dennis Rodman and a book about his own obsession with game, entitled *Hoop Roots*. But it is useful to begin this section with a discussion of a piece he did on his daughter, Jamila, titled "My Daughter the Hoopster," which appeared in *Essence* in 1996. Ironically, given John's own ambitions for himself and his sons, she is the most successful player in the family. She was a high school All-Star and led her Stanford team to the NCAA Final Four three years in a row. Picked in the first round in the first draft of the WNBA, she played for four years before joining a professional team in Israel, which she led to the national championship. She then attended law school at New York University and became a public interest attorney in New York.

Wideman's essay about her begins almost as a praise song, "I love my daughter and love the game of basketball, and the intersection of these two grand passions astounds, exhausts and tickles me."[34] He describes his excitement at watching her play in the NCAA semi-finals. But this happiness is touched by a sense of mortality. This is a child who almost died at birth, who came three months early.

> Some stories are haunted forever by the dire consequences of what might have been, even though, after teetering on the edge of disaster, things turned out well. Such stories remembered or retold remind you how split-second close good fortune is to calamity, how near things always are to turning out differently. This simple truth—nothing is given without the threat it may be taken away— is reaffirmed for me by Jamila's presence at the other end of the long-distance call or sitting across the dinner table.[35]

But the near-disaster is also a blessing, since she became a highly energetic child who was very athletic from an early age, able to compete in several sports against boys older and bigger. He sees her life as kind of miracle in that she went from that frail infant to a Kodak All-American basketball player by the time she finished high school. She was so talented that she was a starter on the Amherst team when she was still in seventh grade. She is then recruited by all the major college programs in the country.

In the present time of the essay, Wideman is sitting in the stands at the semi-final game of the NCAA championship, cheering and watching his child, proud as any parent would be. The article is a celebration of her achievement and her potential. The skills he emphasizes—intelligence, strategy, hard work—suggest not just her ability at playing this game, but also the possibilities for her life. It is in a sense, despite the memory of her difficult birth, perhaps the happiest piece of writing Wideman has ever done. What he omits from the story is that Stanford did not win the national championship during Jamila's time with the team. That omission indicates his desire to make the story about her personality rather than her success. In a sense, she is the child most like her father— overcoming great odds, defying prejudice (in her case, gender), and accomplishing great things, specifically in an area where he was also skilled.

His short article on Dennis Rodman, which appeared in the *New Yorker* the same year (1996) seems almost intended to be a counter essay to the one about his daughter and an earlier one on Michael Jordan. With Rodman, the emphasis is not on grace or speed but on notoriety. Wideman admits that he did not like Rodman as a player early in his career. He was too crude, too lacking in ability to shoot or run an offense. He compares him to the country cousin brought onto the playground courts of Homewood who was big and energetic but disruptive of the smooth city style. He was what the locals called cockstrong, meaning he tried but had no finesse. Such a player is often a liability to his own team and likely to hurt someone if he had a bad attitude.[36]

What happens over his career is that he becomes cocksure, that is, someone who figures out a place for himself in the game and, in doing so, changes the game. He also takes it to new levels of entertainment, with his cross-dressing, hair-dyeing, affair with Madonna, and visits to gay bars. Wideman notes that just as the women's game was becoming the purest form of basketball, Rodman was leading the professional sport to the edge of pure entertainment. On one side is David Stern, the commissioner of the NBA, who is shaping a corporate image for the league, especially with players such as Michael Jordan, and on the other side is Rodman, reminding everyone that it was only a game. Wideman revives an image he used in *Philadelphia Fire*, of Prospero and Caliban. Stern wants control; Rodman thumbs his nose at respectability; they are also Apollo and Dionysus. The problem, according to the author, is that Stern needs Rodman, both for his abilities and for his entertainment value; without him, the game becomes boring and fans and the media lose interest.

Wideman concludes with a question about why fans, officials, and the media are upset by Rodman's antics:

> Maybe that's what really scares , outrages, and entertains us about Dennis Rodman. He dons the uniform, takes the paycheck, but doesn't exactly go to work. He enters a zone where play is not reducible to anything else. The game we've taken for real disappears, and we're left to deal with the reality of Dennis Rodman in our faces.[37]

Wideman's position on his subject is ambivalent. On the one hand, he talks repeatedly about the purity of the game as it can be played, especially on urban courts. He has compared it to dance and to spiritual experience at various times. It is a sanctuary from the stresses of modern life, and he feels that that is corrupted when younger players are no longer willing to respect and learn from older players. He shows this attitude in *Two Cities*. On the other hand, the professional game, and to a lesser extent, the college game, take away the beauty in the name of control and authority. The game is something to sell rather than something to appreciate. When Rodman enters, all these versions are challenged. He draws attention to himself rather than the team. But he plays harder than anyone else. At the same time, he refuses to be serious about his work; he makes fun of the idea of black manhood with his appearance and behavior off court. For Wideman, this is an uncomfortable situation because he knows that this sport that he loves is, in fact, a children's game. Dennis Rodman keeps reminding him of that fact and for that the author is both irritated and grateful.

At the opposite end from Rodman is Michael Jordan. Wideman opens this essay describing the game as one that is most perfectly played in the air; and it is Jordan who has mastered this way of playing. He compares him to Auguste Renoir, who, according to Marcel Proust, changed the way we see women.[38] The writing takes the form of an interview, but as is so often the case, the author makes himself a part of the story. After the comments above, he tells a story of his arrival at Chicago Stadium, complete with a Jordanian cab driver, an outlandishly dressed, probably drunken prostitute, and a brief encounter with Jesse Jackson, with whom Wideman had traveled to South Africa for the release of Nelson Mandela from prison. Then, he discusses the perspective of the game from his end-line seat, though he never tells us what happens in the game.

He then switches to the interview, which he wants to do in terms of his own concerns, race and playground ball. While Jordan handles this well, it is clear that his answers are often careful, a point that Wideman will return to. He often uses "we" to mean black men or black people in general, but Jordan prefers to speak as "I," keeping the focus on his individual experience. This often borders on egotism and arrogance. When asked about what he likes about the game, he quickly moves into what makes him a superior player:

> I started when I was twelve. And I enjoyed it to the point that I started to do things other people couldn't do. And that intrigued me more. Now I still enjoy it because of the excitement I get from

fans, from the people, and still having the same ability to do things that other people can't do but want to do and they can do only through you. They watch you do it, then they think that they can do it. Or maybe they know it's something they can't do and ironically, that's why they feel good watching me. That drives me. I'm able to do something that no one else can do.[39]

He also recalls that he was on the bench often in high school. When they made the playoffs, he would not cheer for the team because he felt he should be contributing to their success. He actually wanted them to lose, so that they could see how important he was.[40] He also states that he believes that selfishness is part of achievement.

Wideman keeps coming back to his own experience, often in humorous ways. After Jordan's comments on his abilities, the author recalls a game he played with his sons at Camp Takajo:

About six years ago I was only forty-three, so I couldn't understand why the jumper was falling short every time, banging harmlessly off the front of the iron. After a summer-camp game my wife, Judy, had watched mainly because our sons, Dan and Jake, were also playing, I asked her if she'd noticed anything unusual about my jump shot. "Well, not exactly," she offered, "except when you jumped your feet never left the ground."[41]

While the joke is on Wideman, it is also a subtle criticism of Jordan's attitude. It says that we all get old, that our physical abilities decline, and that our illusions about how wonderful we are can come crashing down.

Another key point is the relationship between the public Michael Jordan and the private one. He is careful in what he says on matters outside basketball and works hard at maintaining a positive image, despite his awareness of his own imperfections. He believes that by being a corporate spokesman, he can demonstrate the opportunities available for African Americans in the society. But Wideman again undercuts the point. He goes back to a point before the interview, when he is helping out at a summer camp for high school kids from Springfield, Massachusetts. They are somewhat indifferent until they learn that he is going to interview Jordan. This gets them very excited, and Wideman uses the opportunity to talk about dreams and having the support of family in pursuing those dreams. Suddenly, one boy asks, "What if you don't have no family?"[42] At first, it stops everything. Wideman does not know how to respond. The reality of the boy's life intrudes on the fantasy of Jordan and of Wideman's own little sermon to the boys. The best he can come up with is the advice to find a friend (a "cut buddy") that you can depend on and who can depend on you.

The article closes with thoughts on time, one of Wideman's main themes. The boys want to get back to playing ball:

> I should have brought my sneaks. Should be thirty years younger. But why, seeing the perils besetting these kids, would anyone want to be thirty years younger? And why, if you're Peter Pan playing a game you love and getting paid a fortune for it and adored and you can fly too, would you ever want to grow a minute older?[43]

Michael Jordan gets to live a fantasy life, but, of course, he is not a fictional character. He will get older and have to return to the real world. Meanwhile, the older Wideman and the younger boys are trying to figure out ways to live in that reality every day. Wideman's problem, as will be seen in *Hoop Roots,* is getting older and still wanting to be part of the game. For the boys, the real issue is survival, and the author is not optimistic about their chances.

Hoop Roots (2001) is very much about time, survival, family, and the role of basketball in all of it. A frequent character in the book is his grandmother Freeda, who never saw him play a game. In fact, he tells us, none of the older members of his family, including his father, ever saw him play. And yet, they are part of the story of the game he started playing when he was little and that continues to be important at the age of 60, when the book is published. This is a memoir, in the sense that it focuses on a specific aspect of Wideman's life—his personal relationship to the game of basketball—even though he includes a wide range of other material. He opens by explaining that the book is really for himself at a point in his life when he must quit playing. "A way of holding on. Letting go. Starting a story so a story can end. Telling playground basketball stories, and if I tell them well they will be more about basketball than about me . . . I need the game more than it needs me."[44] He ties the game to family stories—of Danny losing a free-throw contest, of Jake winning a game with his jump shots, of Jamila playing her last college game in the national championship—and to troubles in his life: his marriage to Judy breaking up, his visit to Robby in prison, and the same day a trip to the VA hospital to see his father, who is suffering from Alzheimer's disease. The book, about a children's game, is a way to come to terms with where his life has gone.

He asks himself the question that he expects readers to ask—why is this game so important to someone who has had a successful career as a writer and teacher? He has several answers that he develops through the book. First, basketball was a way to move beyond Homewood and its limitations. Without it, he would not have gone to UPenn or received a Rhodes scholarship.[45] But it also allowed him to separate himself from the problems of the family and the streets while growing up; his second point is that the game requires hard, solitary work, meaning that he had reason to be away from home and to be on the protected space of the playground court. The third point is the beauty of the game. He compares it to music and to writing. The hard work and training often result in play that was almost magical, with the mind and the body working perfectly together. A key fourth point is that he learned the meaning of black manhood by being in the all-male space of the court. Older men taught younger men not only athletic skills but also the rituals of the game. They also told stories and reinforced traditions. Since Wideman's father was absent for much of his childhood, the game became a substitute.

The story itself begins when he is about nine. His father has left the family for the first of several times, and Bette has to move with the children back to her mother's house on Finance Street. It is a house primarily of women, though John French is still alive. Wideman's female relatives—mother, grandmother, aunts—are very protective of him and require that he stay in the fenced backyard or on the front porch where they can see him. On occasion, they allow him across the street into the grassy area below the railroad tracks. The point is that he should always be under surveillance or at least believe that he is. There are no houses on the other side of the street, but there is a factory. One day, he realizes that the white men who work there have set up a basketball hoop. He sneaks off to watch them; at their urging, he takes a couple of shots and then runs back home. While the episode is brief and simple, it teaches him important things—he can escape the attention of the women if he is careful, he can get the attention of men (even white men), and he discovers something that he can work at that might make him different.

While the book is typical of Wideman's writing in jumping back and forth in time, the next episode chronologically is called "Learning to Play." He is now about 12. His mother moved the family to Shadyside after another stay with her parents, but John French dies shortly after. Freeda has a stroke and is bedfast. John offers to stay and take care of her, which will free his aunts to do some of their chores in the house and the neighborhood. Each day, he spends the morning in her tiny room and then, in the afternoon, he goes to the basketball court that is connected to Westinghouse Park. Although he does not say so, this might be considered the beginning of his tendency to break his life into compartments. In Freeda's room, he is quiet most of the time, watching her and looking at early photographs of her. He also brushes her long straight hair and adjusts her pillows and covers. It is almost a sacred place for him.

Later, he goes into the active, vulgar space of men, where there is constant talk and motion on the court. He tells us that he is a different person there. He goes there in violation of the rules of the women, since he walks along the railroad tracks, which they have explicitly forbidden. Also, he practices a confident walk, so that he will appear more manly when he is there. Part of the reason he separates himself this way is fear. He had recently lost his grandfather, John French, and had not yet gotten over that, still feeling that he had been betrayed somehow. Now he has to face the possible loss of Freeda, who was the stable center of his universe. By breaking away from her world, he is each day getting ready for her death.[46] He says:

> After losing two fathers [John to death, Edgar to abandonment], I couldn't afford to love my grandmother too much. Or at least that's how it seemed to me then. It seemed important not to get too close, or rather, I needed to deny closeness, close down the room in my heart where she lived. Running to the court seemed one way out of the room. One way to prevent her from slipping from me.[47]

But the basketball court has its own rules and traditions that he has to learn. He is very careful here and elsewhere to point out that playground ball is not chaotic and purely individual. Its guidelines are flexible, depending on the conditions of the court (the size, location, surface) and the number of players, but everyone is expected to know how to play the game. For example, in selecting teams to start playing, two men who earned the right by making foul shots, alternate picking players until they reach five.[48] Other teams are made up from those not chosen or those who show up later. As long as a team wins, it gets to continue playing. The order of opponents is determined by calling out "Next." Everyone has an opportunity to join the game, and while it is rough, players can call fouls and any attempt to hurt an opponent is a violation of the rules. Older players serve as mentors for younger ones such as Wideman. Ed Fleming, who later played in the early NBA, served as a guide for John, and John's father, Edgar had played the same role for Fleming. Often the mentor teaches by doing, by making the "young-blood" look bad on an offensive or defensive play. But he also passes on stories of the court and great plays that have been made in the past. In this sense, playground basketball is much like the practices of African American folklore, which involve passing skills and tales from generation to generation.

Another important point he makes is that identity is determined by your actions on the court. There were men that he played with for years whose real names he did not know. He was always "Wideman" to Ed Fleming; decades later, when they meet at a funeral home, he calls him "John" for the first time in his life. Wideman does not know how he feels about the change, since it means that the playground is no longer their primary connection.

In addition, the game he plays at Westinghouse Park, unlike the more structured institutional games of school, college, and the professionals, is not limited by time. Teams have to win by two baskets, so they could conceivably go on forever. Inside the game, there are also no clocks for crossing the half-court line or taking a shot. It operates in what Wideman repeatedly, here and elsewhere, refers to as Great Time, meaning that past, present, and future exist simultaneously.[49] The player remembers what has been done before, recognizes the present situation, and anticipates what is coming next. In this flow, the mind is working rapidly, but it is working with the body, so that one does not stop to think and decide, but acts on the knowledge of the game, the players, and the situation instinctively. This is one reason that mentoring is so important, since more experienced players have more knowledge to draw on in that moment. As Wideman suggests, it is very much like "dancing with an invisible partner who's so good at dancing you forget who's leading, who's following, aware instead only of the rhythm, on time, stepping, and your body free, mind free, dancing the steps."[50] In describing this experience, he is referring to what psychologists have called "flow," defined as effortless action that seems outside of time where the goals are clear.[51] Here is Wideman's description:

> You're large, large and tiny too. Time a co-conspirator as you *break* from clock time. Everything happening simultaneously so you don't have to hurry or slow down. The game in its own good time comes to you as you come to understand its rhythms. You're not counting but the count's inside you, heard and unheard. Disciplined by years of experiencing the action, your body responds to the internalized measures, frees your playing mind. You let yourself

go where the game flows. Gametime opens like your mouth when you drew your first breath.[52]

Such an experience tells us why basketball is so important to him. Mihaly Csikszentmihalyi reports that people who go through this say that it gives them great joy, unlike anything in their everyday lives.[53] Given all the troubles in Wideman's life, including those of the time he is writing about and the time he is writing, memories of such happiness would be precious. The fact that he has to give up such possibilities because of his age, makes them bittersweet.

Having established these personal connections to the game, Wideman broadens out to discuss the larger meaning of basketball for the country. In a chapter titled "Who Invented the Jump Shot?" he imagines himself at a popular culture conference where this question is being debated. He is certain that "the fix is in," because he knows that white scholars will claim that a white man is responsible.

He then moves back in time to 1927 for the first road game of the team that became the Harlem Globetrotters. He imagines being the white man driving five black players from Chicago to Hinckley, Illinois, in a snowstorm. The town was directly west of the city. It was to be their first road game. Wideman shifts time momentarily to remembering his own Boys Club coach driving their under-12 team around Pittsburgh in a similar car.

He shifts again to the story of Rastas, the only black person in Hinckley because some years earlier, the townspeople had destroyed the black community and run off all the people. Rastas became part of the town accidently, when his pregnant mother fell off a freight train and died as she gave birth to him. He became a kind of pet or good-luck figure for Hinckley, though they endlessly exploited him. He was made to do all kinds of dirty work, for which he was only given scraps of food, never money. When the crude posters for the Globetrotters are put up, he sees himself in the images of the black men. He anticipates for days seeing them play, only to discover that he will not be allowed into the armory. He wanders the streets and finds a little immigrant girl injured. When he is found over her, the townspeople assume he has assaulted her and they apparently lynch him; we cannot be certain because Wideman refuses to tell the end of the story, though he does have the white manager (who is Jewish) regret the treatment of Rastas:

Our driver's appalled by the raw deal Rastas received. I'd never participate in something so mobbishly brutal, he swears. I would not assume appearance is reality. I would not assume truth lodges in the eye of the more numerous beholders. After all, my people also a minority. We've suffered unjustly too. And will again. I fear it in my bones.[54]

Since the story takes place just a few years before the rise of the Nazis, his fear is a prophecy. But it is complicated by the fact that the hostility against the black man was fed by the Globetrotters thorough defeat of an all-white team in this all-white town. In his effort to use basketball to both entertain and educate with African American athletic skills, the coach unintentionally feeds racist antagonisms. Yet again for Wideman, race and sports in America are a complex mixture.

The memoir then returns to the present. The author is in New York City and decides to take his French female friend Catherine to see playground ball in his neighborhood in Greenwich Village. Since he has been working for two years on what will become *Hoop Roots,* he wants a chance to show her what he has been working on. What he finds is a game much more diverse than when he played it. While the playground has primarily black athletes, it has a significant mixture of others as well, including, on many occasions, women; in this sense, the game has become even more democratic than in the past. He takes time to suggest how this is different from institutional basketball, where many of the racial stereotypes still apply. He notes that the NBA began its rise in popularity with Larry Bird, whom he calls the "Great White Hope."[55] He points out that Bird's arrival coincided with that of Magic Johnson, to set up a tidy black–white opposition. He explains that the actual differences were not between the real players, who were in fact very similar in their abilities and devotion to the game. The point was the selling of racial contrasts. And because, in Wideman's view, the nation was still trapped in racial thinking, the selling worked. White fans could make Bird their hero and Johnson's Lakers the slick, but not substantial bad guys. He argues that those who controlled and marketed the league wanted the West Coast team to be a modern version of the minstrel show, where blacks are made to look foolish and incompetent. The Harlem Globetrotters were a version of this; the problem was that their antics could not hide their real skills, and so, they almost always won their games. The same thing happened with the Lakers; "Showtime" kept leading to worthy competition with the Celtics and a significant number of championships.

Playground ball, in contrast, is a form of folk art, done through practices passed down the generations and not reliant on mainstream concerns. It involves participating athletes much more than passive spectators. Wideman notes that "organized" ball from early on encouraged watching; the first professional league was created only five years after the game was invented. He has an obvious dislike for games played primarily for money:

> When you're paid to play a game, a different game results, many different games dependent on the kind of payment, its scale, who's paying the players, who buys tickets to watch them play, who writes the contracts, who controls the venues for play, who sets the stakes. Playing for pay leads to the NBA, to barnstorming teams like the Harlem Globetrotters, to cutthroat winner-take-all gambling matches and tournaments on ghetto courts, to fixed college games, to millionaire players, to the hypocrisy of so-called amateur college or scholastic players whose labor generates millions of dollars for corporate sponsors and advertisers.[56]

What he sees on the court at Sixth Avenue and Houston Street is a game he does not like, one that is more about entertainment than about the game he remembers. This is emphasized with one particular player who always has to have the ball. He only plays enough defense to make steals and ignores his teammates when on offense. His moves are very impressive, but there is no teamwork involved; all eyes must be on him. Wideman notes that Catherine is constantly watching him, as is everyone else. Wideman tries to explain to her that this is not good playground ball, that there is no flow, only individual display or "showboating." But he stops himself because he realizes that she cannot understand and because he does not want to be one of those old men complaining about how much things have changed, especially since his whole argument is that the game is always changing. Nevertheless, he recognizes that something important has been lost.

He finishes this section with a discussion of playground fashion, of the ways clothing worn to the court and on the court express individuality. He recalls a player named Cook who would play in expensive dress suits, which would often end scuffed, torn, and dirty by the end of the day. Dressing this way was both a personal statement and an expression of disdain for the mainstream society that excluded people like him from opportunities. Wideman compares playground style to carnival, with its costumes and masks that both express and disguise the wearer. In addition, both playground ball and carnival are deliberately designed to mock conventional society and its rules. They emphasize fun and pleasure and reject, for a short time, the world of work and duty.

From celebration, Wideman turns to what might be considered the tragedy of the game. He imagines the naming of the court in Homewood, pointing out that several players went from there to become successful college and professional athletes. He tells the story of Maurice Stokes, a star professional player, who developed an abscess that would not heal. When it was hit once too often in a game, it burst and the poisons entered his system, permanently paralyzing him. He died 12 years later, without ever being able to speak again. While the league held a charity game for him each year, it refused to pay for any of his medical bills.

The contrasting player was Eldon "L.D." Lawson, who was big, but "soft," meaning for Wideman, that he did not assert himself in games and that he was not willing to work hard to improve.[57] L.D.'s father was a drinking and gambling buddy of John French, and Wideman himself tried to do on the court for L.D. the kinds of things that Ed Fleming had done for him. Unfortunately, the lessons did not take. While he grew bigger and his skills improved, he was always considered lazy by other players. He lasted one semester in college and then returned to a life of petty crime and incarceration. His indulgences resulted in diabetes, and he eventually had to have his legs amputated. Wideman's brother Robby would push him out to the prison yard in his wheelchair so he could entertain the men with stories and be, for a moment, the center of attention once again.

So, Wideman proposes the Maurice Stokes/Eldon L.D. Lawson Memorial Playground. It would be both celebration and warning. The name carries the story of how the talented played here, but were brought down by an indifferent outside world and how great potential can be brought to nothing by our own failings. For the author, such a name is the essence of what his book is about.

The last chapter circles back to his time with his grandmother; his question is whether he can make connections with her 50 years after the time in her sick room. He recalls again his disobedient walks along the train tracks. In this version, there something almost suicidal in his thinking:

> When I deserted you every afternoon that summer for the basketball court in Westinghouse Park, I'd feel my self growing larger as I bopped along the tracks, kicking the rocky gravel, getting away with something. wondering if a train would catch me before I clambered down from the tracks, knowing it might if I left 7415 [Finance Street] at the usual time, just a matter of where, the days were so alike, and trains kept a tight schedule, I could almost count

on the moment I'd be overtaken and wiped from the face of the earth by the sound of a train just a few yards away, dropping like a sack over my head . . . I might have gotten away with it for a while, but one day, sooner or later, just a matter of time.[58]

The fact that he talks about going to play as "deserting" his grandmother, when it was, in fact, what his aunts wanted him to do, indicates a level of guilt that he might associate with his father, who had left his own family that summer. Part could be his anger at being now the oldest male around, with his grandfather dead and his father absent. He wants to prove that he takes *his* responsibilities seriously, but he also feels trapped by them. He is 12 and wants to play the game he loves. This conflict, along with the grief connected to John French's death and Freeda's illness, is too much for him. When he says, "I might have played this game [with the train] once too often," we are reminded of the death of Brother Tate in *Sent for You Yesterday* on the same tracks.[59] The child John may well have seen this game as also an opportunity to forever get rid of the unbearable conflicts in his life.

What he also recalls, as mentioned earlier, is that Freeda never went to any of his ball games and neither did any member of his family. He was "high school all-city, all-state hoop star," but they did not bother to support him:

Sports a boys' thing, man thing, *play,* so the women had no interest and no time anyway if they were interested, and where were the men of our clan. If not out in the street playing their own kinds of games, then busy working or if no work, then busy in that all-consuming limbo of hyperactivity, the pressure cooker of indolence, excruciating, helpless waiting between jobs, or the dramatized denial of powerlessness in a thousand devastating little performances daily of power, of ego and worth they could not display anywhere except in these performances. . . .[60]

But this explanation for the men's behavior, shortly followed by a statement about the racist nature of high school education at the time, still does not conceal the child's hurt, though it is expressed in the adult's words: "The beatings they absorb in this society evilly disposed against them does not excuse the men's absence. Didn't make me miss them any less at my games."[61] He recalls the father of a rival putting on an excessive and embarrassing display of pride when his son's team won the city championship. While John would not have wanted his father to do anything like that, he remembers at that moment wanting to reverse time so that his father would have been in the gym each time cheering him on. That his recall is so precise four decades after the events tells us how strong his sense of loneliness and isolation really was. This feeling of being ignored may also help explain why he was so obsessed with his own children's games 30 years later.

He says that he never expected Freeda to be part of his athletic life, that he learned to divide his life into segments, with the goal of eventually escaping from her world. And it is precisely because he was so successful at creating this separation that he now wants to bring things together again. He describes a photograph of her, one that becomes the cover of the book. In the picture, she stands in front of one of their early houses in Homewood; he is not certain whether it is Cassina Way, where much of his fiction originates, or Albion Street, where she and John French lived even earlier. The photo has the year 1923 penciled in the margin. He then launches into a mini-lecture on art, connecting the image with blues music or African folk art or playground ball. He emphasizes the composition and her sense of style in dress and posture.

This leads him to imagine her as an athlete, one who could have played basketball, if that opportunity has existed for women at that time. He also assumes that, given her sense of style, she would have attended dances in the 1920s. He recalls that in those days, exhibition basketball games were often played in the armories and gyms before the dances. Thus, he imagines Freeda watching someone like him playing the game so important to him. He finishes the book by taking her with him to the ancient Mayan ritual game of pok ta pok, which combined features of basketball and soccer. It was said to be related to battles between good and evil.[62] He also invites her to think of the ring shouts, used by slaves and their descendants on the Sea Islands of Georgia and South Carolina as an alternative Christian worship. It was a form of stylized movement in a circle with observers keeping time with clapping, stomping of feet, and singing. It was a way of getting in contact with divine spirits.

This way of concluding the book suggests the ways in which basketball is a form of ritual, connected to the ancient symbol of the circle or the hoop. Freeda is the ancestor who helps Wideman come to terms with the truths of his own life, both the happy ones and those more troubling. The book itself comes full circle, with her at the beginning and the end. The game itself serves as an initiation ritual that, when it works, guides boys into manhood, that takes them out of their childhood world of women, but allows them to return having achieved maturity. Because the outside world does not encourage maturity in black men, they create their own alternative. It is this deep purpose for the game that makes playing it such an important matter for Wideman in *Hoop Roots*.

CHAPTER 8

Wideman's Mash-Ups

Wideman has continued to be a productive writer into the 21st century, despite significant changes in his life. His troubled 35-year marriage to Judy ended in divorce in 2000, though a line in the story "Thirteen" (from *Briefs,* discussed later) indicates that the real breakup had started in the mid-1980s. After the failure of his marriage, Wideman moved to New York City, though he continued to teach at the University of Massachusetts. He soon began a relationship with Catherine Nedonchelle, a French journalist who received her education at the Sorbonne. They were married in 2004, the same year he took a position as Asa Messer Professor in Africana Studies and English at Brown University. His residence in the city and his new, international relationship has led to an expansion of his writing interests. In addition, his father died in 2001; his mother survived until 2008.

His brother Robby lost an appeal for a retrial in 2000, a decision confirmed by the state Supreme Court in 2001. The effort was legally unique, and the family had very high hopes for its success. The dead man's family had successfully sued the hospital where he was treated, claiming that negligence by the doctors resulted in his death. When Wideman's attorneys learned of the case in 1998, they requested that the original judge grant a new trial based on this evidence. The county coroner agreed with the negligence argument. Robby was set to be freed on bail, but his release was halted by an appeal by the prosecutor. Two years later, the Superior Court overturned the judge's order, citing a state Supreme Court decision that if a crime produces a nonfatal injury that leads to death, the person causing the injury is guilty of homicide.[1]

John's son Danny married Maimuna Madhi of Sierra Leone, whom he met on one of his trips to West Africa, and moved with her to Raleigh,

North Carolina, where he became a writer and an expert in electronic publishing. Jamila, after a successful basketball career, went to law school, just as her mother did, and settled in Brooklyn in public interest law. All of the possible appeals of Jake's case were rejected, and he remained in the Arizona prison.

Wideman has also received international attention, especially in France. In 2001, panels on his work were presented at a conference at the University of Nice. He has been the subject of several dissertations in that country, as well as a special issue of the American academic journal *Callaloo,* devoted to his European readers and critics. This helps to explain his pattern of spending part of each year now in France, where his second wife is from.

These changes in Wideman's life are reflected in the books published since *Hoop Roots* in 2001. Two of them, *God's Gym* (2005) and *Briefs* (2010) are collections of short stories, while *The Island: Martinique* (2003) is a travel book and *Fanon* (2008), a novel. In each of these books, he practices a form of mash-up in the sense of putting together different kinds of writing in unexpected ways. While a literary mash-up is usually thought of as taking a classic work, such as a Jane Austen novel, and blending it with another form, such as a zombie story, Wideman's version is more like the slang definition, where different styles are connected to form a hybrid. *God's Gym* tells stories of death and silence. In two of them, Wideman apparently imagines the deaths of his parents, though his mother is still alive at the time of writing. The story "Weight," which was first published in 1999 in *Callaloo,* won the 2000 O. Henry award for best short story. "Weight" opens with the narrator saying, "My mother is a weightlifter."[2] By this, he means that she willingly takes up the burdens of family and community. She expects life to be difficult, so she is always prepared for it to cause her problems. The narrator admits that he is one of the weights she must carry. In an extended sentence, he shows the extent of her burden and her way of bearing it:

> In spite of a son in prison for life, twin girls born dead, a mind-blown son who roams the streets with everything he owns in a shopping cart, a strung-out daughter with a crack baby, a good daughter who miscarried the only child her dry womb ever produced, in spite of me and the rest of my limp-along, near-to-normal siblings and their children—my nephews doping and gangbanging, nieces unwed, underage, dropping babies as regularly as the seasons—in spite of breast cancer, sugar diabetes, hypertension, failing

kidneys, emphysema, gout, all resident in her body and epidemic in the community, knocking off one by one her girlhood friends, in spite of corrosive poverty and a neighborhood whose streets are no longer safe even for gray crippled-up folks like her, my mom loves her god, thanks him for the blessings he bestows, keeps her faith he would not pile on more troubles than she could bear. Praises his name and prays for strength, prays for more weight so it won't fall on those around her less able to bear up.[3]

He makes the joke that she should have a T-shirt that says God's Gym. She is very similar to the mother in "Solitary," though that version was only faced with the specific problem of an imprisoned son. Here, Wideman extends that sense of responsibility and seems to exaggerate it. This mother is a kind of superwoman.

He follows this general statement with a small everyday example. He remembers, as a child, going with her to the grocery in Shadyside, the white neighborhood the Widemans lived in for several years. The cashier, who had never seen him before, blurts out, "Is this your son?"[4] She covers herself by commenting that he is very tall, but they all know that she is confused by a very light-skinned woman with a dark child. One thing the narrator realizes at that moment is the importance of race and how this mother–son combination causes problems for people who believe in the separation of the races. But more important for the story, he sees how his mother handles that situation, how she must face similar moments each day, and yet manages to keep her temper and her dignity, something he is certain he could not do.

He stops at this point in the story because he is not certain where it will go next. He calls his mother to tell her about it and read to her what he has written so far. Given what he has told us about her, we are led to expect that she will find a way to praise his work: "Mom's always been my best critic. I depend on her honesty. She tells the truth yet never affects the holier-than-thou superiority of some people who believe they occupy the high ground and let you know in no uncertain terms that you nor nobody else like you ain't hardly coming close."[5] Instead, she is angry. At first, he does not understand: "Was it the weightlifting joke, Mom. Maybe you didn't think it was funny." But she makes it clear that the issue is deeper: "Sorry. Tell the truth, I didn't see nothing humorous about any of it. *God's T-shirt.* Ought to be ashamed of yourself. Taking the Lord's name in vain."[6] But she goes on, accusing him of making fun of her, lumping him with those who cause themselves and others real harm. The only difference is that he uses words. He makes jokes of her endurance and of her faith and then seeks her approval. In addition, she thinks he is questioning her intelligence: "What makes you think a sane person would pray for more weight. Ain't those the words you put in my mouth. More weight."[7]

We can easily imagine this scenario in real life. Since Wideman has repeatedly told us that Bette and her sisters were the family's best storytellers, he might well want to try out a new piece of material on her. He even tells us at the beginning that "I called it a story but Mom knew better."[8] The physical distance between them mentioned in the story, 550 miles, is almost exactly the distance between Homewood and Amherst, Massachusetts, where Wideman was teaching at the time of the story's original publication. Certainly, the character of the mother is consistent with the way Bette has been presented in both his fiction and memoirs. While he does change some details about himself, saying, for example, that he was a bachelor with no children, these details have some truth, since all his children were now gone from home, and his divorce from Judy takes place during the year after the magazine publication (1999).

The connection between life and fiction is important because of what he does with the rest of the story. Having been shocked that he can actually hurt his mother with his words, the narrator quickly falls back into his self-satisfied attitude. He talks to her again and reports that she seemed fine; there is no indication that they return to the topic of his story. But then two days later, there is no answer when he calls. He tries again later, then contacts family in Homewood. Eventually, the supervisor and a neighbor find her body in the apartment. He goes home for the funeral, but cannot be a pallbearer, even though he is the oldest child. Her death has overwhelmed him.

He suddenly realizes what offended her about the story. It was not so much the issue of faith as an introductory comment he had made, saying the story was about a man who might not survive the death of his mother. In other words, he had added yet more weight to the end of her life by not allowing her to die in peace. The remainder of the story is an attempt to receive forgiveness for his selfishness and insensitivity. He expresses his lifelong fear of losing her and his need for her approval. He somehow wants that to be part of the story as well. He seeks, in other words, to take up some of the burden that had always been hers.

The story would have been strange for Bette to read, since she did not die for several years after it came out. It can be seen, as the narrator suggests, as a rehearsal of her passing. The question is why Wideman would want to tell such a tale that his mother could read. One answer would be the tendency of both the real and fictional family to not speak their private thoughts, even to each other. As the narrator says:

> It's just that I should have confessed sooner, long, long ago, the size of my fear of losing you. I wish you'd heard me say the words. How fear made me keep my distance, hide how much I depended on your smile. The sunshine of your smiling laughter that could also send me silently screaming out the room in stories I never told you because you'd taught me as you'd been taught, not to say anything aloud I didn't want to come true. Nor say out loud the things I wished to come true. Doesn't leave a hell of a lot to say, does it.[9]

One way for Wideman to overcome the emotional privacy of the family, at least in order for him to say something important about his mother, is to create a fiction in which a character does the work for him. He can give that character (the narrator) an attitude that may be some part of the author's own thinking, but a part that he does not admire. Certainly, we can see Wideman believing that his mother was the one stable force in his early life, especially with a father who was emotionally unreliable. Given everything that Bette had to endure, it would be easy to think of her as superhuman. But doing that deprived her of some part of her humanity. By killing off the mother in the story, Wideman can push his character past his denial of his fears to a more mature understanding of his mother's life. In this way, the author can say to his own mother how much he values her as a person before it is too late.

In "Are Dreams Faster Than the Speed of Light," the protagonist again is identified with the author. Near the end, his father is called Mr. Wideman, and he tells us that his own name, John Edgar, comes from his grandfather and his father. But the story shifts between first and third person, so it is difficult to call him a narrator. The reason for this shift is related to the plot. On the first page, the protagonist/narrator is told that he has a terminal disease. He has at most a year, but most of that time will be spent in terrible pain. He then makes a list of things to do before he dies. The list becomes very long, so he changes it: "When he switched the list to *must do,* he was relieved by its shortness. Only two items: he must die, and before his time's up he must end the bad ending of his father's life. Couldn't leave his poor daddy behind to suffer any longer—how long, how long. He must take his father's life."[10]

This shocking duty is the result of his father's illness, Alzheimer's disease. He goes to see him at the VA hospital, without knowing whether the old man will be able to speak or remember anything on a given day. He sometimes tells stories of how the staff treats patients, but it is not clear whether or when they happened. Since John Edgar is the only direct relative (he has a half-sister), he is concerned about what will become of his father if he survives the son. So, he tells his father of his plan to take care of both of them through murder–suicide. The father has trouble understanding why he is going to be killed: "What I'm trying to say is I know you already told me once, but I can't keep nothing straight in this feeble-ass mind of mine anymore. So tell me again, son. Why do I have to die. Why you have to kill me."[11] It is not clear that the father's confusion is related to his disease, though the narrator thinks this. It could well be that he simply does not want to die.

What happens next indicates that the father is capable of thinking things through. John Edgar gets a call that his father has fallen, shattered his hip and has internal bleeding. If we do not want to believe that this is coincidence, then it is probable that the old man has taken things into his own hands and tried to kill himself so that the burden will not be on his son. Just as in "Weight," the narrator has a revelation and realizes that he has been thinking only of himself and not of his parent. At the end of the story, he wants his father to live and sits feeding him: "I keep Lil Sis busy wiping vanilla drool from our daddy's chin as I ladle what I can into him, down him, and nothing, nothing else matters."[12] Life is precious and must be cared for. This father with whom he never had a good relationship is still, at the very end of his life, willing to sacrifice for his son. The son must now take responsibility.

Such a tale is peculiar for the moment it comes in Wideman's life. Edgar Wideman had died in late 2001, and the story is first published in 2004—the same year John married Catherine Nedonchelle. So, at the same time that he is beginning a new phase in his life, he is writing about his own death and making it a particularly painful one. He has gone back in this piece and "Weight" to settle accounts with his parents.

He does something similar in "What We Cannot Speak About We Must Pass Over in Silence." Here, he revisits the story of Jake, but from a very different perspective. The narrator is a friend of sorts of a man who has a son in prison in Arizona. The father describes in detail visits to the facility, in much the same way Wideman has previously in fiction and nonfiction:

> The moment that's not easy, that's impossible, he said, is after three days, six hours each, of visiting are over and he passes through the sliding gate of the steel-fenced outdoor holding pen between the prison visitation compound and the visitors' parking lot and steps

onto the asphalt that squirms beneath your feet, oozing hot like it just might burn through your shoe soles before you reach the rental car and fling open its doors and blast the air conditioner so the car's interior won't fry your skin, it's then, he said, taking your first steps away from the prison, first steps back into the world, when you almost come apart, almost lose it completely out there in the desert, emptiness stretching as far as the eye can see, very far usually, ahead to a horizon ironed flat by the weight of blue sky, to the right and left zigzag mountain peaks marking the edges of the earth, nothing moving but hot air wiggling above the highway, the scrub brush and sand, then, for an unending instant, it's very hard to be alive, he says, and thinks he doesn't want to live a minute longer and would not make it to the car, the airport, back to this city if he didn't pause and remind himself it's worse, far worse for the son behind him still trapped inside the prison, so for the son's sake he manages a first step away, then another and another.[13]

This one continuous sentence creates a sense of the dread that the father feels by stretching out time almost to the breaking point. It is a version of hell, with its heat, emptiness, and weight It does not attempt to tell us directly his emotions, except that he has become, in effect, the walking dead. He is helpless, isolated, frustrated that he can do nothing for his child. But he is also burdened by the fact that it is worse for his son, whom he will not see for another year.

This passage is important not only because it hints at Wideman's own feelings on his visits to Arizona, but also because it is so precise about the experience, an experience that may never have occurred within the story. The narrator gets a letter from a lawyer telling him that the friend has died. His response to this news is somewhat complicated. After all, this was someone whom he had known only a couple of years and with whom he was not really that intimate. He discovers that he feels sorrow for the son, who has no other relatives. So, he contacts the lawyer, so that he can send the young man a letter of condolence. He is surprised to learn that the attorney is not aware of any son. He then works with a paralegal to locate the boy; he gets a very rude reply to his letter saying that the boy has no idea who his father is.

Instead of ending the matter there, and assuming that the friend, for his own reasons, had been lying, the narrator becomes obsessed with the prisoner. One of the things that results is a relationship with the paralegal, whose own father had committed suicide. Together, they track down the young man's location, and the narrator decides to go to Arizona. He writes another letter and this time receives a more polite response, with the suggestion that he claim to be the father in order to speed up the paperwork. At this point, the protagonist steps back. He uses Suh Jung's paralegal skills to find out everything he can about the prisoner; what he learns is that he has done many cruel things and probably deserves to be incarcerated. He is no longer the wronged child that the friend had suggested he was. This disappointment also leads to a weakening of the relationship with Suh Jung. Since the narrator had linked the two younger people as possible children of his own, his disappointment with the "son" seems to carry over to the "daughter." They are not who he wanted them to be.

He finally decides to make the trip, but even then delays so that by the time he gets to the prison, only one of the three visitation days is left. He worries that his false claim of fatherhood might be discovered, but then realizes that the system really does not care. He then takes us through the reverse procedure that he offered at the beginning. We see all the complications of getting into the facility. This covers most of the last five pages of the story. At the very end, we learn that there has been a mistake. The son is apparently not in this prison, and he is told that he can check with the warden's office the next day and then is asked to step aside for the next visitor.

"What We Cannot Speak About" has many of the qualities of a Franz Kafka story. The narrator gets involved in a situation he knows nothing about, but that seems to be controlled by others who want to cause him difficulties. Who is lying and who is telling the truth is not clear. Why they want to do this is also unclear. By taking the point of view that he does in the story, Wideman can give readers an innocent angle on the workings of the prison system. Unlike himself, the narrator has no experience of the complications, bureaucracy, and absurdities of that system. The readers take the journey with him and feel the same doubts and frustrations, especially when there is no resolution at the end. It is a mystery without a solution.

The final story in *God's Gym*, "Sightings," looks back at Wideman's time teaching at the University of Wyoming. It is one of the few pieces of writing, whether fiction or nonfiction, that discusses this period of his life. Like the others in the book, it is concerned with death. In the present time of the story, the narrator is living in New York City and teaching at a university in Massachusetts, just as Wideman was until shortly before *God's Gym* was published. The story opens in a moment of confusion; he briefly mixes up a colleague with someone he knew at the university in Wyoming several years earlier. He knows that it is a mistake because the Wyoming man has been dead for a while. He adds more confusion by telling us that he sometimes calls the building they are in Bartlett Hall, which he says was the name of the office building in Laramie. This is a little joke Wideman plays in order to confuse readers. Bartlett *is* the location of the English Department at the University of Massachusetts; the name he gives it in the story, Logan Hall, was the location of Arts and Sciences block at UPenn. So, from the beginning, mistaken identities are piling up. We learn that the Wyoming colleague had committed suicide up in the mountains.

The narrator then makes connections to another person from there, Molly, who suffered from bouts of insanity, caused in part by a terrible sexual assault that took place once in Africa. Later on, he confuses her with another Molly from his present life. Time is also mixed up, as the story shifts quickly from present to past and back again as we follow the track of the narrator's mind:

> I hadn't thought much about Roger or Molly for years. For some reason never paired them, though they knew each other well and were linked by the obvious fact of suicide. I'd been long gone from Wyoming when I heard they'd taken their lives, Roger first, then Molly, each death a kind of postscript to a portion of my life I thought I'd laid to rest until these painful footnotes forced me to raise my eyes to a text that hadn't disappeared just because I'd stopped reading it.[14]

This narrator sounds very much like the young John of *Hoop Roots,* who would compartmentalize parts of his life so that he could move on to whatever was important to him. The deaths of two of his friends have been put aside so that he can go on to the next stage of his life. The problem is that life does not always stay in neat boxes, and it is this messiness that the story is about.

Hunting becomes the symbol for trying to sort things out. He recalls various trips in Wyoming with friends from the university and with local people to hunt antelope. Part of the point is to see how the narrator, a black man from Pittsburgh and Philadelphia, will handle himself in the Wyoming wilderness. They make fun of Roger, who tries to fit in, but clearly cannot:

> Forget it, Roger. No matter how crudely you act or talk up here, no matter how many notches on your gun or spots on your slovenly khakis or how much grime under your fingernails, you'll never

fit in—too much Eastern prep school, too much Eng. Lit. professor whose existence insults the others even as you dispense a desired patina of knowledge and culture, red-pencil their B/B-essays, too much stern, thin-lipped, narrow-hipped spinster, New England rectitude and ruling class and old money. Money proved by your poor church-mouse lifestyle, your disdain for stuff other folks work their tails off to own.[15]

Part of Roger Wilson's problem is that he likes to be part of the group, but he cannot accept their thinking. For example, he refuses to shoot any game. And while the others tolerate him, in part to have someone to make jokes about, he can never be a part of their community. They also suspect that he is responsible for bringing the narrator into the university—a situation that makes them uncomfortable, since race is an issue they do not want to address. In the end, we have some sense of why Wilson would kill himself.

The narrator returns to the hunting scene to show us an actual kill. Like Ernest Hemingway, William Faulkner, Toni Morrison, and a number of other writers, Wideman uses hunting as a kind of ritual. Part of the dressing of the animal is intended to test the rookie, to see if the exposure of guts and blood make him sick, to see, in other words, if he is a *real* man in their terms. He nearly fails, but not for the reasons they think:

No, fellas, I don't gasp when John opens the antelope's distended water-balloon belly and yanks out steaming viscera. I'm digging erotic pinks and vivid lavenders, delicate mauves of stretched, moist skin, the smell discharged with a palpable hiss, engulfing me, not in fetid nastiness of bile or vomit but sage perfume, so familiar, ungent, and intimate I've never forgotten it, and that nearly-falling-in-love swoon as close as I came that day to losing my composure.[16]

What unexpectedly overwhelms him is not the rawness or ugliness of the moment, but its beauty. It is full of colors, textures, sounds, and smells that please rather than nauseate him. The fact that it is an instant of poetry for him marks him as different from the others—a difference that has nothing to do with race or any factor that makes Wilson an outsider. His experience is that of a writer, something none of them will ever be. The fact that he has never forgotten it reconnects to the blending of past and present, since in the present, he is telling the story of Wyoming and trying to sort out the confusions and coincidences running through it.

The final blending moment comes when John, his colleague from Wyoming and the one who killed the antelope, calls to say he is visiting New York. This occurs while the narrator is writing the story. He ends by imagining what their meeting will be like. How they will catch up, but never talk about the dead. They will do what the narrator has been trying to break away from, separating the parts of life that do not neatly fit together.

The mixing of life and fiction apparent in *God's Gym* raises questions about the importance of the theme of death running through the stories. Wideman turned 65 the year after the book came out, and we know from *Hoop Roots* that he had reluctantly given up playing playground ball a few years earlier. This is also the point at which he must have realized that he was never going to be a popular writer. Though his books had always received positive reviews, they had never turned up on a best seller list nor been made into films, as had the work of his contemporaries Toni Morrison (*Beloved*), Alice Walker (*The Color Purple*), and Ernest Gaines (*The Autobiography of Miss Jane Pittman* and *A Gathering of Old Men*). So, it is possible that he was beginning to think about his own mortality and his legacy. Having written about the deaths of individuals, groups, and even communities (such as Homewood) for his entire career, it was time to turn inward, to come to terms with death in his own life. The conclusion he seems to come to is that we have to face the reality of it, but neither obsess about it nor deny it. We must value the life that we have and the humanity around us. Our tidy answers to big questions will never work, because life and death are too mashed-up together to ever make easy sense.

The Island: Martinique (2003) is part of National Geographic's Literary Travel Series, otherwise known as Directions. The series began in 2002 with the idea of using authors who did not usually write about travel to select a place to tell readers about.[17] Writers were given the freedom to choose the location, with the expectation that they would incorporate material about history and culture and create a work that was nonfiction. In other words, we should expect a book that fits the ancient genre of travel writing. But since we are dealing with John Wideman, we should not be surprised when he says in the introduction, "the reader should expect improvisation, spontaneity, play, breaking rules to rule here."[18] He does make some attempt, early on, to follow rules. He provides a map, a brief chronology of the island, and a discussion in the introduction of his reasons for choosing Martinique. From that point, the text takes off in its own directions, blending history, political comment, autobiography, and fiction. It is also, in several ways, a ghost story.

Wideman begins by describing how he has set up the characters in the book. There are John and Catherine, clearly the author and his new lover, Catherine Nedonchelle, then John and Katrine, who are a version of the first set, and finally Paul and Chantal, who are fictional creations that the author uses to examine certain conflicts that he does not want to connect to the others, since he wants their stories to be happy. The John–Katrine pair seems to be necessary so that he can tell things that may or may not have happened to the real people, as he has done so often in his writing. He can seem to reveal secrets, while maintaining privacy. For example, they arrive on Christmas Day; he goes on to discuss the importance of the holiday in Western culture and its implications for others:

> This Christ robed in a milk-white mantle in whose name human-kind has committed every conceivable cruelty upon itself, a creed no better or worse than others, I suppose, that grant believers permission to treat nonbelievers worse than dogs, creeds whose tangled heaps of prohibitions, incitements, and license pile up mountain high and we spend far too much of our precious time on earth groveling up, groveling under them.[19]

While Wideman has little use for religion, though he is aware of its symbolic importance for writers, here, he can disguise that attitude by assigning it to John the narrator and thus not offend readers of the National Geographic series.

He makes use of the symbolism right away. The morning after they arrive, Katrine has a miscarriage. Whether or not it actually happened (since this is Katrine and not Catherine), the death of the child on the date associated with divine birth indicates that the author sees this as a fallen, troubled world. They had not known about the pregnancy, but the narrator says that they speculated about the possibility, though John already had grown children and Katrine was on the edge of menopause. When the loss occurs, she has a short period of mourning for a child she did not think was possible. In other words, Wideman presents this as an anti-miracle, the reverse of the birth of the Christ child.

The lost child is also the first of the ghosts of the book. On the first page of the introduction, Wideman refers to *revenants,* a French word meaning those who come back. He uses this meaning to talk about Martinique as a place that people like to return to, for a vacation perhaps, or a place of retirement. In his own case, the book is his return. His real visit occurred during the time period indicated in the journal that makes up the first chapter. He points out that between the real and the literary visits, many things happened: "In the months since my first visit I've lost my father, the World Trade Center has been attacked and destroyed, I've moved from a rural area to the big city, and I've fallen deeper in love"[20] For him, even a virtual return to the island is welcome, both as an escape from troubles and as a romantic getaway.

But the second meaning of *revenant* is also relevant. It refers to those who have returned from the dead. For him, Martinique is haunted as well as beautiful. Its history is filled with ghosts. There is Père Labat, a priest who was the cruel overseer of a church-owned slave plantation. There are the slaves themselves, who suffered and died on the island—a history that an African American such as Wideman would find especially important. There are the Caribs, the native islanders who were wiped out in order to establish the plantations. Then, there is Franz Fanon, born in Martinique, but devoting much of his life to the liberation of Africa. Learning more about the island, its people, its history, and its culture only leads Wideman deeper into the world of ghosts. It is no wonder that he says that this is not going to be an ordinary travel book.

Part of his breaking of rules is connected to his concerns about being a tourist. The tourist for him is someone who is interested in the surfaces of a place, not in matters like a haunted past, unless, of course, that past is entertainment, which is something that the islanders try to provide with dances and pageants. Wideman wishes to be something else, someone who understands the real people behind the masks and the costumes. But he realizes that this is impossible, since he shows up from someplace else, not speaking the local language, with a white woman and credit cards. In fact, he comes to believe that in some ways he is worse because he is a writer, a person who wants to get at their secrets and invade their privacy. He wants to look at the ghosts they have carefully locked away and then go tell others. In other words, he will exploit them at least as much as any tourist. He also comes to see the tourists as people who are locked into a way of seeing the island through the manipulations of others. Travel agents, guides, and local organizers control the use of time and the access to space so that only a certain version of the island and the natives is visible. He suggests that a place such as Martinique is a stage set carefully designed for the visitors so that they take away only the right images and memories. Even with his relative independence as a traveler, Wideman cannot get far below the surface because no one wants him to go there.

A key to what he wants to accomplish here in defiance of the travel book idea is found in his discussion of Thomas Jefferson and Monticello, his plantation in Virginia. For the "3 January 2001" entry, Wideman thinks about their forthcoming return to the United States and the inauguration of a new Southern president (George W. Bush). This leads him back to Jefferson and the promises of the nation that did not even exist when the French first came to Martinique. He recalls the promises made for the country of equality and opportunity, but also the tendency to forget Jefferson's status as a slave owner. Instead of his portrait on the two-dollar bill, Wideman suggests something else: "Why not a five-dollar bill with Massa Tom kissing Sally Hemmings, his beige mistress, behind the barn."[21]

He sees Jefferson in the same terms as those Europeans who turned tropical islands into slave plantations:

> . . . Jefferson's dream for a new nation is among other things a sugar-coated riff on the same ole, same ole European power trip of conquest and exploitation, theft and enslavement, a plan for transforming the tropical isles of the New World into cash cows for investors, demi-paradises where white men who choose to settle would be enthroned as masters of Eden, top dogs in the chain of being, reigning over the rest of creation.[22]

He imagines a version of Fanon's anticolonial violence when he dreams of blowing up Monticello, Jefferson's symbol of Western civilization and the Enlightenment. He considers whether history would lose anything by such an act of destruction or whether it might be an opportunity to rethink what matters in history. His alternative would be to turn it into ruins, a reminder of the fate of those who presume that they have the right to enslave and control the lives of other human beings. He reminds us that Monticello worked only because of the daily forced labor of slaves. Wideman wonders what it must have been like to be Jefferson faced with all those contradictions. He wonders in part because, as he says, he himself has been granted "honorary white-guy status," which makes his position in Martinique so complicated.[23]

He tries to overcome the problem by telling stories, both historical and fictional. Chapter Two takes up Père Labat's career. Jean-Baptiste Labat, who went to the West Indies in the 1690s, was a Dominican priest, an engineer, and a botanist who designed defenses against the British and devised new methods of turning sugar cane into rum. He spent about 10 years in Martinique and Guadeloupe before returning to Europe. One of the things we learn about him is that he continues in the local folklore as a bogeyman; mothers warn their children that, if they do not behave, he will come and take them away. The reason for this becomes clear as we enter his mind, both before and after he arrives on the island. While still in France, he sits in a tavern waiting for his ship. He has no use for the people who enter there and he wonders why they come, since it is a dangerous place where they might be robbed or killed or perhaps impressed into duty on a ship. But beyond them, he is scornful of the wealthy who come to such places to satisfy their own guilty pleasure. Furthermore, he believes that the priests sent to places such as Martinique are worse than useless; they are not competent to manage plantations, and their efforts to convert native Indians and African slaves are only excuses to indulge in eating and drinking and sensual activities to excess. He alone is capable of doing what needs to be done, which is to make money for the church and the nation.

When he arrives, he takes firm control, and while he believes that Africans are the devil's children and unable to understand either civilization or Christianity, he does have a sense of justice. He tries to match punishments exactly to crimes. This attitude can be very cruel:

> Flay this bird. Then tie it to a stake. Roast it. Display it as an example to others. Hang the empty skin on a rack facing the stake and burn it, too, as you burn the creature. Let it, let them watch the infernal blackness of its pelt shrivel to ash . . . If we are to succeed here, if God's feast is to be served to those few able to recognize and love his power, we must deafen our ears, harden our hearts to pests we cannot convert, only exterminate. Off with this one. Let its cries ring out like sweet bells summoning the faithful to worship.[24]

This statement is made about a slave who has repeatedly tried to run away and been tortured each time he was captured. Labat points out that such treatment has made him useless for any kind of work and shows the ineptitude of the managers. The best that can be done is to make him a warning to others through torture and death.

It is no wonder that this priest would become the bogeyman. But it is also clear why Wideman would draw attention to him. After all, there is no hypocrisy here. Labat does not claim that slavery can be justified by claiming to convert or civilize Africans. The only point is making money in the most efficient way possible. This wealth will then be used to ensure the power of the church and the state. This approach also has racial implications, as indicated by the word "exterminate." Here, the author links the activities of the colonizers in the New World to the Holocaust of the 20th century.

The third chapter is a work of fiction that appeared in *God's Gym* as "Fanon," which is also the title of Wideman's next novel. In it, the two characters mentioned in the introduction to *The Island,* Paul and Chantal, have come to Martinique, in part because Paul is writing a book about Franz Fanon. In the story, they visit some of the same places as John and Katrine, including an old building with an image painted on it that turns out to be Fanon. To understand the story, it is important to know two things. One is that Paul is black and Chantal white. They racially match John and Katrine and John and Catherine. The second thing is Fanon's view of the relationships between black men and white women and the other pair of white men and black women. In *Black Skins, White Masks,* he argues that blackness is so negative an idea in the minds of whites in power that blacks who seek to become part of Western society (such as Fanon himself) often take on some version of this belief about race. They are then attracted to white individuals as a way to enhance their own self-esteem. But they are always insecure in these relationships because they secretly believe in their own inferiority.

One indication of this problem in Paul is his attitude toward African names. He and Chantal go to see a movie about Patrice Lamumba, the first prime minister of the Congo after liberation:[25]

> I imagine Chantal beside me, imagine us going to a bar after the movie, and maybe I'd attempt to explain my reaction when I was a kid and first heard Lumumba's name. His name and the others— Kasavubu, Motubu, Tshombe. Names embarrassing me, sounding like tom-toms, like jibber-jabber blabbered through big African lips at Tarzan or Bwana in Hollywood movies. Black sweaty faces. Fat eyes rolling and showing too much white. Would tell her I'd heard my white friends giggling inside my skull at the funny names . . .[26]

Paul hears the giggles inside his head, which means that he feels ashamed not because of what his friends have actually done, but what he believes they will do. And, instead of being angry, he is embarrassed. Given his way of thinking, it is not surprising that he would want a relationship with a white woman like Chantal.

Back on the island, they go one day to a nude beach, where they spend time in the water, but mostly lie against a large tree. A European man puts out his towel nearby and cannot stop looking at Chantal's body. Paul knows this because he keeps watching the man. He believes that his lack of jealous reaction is a kind of history: "I thought I mught have slain my demons that day watching another man's eyes on you, a white guy no less."[27] But unfortunately, this is not true. She later tells him about an old relationship, one that has been over for several years. Now, he reacts jealously, saying that it must have been more important than she indicated if it lasted so long. No matter what she says, he interprets it negatively and effectively ends their affair.

One of the ironies of the story is that Paul is interested in the Fanon who was a political radical and largely ignores his insights into personal relationships. He can talk about the arrogance of Chantal and her white boyfriend in black environments such as the West Indies, but he fails to see that the psychological side of Fanon's work applies to him. One way to apply this to Wideman is to think of it as a reminder to himself that he needs to understand his own motivations for his choices in life. After all, he married a white woman many years earlier, and he was the product of the marriage of a light-skinned woman and dark-skinned man. In the present time of the book, he is living with a white French woman whom he will marry about a year later. The story suggests that his own reasons for focusing on race matters may be more complicated than he would like to believe.

"Fanon" ends with another ghost story. Marilyn Monroe and Frantz Fanon were born and died within a year of each other, both only 36. Wideman imagines them meeting at the end of their lives on a slave ship. They try to understand what has happened to them and why people are staring at them. The ship is suggestive of their being trapped in a world of media attention that has denied them their human reality. They have become the Black Devil and the White Sex Symbol, not real people. But in their last moments, they each recognize the humanity of the other, which for Wideman is a form of love. It is this story, rather than Paul's story, that the author wants us to believe in.

This message comes through as well in the book's last chapter. Here, he records the volcanic explosion of Mount Pelee in 1902, which destroyed the capital city of Saint Pierre. He tries to imagine what it was like to be one of the people in the town who went to the cathedral for refuge, only to have it destroyed in the eruption. He recalls that the local politicians had discouraged people from fleeing because an election was coming up. But connected to this tragedy is the beauty of the setting. From this place up on a hill, he and Katrine can see the harbor as the sun sets. He also recalls the Gauguin Museum that they visited on the way up, with copies of paintings he had made in the 1880s. He additionally ties his complicated reaction to Martinique to his experience as a Rhodes Scholar, an opportunity paid for by wealth gained by Cecil Rhodes and his exploitation of Africa. He seeks forgiveness from both the living and dead of Martinique for his limited ability to understand them. But more important for him personally, he realizes the he must accept Katrine's difference from him and that he cannot and should not make her either into an idol or a scapegoat based on her race and gender. She is simply herself, someone he can love. By the end of the book, that is enough.

The person who comes up so often in *The Island,* Frantz Fanon, is supposedly the subject of Wideman's 2008 novel, *Fanon.* He is supposedly the subject because the author talks all around him without ever getting down to the business of telling Fanon's story. It is not unusual to write fiction about historical figures. Some books in the category of historical fiction try to stay as close as possible to the facts of the life, while others go off into fantasy. We can have Robert Penn Warren's *All the King's Men,* Barbara Chase-Riboud's story of the affair between Sally Hemings and Thomas Jefferson, or Seth Grahame-Smith's *Abraham Lincoln: Vampire Hunter.* Such authors take parts of the historical record and then spin a story around them.

What Wideman has chosen to do is to write about writing a novel on Fanon. He has a narrator named John, (who is working on a book on Fanon) who creates a writer named Thomas who is also writing such a book. But John and Thomas sometimes meet to talk about their shared subject. Thomas is somewhat like Paul of the short story "Fanon" and the section of *The Island* with that title. The difference is that Thomas does not have the personal issues that Paul has. One question that we will explore is why Wideman needs to complicate telling Fanon's story so much. Why is it so hard for him to recreate a man whom he so much admires?

The book opens with a letter that the narrator/author is writing to Fanon. Like so many letters in Wideman's work, it is one that will never be delivered, since, in this case, the addressee has been dead for almost 50 years. The writer sits in a garden in Brittany, sipping a glass of wine, aware of how different his life is from that of Fanon, who came to France to fight in World War II. He describes in the letter how his life was changed when he read *The Wretched of the Earth* for the first time:

> Although the worrisomeness I'm calling a Fanon project has as-sumed various forms, it began clearly enough as a determination to be like you, that is, to become a writer committed to telling the truth about color and oppression, a writer who exposes the lies of race and reveals how the concept of race is used as a weapon to destroy people. I wanted to be somebody, an unflinchingly honest, scary somebody like Frantz Fanon whose words and deeds just might ignite a revolution, just might help cleanse the world of the plague of racism.[28]

Since he says that he read Fanon's book at least 40 years earlier, that would mean that he was finishing or recently finished at Oxford and working on *A Glance Away* or perhaps *Hurry Home*. None of that work suggests an author busy exposing lies about racism; in fact, that idea of writing sounds more like the Black Arts Movement peo-ple that Wideman wanted nothing to do with, precisely because they wanted literature to serve political rather than artistic goals. While his work from that time was "honest," it was also about the private lives of its characters, not their social concerns. He admits that his ambitions changed over time, that he took up different kinds of books, but, even then he "was hoping they didn't dishonor Frantz Fanon nor compro-mise unforgivably my original project."[29]

He then describes the experience that became the subject of *The Is-land* and especially seeing the image of Fanon on the building, an image that no one there seemed to recognize. It was at this point that he de-cided that, since he could not write *like* Fanon, maybe he could write *about* Fanon in his own way. His way is to introduce Thomas, a fiction writer living in New York. The purpose of this character would seem to be similar to the reason for having Paul in the story "Fanon." He is a way for Wideman to explore some of the issues of his relationship to Fanon from a distance; he puts certain ideas and concerns in the charac-ter's head, so he can look at them somewhat objectively.

He also introduces a mystery into the story; Thomas receives a pack-age from UPS that he believes holds a human head, though he never actually opens it. He believes this because the narrator states it as a fact—one that is never verified. The narrator then talks to Thomas about the contents of the box, telling him that the head is a warning, a reflection of the terrible things happening in society. He tears apart the box to find something wrapped in plastic; the narrator keeps encouraging him to take the next step, even calling him a coward for not ripping off the plastic. Along with the "head," there is a note that is a quote from Fanon: *"We must immediately take the war to the enemy, leave him no rest, harass him. Cut off his breath."*[30] These words add to the mystery, since no one knows that Thomas is writing a book about Fanon. Then, the narrator and Thomas debate whether this is the best Fanon quote to use, which suggests to us that this whole scene is just something that Thomas is making up as a story. The problem is that it comes back again later, and haunts the novel.

Wideman goes further by discussing various ways of telling a story. For example, he describes his mother's technique:

> Her stories flatten and fatten perspective. She crams everything, everyone, everywhere into the present, into words that flow, intimate and immediate as the images of a Bearden painting. When she's going good my mom manages to crowd in lots and lots of stuff without creating a feeling of claustrophobia. She fills space to the brim without exhausting it. Without surrendering the authority of her long life, she always talks about the precise moment she's inhabiting. Makes the moment present and large enough, thank goodness, to include everybody listening.[31]

In contrast to this spontaneous way of telling, there is the class that Thomas teaches at a university. On the first day in creative writing, he puts a list of rules on the board, especially for point of view. While he states that following these rules will not guarantee a good novel or story, they at least provide some method for what he calls "the writing madness."[32] At the same time, he remembers a photograph of himself in front of a class at UPenn 35 years earlier, putting the same rules on a chalkboard. There is, in fact, a photo of Wideman from that period teaching a class.

Eventually, the story gets around to Fanon and his time in Africa during the Algerian rebellion against the French during the late 1950s. One of his ideas was to create a supply route for the rebels through Mali, south of Algeria. In the novel, the Algerians are doubtful of the scheme, saying that the ancient supply route may or may not exist and that they cannot waste time and resources to try to locate it. Finally, Fanon is given an eight-man commando team and two vehicles to try to find it through the desert. We follow him along the rugged terrain as they hit one dead end after another and as he notes its similarity to the rocky trails in parts of Martinique. He also recalls his time in Paris, where he could only be happy at night because, despite his military service to France, he had to every day deal with the racial insults of the French.

The story then jumps to Pittsburgh and a visit to Robby in prison. Their mother is now in a wheelchair, which complicates the trip. The narrator thinks about time and how it is different for those in and out of prison. It has a monotonous sameness for Robby, whose routine is the same day after day, year after year. Even when there is variation, such as visitors, the system conspires against it. The chairs in the visitors' area are bolted down in straight rows, so that in order for Robby to talk to his mother, whose wheelchair is at the end of a row, he must turn his back on his brother, who is then excluded from the conversation. They try to make the situation as normal as possible, with stories about the old days and private family jokes. But it is clear that, for Wideman, the situation is similar to that faced by Fanon, in that the state seeks to control people and make them feel responsible for their own condition. Part of this is his interpretation of a story that his mother tells of a friend of hers who died after being warned not to eat pork rinds because of her poor health. But she could not stop herself. The narrator sees the incident as one more example of what he calls "a war being waged against people like us all over the world," a war in which Esther Morris was one more casualty.[33] His mother argues that Esther knew better and so paid for her own failings, not the actions of some invisible enemy.

In this scene, which seems much more part of an autobiography than a novel, he introduces a fantastical element. He and Robby talk briefly about his work on a Fanon book, then John says that their mother claims to have met Fanon during one of her hospital stays in Pittsburgh. Robby has trouble believing it; after all, Fanon was never in Pittsburgh, and he died in 1961. Their mother becomes angry when she is challenged, and they say that she never lies. At a later point in the book, Wideman will recreate his version of the meeting. In that meeting, the mother sits in her wheelchair at the side of Fanon's hospital bed, one hand rubbing his shoulder, the other switching television channels with the remote, hoping to find something that will ease his pain. The narrator shifts between the experience of pain of the leukemia that is killing him and the mother's thoughts of what she might do to relieve him of his discomfort. They both believe that these are the Last Days, the end of the world as we know it. She believes because of biblical prophecy, confirmed for her by wars, plagues, and the Southeast Asian tsunami of 2004. He believes, for political reasons: "Never forget this simple fact, he warned her one day: always some person or persons at the controls monitoring what you read, hear, see. Never underestimate the power or ruthlessness of those at the controls, Fanon had taught himself and instructed his patients, as he's instructing her."[34] For him, it is not necessary to involve God in the world's troubles because those in power are capable and willing to do harm to both nature and the human beings they consider their inferiors. The scene ends as the mother mops his sweating brow as he drifts off into another fitful sleep.

With another radical leap in storytelling, Wideman returns us to Thomas and his new desire to find a French director to film the life of Fanon. His problem is that he has not yet gotten far enough in his project to describe to anyone what the story might be. He goes to France with the idea of locating the right filmmaker, but does not succeed. Instead, the narrator finds for him a love interest, a woman like Catherine he meets in Paris. Later in the novel, the narrator invites Jean-Luc Godard, the famous French director, to come to Homewood to consider it as the setting for a Fanon movie. They walk the streets of the decimated neighborhood, which looks much the same as it did in the story "Tommy" from 20 years earlier. Yet again, this plot point goes nowhere. But this scene is much more about Wideman's history than it is about Fanon. At one point, he presents dialogue as though it were in a movie script; the characters talking are labeled JLG (for Godard) and JEW, with the note added that "JEW" is named for his father (Edgar) and grandfather (John French). JEW talks about his mother witnessing the killing of a young black man across the street from her high-rise apartment and also recalling her life in Washington, D.C., just before and after John's birth; what is most important is her relationship to him as her first-born:

> She must feed and cradle and comfort him in her arms, sing to him not because anyone tells her she must, she has no choice, understood from the first instant that her arms, her legs belong to him, his puny limbs and blind fingers are hers, preciously, forever hers like certain expressions on his tiny face she sometimes coaxes from him are hers, expressions mirroring her huge face hovering, breathing into his, speaking to him without words in a language her body had learned from others to express with the muscles of her face, passing on family looks becoming his looks and though she understood she must be the source of much of what he saw then she saw spreading across his features, she also discovered new likenesses she had never perceived in herself. She was beginning to know herself in a different fashion, recognizing features she carried, looks taught by glances she exchanged with this baby. Not

exactly as in a mirror. He was so different, far more precious than she was. Except watching those big eyes, small ears, that nose, that mouth, strangely she suffered his pains and pleasures deeper inside herself than the truth of her own sensations.[35]

This passage is worth quoting at length because it tells us so much about Wideman's relationship to his mother. It is one of the most emotionally sensitive statements in all of his writing, matched only by his discussion of the infant Jamila. The mother and child take their identities from each other, learning from each other their relationship to the world. She is presented as a model of unconditional love, actually feeling his "pains and pleasures" more than just knowing about them. We can also see why he would identify with the French side of the family, which was, for him, a world primarily of women like his mother. We can also see why he would react with angry words to a world that did not appreciate such love and that seemed committed to destroying relationships. Here is the ideal against which everything else is measured. He even imagines her young again and giving birth to Fanon, so that he can experience what John did.

Wideman begins Part 3 of the book with a monologue aimed at Fanon, much like the letter that opened the book. He is sitting again in the garden in Brittany with his wine as night falls. He hears Catherine cleaning up in the kitchen from the dinner he made for them. He discusses the book he is trying to write and begins to imagine writing as something like music. Ideally, it is music made by master artists who, in a magical moment, respond perfectly to each other. For him, the other performer is Fanon, despite the differences in time and place. Over seven pages, he "plays" words, picking up and connecting various motifs, including the coming of night, Catherine and his love for her, his book project, his mother's belief in God, and the miracle of snow in July. He is a man at peace with himself and the world, at least for the moment. He hopes that Fanon had an experience like this, even in the midst of war, perhaps when he first saw snow in France.

At this point, two-thirds of the way through the book, Wideman actually begins what can be considered a Fanon novel. He begins with the myth of the Fates, the three sisters who determine the destiny of human beings. What is important to Wideman here is the symbolism of weaving, measuring, and cutting the thread of life for each individual. In order to leave Martinique to go fight for France, Fanon stole a bolt of cloth that his father had bought to make a suit for a wedding. Thus, his fate is literally connected to threads. The author follows him from his home island to Dominica, back to Martinique, then onto a troop ship (the *Oregon)* that is supplied in Bermuda and finally heads to Casablanca, arriving on March 30, 1944.[36] The ship transports only dark-skinned volunteers; the *beke,* white descendents of the original French settlers, decide not to fight for France.

Wideman plays with the names linked to this journey. Oregon is the name of an American state, the same country where Fanon died; Bermuda was the island setting for *The Tempest,* in which, as Wideman has repeatedly noted during his career, Caliban, the black man, is controlled by Prospero the white magician, and Casablanca is the Spanish word for "white house," meaning both the American center of power, but also the castle, the Big House, the mansion of those who gain their wealth and power by exploiting slaves, peasants, serfs, the poor.[37]

He then flashes back to Martinique, to a saint's day parade in Fort-de-France, which includes all the different groups of people. Some of the music played is from Brittany, where Wideman is located while working on the book. The reason for this music is that many of those involved in the French slave trade were Bretons and became the *beke* of the island. So, the author links himself not only to Fanon and the black population of the island, but also to the whites. He then imagines a soccer game on the parade grounds with Frantz and his brothers as one of the teams. In describing the play, he compares Fanon to Michael Jordan and the idea of "flow" discussed earlier. For the brothers, time stops and they maneuver the ball perfectly toward and into the goal. The writer compares this to the life Fanon lived and the one he is trying to write. It is beyond words and the standard ways of understanding life.

He also adds a ghost story to suggest Fanon's thinking about racial issues. Sent away from the city to a rural school at the beginning of the war, Fanon and his brother are taken on a field trip to a local chateau. According to legend, the *beke* who owned it accumulated treasure chests filled with gold. One day, he had one of his oldest and most faithful slaves dig a hole to bury one of the boxes. After the old man dragged the box into the hole, the *beke* shot and killed him so that he could never reveal its location. He then spread the story of the murder so that those who believed in ghosts would not search for the treasure. Apparently, Fanon the next day wrote a short story about the incident, but turned it into a ghost tale where the slave gets his revenge. Wideman then speculates how this becomes relevant later on:

Years later, composing *Black Skins, White Masks,* Fanon must have recalled the legend of the *beke* who sentenced Old Tom to eternal servitude. Wouldn't Fanon have admired begrudgingly the *beke*'s cold logic. Slaves belonged to their owners from cradle to grave, the law declared, but the *beke* had demonstrated that a slave's usefulness could be extended beyond the arbitrary limits of birth and death.[38]

This insight would make the master godlike in the eyes of the slave, or in the case of Fanon's Africa, in the eyes of the natives who had been colonized by the Europeans.[39]

We also learn Fanon's reaction to snow when he sees it for the first time; this experience is important because it challenges what the narrator had said earlier about what he hoped that response would be. It happens in France while he is part of a convoy. The snow comes in the middle of the night and is accompanied by freezing rain. Its effect is fear and suffering, since the troops are not prepared for it and have no means of protecting themselves from it. In addition, Fanon associates it with the white ash that was part of the Mount Pelee eruption that killed so many people in Martinique. Wideman then extends this to the white blood cells that pour through Fanon's body with the leukemia. The snow represents, not a miracle, as it did with Wideman sitting with his glass of wine in Brittany, but with death. It is a kind of horror.

Wideman tries to imagine some other option by having his brother talk about the interconnectedness of all humans:

> You got this one human trying to make a life for itself on the planet. Seems like a lotta us, but we's all the same one, doing the same thing—hunting for something to eat every day, a safe place to lie down at night. Wanting good loving and good talk. Some singing and dancing and maybe getting a little high now and then. We stay alive by having babies, growing new cells cause the old cells get tired and wore out. You and me and everybody else rolled up together into one big One. But the trouble is the hands of the body done forgot each other . . . People so stuck up in they own little worlds they forget they live in the same body and got to depend on the same two hands.[40]

Wideman, through Robby, brings us close to what the Buddhist master Thich Nhat Hanh calls "interbeing," that is, the connection of all living things.[41] This philosophy says that everything in the world is related to everything else. The example is the paper on which such words are written. The paper comes from trees that are nourished by water that comes from clouds, so we can say that the spiritual master needs clouds in order to communicate his words. Such an organic view of life requires respect for all living things. Wideman's view can be said to be more limited because he is concerned only with human beings, but the principle is the same. In this way, he can offer the positive side of Fanon's argument against racism and colonialism. If human beings could see how they need each other, instead of focusing on how they can exploit each other, then there would be a way out of the problems that Fanon wrote about 60 years ago and that Wideman sees as still causing so much suffering still today. In other words, the solution is love.

But before we can arrive at that conclusion, the author must resolve some of the issues in his story. There is, for example, still the unresolved mystery of the severed head that opened the novel. To tie up this loose end, he has Thomas put the head into a black garbage bag and toss it into the East River during one of his walks. The character remembers writing once a short story called "Damballah," in which, as we know, a young slave boy carries the head of a murdered African to the river, where he sends it on its way back to Africa. Thomas hopes that, if the ending worked once, it will work again. The problem is that, as a writer, he no longer believes in tidy endings. He points out, for example, that the East River is a tidal waterway, so it sometimes flows inland rather than out to the ocean. Though he does not mention it, the question remains whether the package in fact contained a head, since he never fully opened it. So, this solution seems more about the character's fear than about how to resolve a story.

We then turn, as the story winds down, to Fanon's own writing. As a psychiatrist, he is interested in people's heads and, in a way, how those heads have become disconnected from bodies in the sense that his clients do not know what to think of what is going on in their lives. One group he worked with were the French officials who tortured Algerians to try to get information. They find themselves unable to leave their work behind, so they are sometimes abusive to their families without understanding why. In writing about them, Fanon is very concerned that he allows them to speak in their own voices rather than presume to speak for them. In other words, he wants to do the very opposite of what he sees whites doing to blacks. In presenting this idea, Wideman is having his hero do what he tries to do in his own work—allow all the stories to be told, in the voices of the people who have the experience. In other words, he is saying that Fanon is a version of himself.

At the end of the book, he returns to Fanon and his mother. In this version, they never meet because he is constantly guarded by the police. She wheels back and forth in the hallways, trying to figure out who is in the room. Inside, Fanon comes to expect her to ride by each day and tries to see who she might be. The mother questions one of the nurses, who says that he must be some dangerous person to get so much attention, although his serious illness makes the security pointless. They also have a conversation about the premature baby unit, which seems to be Wideman's way of introducing his family back into the story, since Jamila would have been in such a place after she was born.

In an epilogue of sorts, Fanon is preparing to speak at a conference somewhere in Africa. Most of the episode is devoted to the busyness of the delegates as they run in and out of the hall, looking for prostitutes or pontificating to a small band of believers. Fanon wonders how he is ever going to be heard above the chatter and the slamming of limousine doors right outside. He wonders if his words will matter at all. He is also curious about the white members of the audience, wondering about their role, their relative importance. Do those few give the conference importance, since without them, no one in the larger world would pay attention? Wideman ends this section with the image of a map—one on which traditionally the only part that mattered was the part occupied by whites. Fanon's idea, Wideman says, is to draw a new map, where everyone has a place that matters.

The key question for this novel is why the author decided to make it so complicated, with more attention paid to himself and his family than to Fanon, with plot elements that do not go anywhere, such as the severed head, with a writer (Thomas) who is clearly a version of the author, but who disappears for long sections of the book, and with fantasy elements, such as the movie director and the meeting of his mother and Fanon. It would make sense to do a more or less standard historical novel, given the fact that Wideman had access to the main biography of Fanon's life and that the issues that Fanon raised are important to Wideman. Fanon is clearly someone he is obsessed with, having written a short story, large parts of *The Island,* and this novel about him. The imprisoned brother asks, "Why Fanon?" and that question would occur to many readers. So, why not give us a straight answer?

One response has to do with *what* rather than *why.* Wideman is not so much interested in Fanon the man, who lived in various places during a specific time period and did a number of things. It does not matter that some of the places—Martinique, France during World War II, Paris after the war, Algeria—would be colorful and exotic locations for Americans to read about (or to see if Jean-Luc Godard had actually wanted to make a film). It does not matter that this could be an inspirational story of a poor child from the islands growing up to be a world-renowned figure, nor that he went through various adventures and narrow escapes, nor that it is a tragic story of a man dying far too young of a terrible disease far from home. All of those elements would make for a good story, maybe even an inspirational one. But that is not what Wideman wants to do.

Instead, he is interested in Fanon and his ideas. So much of his writing, as should be clear by now, is about what happens when people do not recognize or respect the humanity of others. We see this in his work on Homewood, on the yellow-fever epidemic, on MOVE, on prisons, on violence and racism. Most of the time, he has no good solutions to the problems; he sometimes seems to be saying that we are doomed to do the same terrible things over and over. His question in this book is whether Fanon might offer a way out, whether the work of a mid-20th century radical thinker might help us to change the world in the 21st century. To test this thought, he decides to tell the story of how one can write about Fanon in our time. Part of that work involves presenting the world as it exists today, especially as it exists for people at the bottom of society, those that Fanon most wanted to help. As always, Wideman goes to his family for those experiences. How would his mother and brother respond to this West Indian revolutionary? And since he is often in his own stories, since he does not want to pretend that he necessarily has the right answers just because he can write better than most people, he talks about the problems of turning this effort into a novel. While he is interested in ideas, he wants them to be meaningful in real lives, so he introduces severed heads to symbolize the dangers of separating our thinking from our feeling, our heads from our hearts. *Fanon* can be said to be a maddening book, because of all its complicated parts, but that is because Wideman considers the world to be a maddening place. He wants to be honest about the madness, but also wants to bring sanity, so he tells us about the revolutionary and psychiatrist Fanon, who might point us in the right direction.

It is also the case that Wideman has from the beginning of his career liked to experiment as a writer. We can see him doing this as early as *A Glance Away*. The most radical experiment is his 2010 collection of stories called *Briefs: Stories for the Palm of the Mind*. Here, he creates what he calls micro stories. They are a version of what is more generally known as flash fiction. The Oxford online dictionary defines it as "fiction that is extremely brief, typically a few hundred words or fewer in its entirety."[42] Some sources put the maximum at 75 words, while others allow it to be 1,500 words.[43] Since a published page of print is approximately 400 words, this means that the longest of these stories would be less than four pages. The longest story in *Briefs* is a little over five pages, but it is broken into three parts that are really separate stories.

The other experimental part of this project is that it is being published by Lulu, the largest self-publishing company. Wideman has traditionally had contracts with large publishing houses, such as Houghton Mifflin, which produced *Fanon*.[44] The problem for publishers is that, while Wideman is a highly respected and honored writer, his works have never reached the level of blockbusters or even the success of serious literary artists such as Toni Morrison. He sees self-publishing as an alternative: "I'm very, very attracted to a situation where I have more control over what happens to my book, where I have more control over who I reach. I like the idea of being in charge. I like the idea of being able to speak to people, have a conversation even as the book enters the world." He also points to another problem for the audience for his works in the same interview: "My books suffer because there's an African American category and they're sold on a particular shelf. That shelf can become a kind of prison. Readers get into the habit of going to a shelf and thinking that literature is divided in that way. You miss the opportunity to reach new readers."[45] Since Lulu sells online rather than through the kind of distribution system used by large publishers, a key question would be how new readers are going to find his writings. But since the company is print on demand, it does not have to invest in printing copies that will never sell. In addition, it can make the book available in either print or e-book format, thus potentially attracting readers who use the internet as their access to reading material.

Another factor is that his son Daniel was Director of Product Management for Lulu and thus in a position to assist his father in publicizing this and other books. They have created the John Edgar Wideman Microstory Contest. The winner may have the story published in new editions of *Briefs*. Lulu also created a VIP service, with Wideman as their first customer. While basic Lulu publishing is free, VIP offers a professional package for design and marketing for a fee. Thus, Wideman was able to control the process of getting his book into print, while not having to involve himself in the mundane details. One thing that he did to publicize his work is create a blog on Goodreads.com. His two posts, one describing the book and the other reproducing the Lulu interview connected to the publication, were both posted on March 13, 2010. While there have been some views, his entries have generated no comments. This may suggest the difficulty of self-publishing—how are readers, especially potential new ones, going to find his work?

Briefs is made up of exactly 100 stories over 155 pages. In the blog, Wideman describes what the stories are about:

> The micro-fictions in my collection are about losing time, saving time, enduring time, fearing and escaping time.
>
> About the ubiquitous, silent pulse of time and how people learn to dance to it or not, to stumble through or find themselves graced by time or ignored or get their asses kicked.
>
> Time, the immaterial medium nobody can see, hear, smell, taste, touch, a vast neutral sea containing all creatures living and dead, a mysterious presence allowing us to move and speak and suffer our collective being.[46]

Some of the stories talk about the idea of time, almost philosophically, while others describe moments of change, such as birth and death or the nature of relationships. Some are about growing old, and others about remembering earlier days. In a move unusual for Wideman, some are about nature.

The focus of this discussion will be on stories that cover the themes we have seen throughout his career—family, social issues, and storytelling. The family stories as a whole span several generations, though each one tends to have a tight focus. "Party," for example, is devoted to Aunt May, who has been featured as a storyteller in several works. One of the things that we learn is that she was Freeda's first cousin. The party of the story is for her 83rd birthday. The narrator is some version of Wideman, since May calls him Mr. Doot (his nickname from *Sent for You Yesterday*) at the end. Though she is now in a wheelchair, he remembers a picture of her from many years earlier and imagines dancing a jitterbug with her. He also projects the story backward and forward at the same time: "May smiles at me from a sepia-toned photo. No. That's not true. Same smile but May smiles it here, now, her hand in mine, during the celebration of her 83rd birthday, although unbeknownst to everybody at the party (and everyone at the party in the old photo) the surgeon forgot a metal clip in May's gut last week that's festering and will kill her next Christmas Eve."[47] The glow of memory is tempered by the harsh reality of death. For Wideman, they are never far apart.

Death, aging, and memory play a part in several family stories. In "Answering Service," the narrator, having just talked to his mother, decides to call his father, then suddenly remembers that he died six years earlier. His habit, developed over many years, of calling them back to back, momentarily cancelled out a basic fact of his life. Another story,

"Passing On," takes him back to that death and his relationship with his father. In this case, the narrator is a man with grandchildren who is trying to pick out the appropriate suit for a funeral, presumably his father's. He feels that he has been defeated by the world, despite his pride and abilities: "Only prickly pride remained, pride in how he dressed, how he spoke the language, pride he hoped would allow him a dignified passage through final disappointments and fickleness." He wonders if there is anything that his father taught him that might help him now: "In other words he was aching to remember any occasion when or if his father had granted him permission to enter the unknown world his father inhabited a world that intersected only rarely with rooms shared with a wife and children."[48] The sad reality is that there is no such time; instead, there is something much crueler: "Teaching the shame of bearing an inexhaustible bag of useless tricks he knew better than to pass on."[49] The story plays with the notion of "pass on" as both dying and leaving a heritage. In this case, the death of the father leaves the son with nothing meaningful that he can leave to his own children and grandchildren.

But this harsh truth has not destroyed a sense of love. In "Automatic," the son comes to the father's apartment to take away his car keys, since the family is afraid of his driving. He has always resisted their request, claiming that he knows the car and the city so well he could "Drive this city blind-folded."[50] He creates a distraction by complaining about the contests that he keeps entering that never produce any prizes, even when he is told he has won. The son refuses to play this game, but is saddened by the reaction to his asking for the keys: "A slightly puzzled glance, a smile breaking my heart, *No, Daddy, no. Don't do it,* I'm crying out helplessly, silently, as he passes me the keys."[51] This sacrifice of independence and pride means that the father has resigned himself to old age and reliance on other people. To paraphrase Dylan Thomas, he has chosen to go softly into the night of death. For the son, the moment is incredibly sad.

Two other father stories relate to earlier days. "Work" tells about garbage men, one of the jobs that Edgar did as a way to make a living to support the family he often did not live with. As one of the senior workers, he always has the choice of the truck he and his partner Eduardo use. He regularly picks one of the oldest ones, because he says that it is "old and reliably undependable in predictable ways."[52] For the two men, this means that they can repair the truck themselves while out on their route rather than lose pay while waiting to have one of the newer trucks towed in for more complicated mechanical work. This passage suggests the subtle ways Wideman believes men of color (Eduardo is Latino) are exploited. Their employer docks their pay for the failure of the equipment, thus saving money by penalizing the workers.[53] But the story is not about anger at the situation. It is first about the pride of work, of being able to do what is necessary to get the job done. The second point shows the limited perspective of the father; he imagines his sons doing this work some day: "one load a day his contribution to peaceful streets, peaceful country, a promising life for boys like his sons who will ride up front one day, a good job, a family, a future."[54] What is striking here is the fact that Edgar Wideman wanted to become a dentist and moved his family to Shadyside for a better education for his children; yet, his son, in writing the story, sees the character who is clearly modeled on his father as having such a narrow view of the world. It seems almost like revenge on Edgar for being the kind of father he was.

A further complication comes in the last of this set, "Mercury," which immediately precedes "Work." The central character, Tommy, who in previous work had been a version of Robby, now is John. We know this because the narrator tells us that Tommy was the same age as Emmett Till, who was murdered the same year the story is set. A neighbor, Big Jim, has bought a new "streamlined F-86 Sabre jet slick Merc."[55] One morning, his father yells at him for being out late the night before. The boy tries to explain that he was just across the street sitting in the new car, that he was where his mother could see him. The father is not interested in his explanations; he grounds him and plans to talk to Big Jim. He prohibits him from being anywhere near the other man or his car, which we are told is "three-toned green." The child has no sense of what is happening. Only years later does he begin to connect the actions of that day to the Emmett Till killing. That terrible event produced fear in black parents about what might happen to their sons. Of course, this was something that could not really be explained to the children, in part because it was so traumatic for the parents. In addition, it was not the way of the Wideman family to explain anything directly.

If the stories of the father are troubled and complicated, those of the mother are far fewer and more straightforward. One of them, "Witness," is taken more or less directly from *Fanon*. It is a condensed version of the episode in which she sees a teenage boy shot by other boys, and then the next day, sees his parents come to the very spot where he died. Telling it in this more focused way brings the attention of the reader to the mother and her sympathy for that family: "How'd his people find the exact spot. Did they hear my old mind working to lead them, guide them along like I would if I could get up out of this damn wheelchair and take them by the hand."[56]

The only other story that fully involves the mother is "Pills," which, in a way, is the reverse of "Automatic," the story of the father and the car keys. As in that piece, the children, though sympathetic, have come to believe that the parent is no longer competent to handle life. In this case, the daughter comes by regularly to set out her mother's medication so that she will take the right amount in the right order. The task is difficult for an old woman—there are 23 pills to be taken each day. About once a week, she flushes a day's worth of medicine down the toilet, and in this way, takes control of the end of her life. Dumping the pills is "her prescription, her cure. She's the doctor." Unlike the father, who finally surrenders, she secretly makes her own choices:

> Happier dumping pills than swallowing pills one by one to the last burp and gag and bitter aftertaste, happier flushed away hand in hand in the colorful swirl down the drain than when she takes pill after pill and they make her sick, or as well as she's ever going to be, the doctor says, but I'll get better soon, she smiles to herself, watching the last pill disappear.[57]

Her form of control is to speed her death. The medicine may extend her life, but it robs her of any real meaning for that life. She is being artificially and uncomfortably kept alive. As a woman of faith, she chooses to believe that God can better decide than doctors what the end of her life should be. She prefers days of clarity and relative ease, even if it means shortening her life.

Some of the stories concern the children. "Divorce," for example, is about a father meeting with his grown daughter to talk about his divorce from her mother. He worries about what to wear, almost as if this were a date. He wants to believe it can be a pleasant meeting, but he knows better. When the waiter spills a little coffee, he realizes the situation:

> Nobody's fault, really, that their table happens to be at the foot of a mountain range with jagged peaks looming above them, obdurate and unimpeachable as annular rings of a tree. The crack, the fissure begins under there, under the stony folds of mountains stacking up, stacking up. Too much weight, too many years. The

earth shudders, dances the rug under the poor, pompadoured waiter's feet, *Sorry . . . sorry . . .* he faintly warbles, . . . *excuse me,* a
canary dying of what's to come.[58]

The images here pile up like the mountains. There is the weight of years
of relationships, the weight of emotions, the weight of responsibilities.
There are the cracks in the family that run deep, causing the tremors like
an earthquake. The poor waiter is like the bird sent into a mine to see if
there are poisonous gasses; and we know there are because he is "dying."
    While none of the characters are named, Jamila would have been
25 at the time of John and Judy's divorce. Given the difficult nature of
her birth, the troubles of her brother and uncle, the complexities of her
parents' marriage, and her own success in the sport associated with her
father and her desire to follow in the footsteps of her mother and become a lawyer, it is easy to see this story as expressing an emotional, if
not factual, truth about the family.
    Two of the stories return to Jake and especially his father's relation-
ship to him. The first of these, "Thirteen," was the 13th story published
in a set of micro stories in *Harper's Magazine* in October 2008. It is also
Jake's date of birth—February 13, 1970. The narrator also notes that it
was the date (August 13, 1986) on which Eric Kane was killed in Arizona. He then takes us back to that time: "With two Arizona lawyers,
my son, his mother I'd stopped loving and me in it, the car speeds south
to north, Phoenix to Flagstaff."[59] This event follows what we know happened when Jake contacted his parents after several days of running.
Because Arizona wants to start executing juveniles, the only chance to
save him is through a plea bargain. Thus, the case is, in a sense, lost even
before it begins.
    He steps back to recount briefly the killing and flight, then endures the
radio playing his son's favorite song as they drive. At the end, he takes
on some of the responsibility he had not fully accepted before:

You only get one chance. That's all a father gets with a son. A
child's life in your hands once. That's it. Once. He was born in
New Jersey and I took classes to assist at his birth, but some clown
passed out the day before, so on the 13th the delivery room off
limits for fathers and I missed the moment the earth cracked and
she squeezed out his bloody head.[60]

Even in this moment of responsibility, he shifts the blame. His opportunity, if we believe the story, was only at the actual birth, and some

"clown" spoiled that. But, of course, he also had the next 15 years of his son's life to make a difference. He makes the tale about luck and chance, and so "thirteen" becomes a sign of bad fortune. He takes himself off the hook once again.

"You Are My Sunshine" begins as a comment about writing, but turns into a story about family. The narrator reports getting an email from his French translator, Jean-Pierre Richard, who has served as both a translator of Wideman's fiction and a bibliographer of all of his work. Since the first question is about the relationship between actual family history and the fictional version, it provides the narrator the opportunity to describe himself as a kind of translator between the two: "I'm just a mediator with no answers or changing answers, always more questions than answers, as curious as you are, Jean-Pierre, a translator like you, who at best attempts to mediate irreconcilable differences."[61] Here, Wideman claims that he does not know himself exactly how he makes the choices in his work between what is from his imagination and what is from his actual life and those of his family.

He offers an example in response to Richard's second question, about the song "You Are My Sunshine." He explains that it was a favorite of John French and even mentions where his grandfather was originally from. He can offer no help in translating the emotional experience of listening to the song when he was a child. He then compares trying to communicate its effect to "translating love into words and sending it in a letter to my son in prison." He exercises his imagination by referring to the 1957 cover of the song done by Richard Berry and the Pharaohs, which Wideman would have listened to as a teenager. He says that Berry "got much of the song right because his version playing in my head brings my son here right beside me, with me, wherever else he must be."[62] Through the exercise of his imagination, Wideman can create a connection with Jake that is impossible in real life, and he does it through engaging a real person in the present who helps him remember a real event with his grandfather in the past. Fact and fiction blend neatly here.

The remaining stories about family are about himself and various moments in his life. "First Love" describes a visit to Atlantic City in 1960, where he met a young black girl who spent the day with him. They spent a lot of time kissing; he even recalls stopping the count of kisses at 22. Then, she leaves to go to work, promising to return the next day. But he never sees her again. But since he can recall the day years later and still label it his first love, she had a strong effect on him. He still wonders if she simply lied or if perhaps the problem was his:

She doesn't return the next night—or next or next or next—no matter how long I stand getting wetter and wetter staring at the sea. Or I don't stand waiting on the beach long enough. Or maybe I'm still standing there and it's still raining and she knows better than to trust her heart to a fool who'd venture out in awful weather like this looking for love.[63]

He is 20 at the time of the story, so if this is his first love, then she may well be right in considering him a "fool." His own insecurities come through in the story.

Another kind of memory is at work in "Equals." It tells of John in fifth grade math with Mr. Brooks. The teacher actually likes him, though he is one of the few black kids in the school. One day, John is unable to grasp a key concept, multiplication by zero. Instead of recognizing his lack of skill, he persists in arguing that the idea makes no sense. Finally in frustration, "Mr. Brooks whacked me with a ruler for being stupid or obstinate or arrogant or a smart aleck or whatever combination and permutation of the above he figured I was displaying to the class."[64] The narrator says that it took him 40 years to recover an interest in numbers. It took longer to deal with the teacher; at a reading, Mr. Brooks appears, but instead of embracing him, the writer "reminded him he'd hit me long ago and called me Jack, his name for me though my name's John." Though he wants to go further, "I shut up because given the look in his eyes, I'd stung Mr. Brooks enough, though not as much as his ruler stung the back of my hand."[65]

The real source of anger here is not immediately clear. Does John hit back decades later because he was embarrassed by the punishment? After all, his behavior in the class does not appear to have been respectful of the teacher, who is right about the concept. He does not indicate that he was treated differently than other students; in fact, he seems to have been a teacher's pet before the incident. Was he upset for being "called out of his name," a folk expression meaning that a derogatory term was used instead of his name? But "Jack" is a nickname for "John," and so would not be truly insulting, especially if the teacher is trying to be friendly. The difficulty of answering the question does not mean that it does not matter; 40 years later, John uses his power as a celebrity to sting his former teacher and seems to feel justified in doing so.

There are also a few pieces that discuss his more recent life, specifically his time spent in Brittany near the French coast. Interestingly, two of them are about birds, a subject seldom seen in Wideman, in part because he virtually never writes about nature. In this sense, he is truly a man of the city. In "Coo Coo," while he sits in the garden writing, he hears the birds and recognizes them as some variation of mourning dove, though he does not know the French name for them. He does not care about the names because he claims to be learning their language: "I'm too busy teaching myself the birds' language. Not phrases or sentences yet. A single word at a time. *Loneliness* the first." His language becomes poetic in this description:

> Only the frantic beating of wings, endless chasing, one coo-cooing at another whether another listens or not, each solitary cry a sounding of this world's silence that vanishes in another world's silence, every cry the same and different, an eloquent, careful repetition and mocking echo of itself, a language of mirrors I'm trying to learn: coo-coo, coo-coo, coo-coo."[66]

We get the sense that Wideman is talking about himself here, sending his writings into what he thinks of as the world's silence, with perhaps no one listening.

"Wolf Whistle" takes place in the same neighborhood. When he walks down a certain street toward the tavern or the beach, he hears what he first thinks must be a "mad boy." What he hears are whistles that he first takes to be racial insults, but then realizes that the sounds are made by a duo of parrots caged in a yard. Once he realizes his error, he begs forgiveness of the nonexistent boy. He also calls the birds "lynched" because they are trapped in their cages forever. He tries to teach them to say "Emmett Till," but they ignore him, so he gives up. The story can be read as a self-criticism, a tendency to see racial attacks in everything. Most of the story is devoted to the beauty of the coast and the everyday lives of families, but he misses part of the pleasure of it because of his obsession.

The question of race emerges in a story entitled "Manhole." In it, an African American jogger makes a joke about workers coming out of a manhole: "So that's where you white guys come from."[67] The workers are angered, and one of them pulls a gun and starts firing at the narrator, who manages to escape. In an act of revenge, he then elbows in the face another white sitting on a bench. He ends by saying that New York is the "biggest, baddest apple in the world."

A similar story, "Quiet Car," describes Tommy's response to a woman using her cell phone in the quiet car of a train. The first time, he reminds her of the rules, the second time, he is silent but angry, but the third tame, he stands over her, and when she tells him to "Fuck off," he grabs the phone and smashes it. When he later tells his lover, who is white, she is shocked at his stupidity:

> A big black man snatching a white woman's phone. Did you forget we still lynch negroes in America.
>   C'mon. Wasn't about race. I admit I behaved badly, but the whole thing's kind of funny, too.
>   Hope you convince the judge it's funny. Here's funny. Me, blonde and white and female, schooling a grown-up black guy about race.[68]

What is distinctive about both stories is the aggressiveness of the narrators in response to white behavior. In most of his work, blacks are either victims or self-destructive, They virtually never act out righteous indignation at the insults or conditions they have to endure.

"War Stories" indicates one source of this anger and frustration. It is addressed to Tim O'Brien, the author of *Going After Cacciato* and, more important for this story, *The Things They Carried*, a collection of short fiction about the Vietnam War. The narrator wants to ask O'Brien about "the war here in America," by which he means the imprisoning of minority and poor men, the conflict between wealth and poverty, the dumbing down of education, and continued racial and ethnic tensions. He wants to know what people have to "carry" in this war and how they will tell who the enemy is. He sees conflicts the nation is engaged in elsewhere as an extension of this one:

> Not separate wars, really. No more separate than different colors of skin that provide logic and cover for war. No more separate than the color of my skin from yours, my friend, if we could meet again and talk about carrying the things we carry, about what torments me, an old man ashamed of this country I assume you still live in, too.[69]

Here, we have the deeper meaning of the incidents in the earlier stories. They are not isolated cases of impoliteness or bigotry or acting out, but rather, skirmishes in a war that everyone is caught up in, whether they know it or not. The shame comes from a sense that the nation has not only failed to live up to its principles, but that some people benefit—socially, politically, economically—from that failure and have no desire to change things.

One particular target of Wideman's anger is religion, which he has recognized as important to his mother and her ability to survive, but which he has had little use for. Here, that indifference becomes hostility. "Giblets" begins with humor that quickly turns into horror. Clara Johnson's dog Giblets has four legs, "one leg for each day of the week."[70] She only counts four days because her mother insisted that Friday, Saturday, and Sunday were to be devoted to religion. On those three days, Clara would often be beaten by her mother because she could never be good enough. So, when she is finally away from her mother, she counts only the four "good" days as part of the week. When she learns that some local church has decided to add Thursday to the holy days, she cuts off one of Giblet's legs.

In "Martyr," Wideman appears to be describing the persecution and torture of Christians in Japan. The story is told by a Jesuit priest. He reports the suffering of a child who has boiling water poured over her by the shoguns, but who cries out that she is happy to rejoin her family in the afterlife. He compares her bravery to his own behavior: "A child's pure soul undefeated by the fires of Hell, though I, King's envoy and Chief of the Jesuit band, quake and cringe, hung by my heels above a pit of steaming dung, and renounce my Father's name."[71] The innocent child, who knows nothing of theology, is braver than the man who has years of experience in the faith. Wideman's point is not about the evil done to Christians, since, as seen in the previous story, evil is everywhere, but about the uselessness of faith. It produces cowardice and cruelty, not only in believers, but also in others, as in Clara's treatment of Giblets. For the author, it is just one more weapon in the war he sees going on.

No discussion of social issues would be complete for Wideman, of course, without basketball. "One on One" continues his ongoing lament for the deterioration of the playground game seen in *Two Cities* and *Hoop Roots*. In this version, an older man regularly replaces the nets that are torn down by what he calls "wannabe Shaqs."[72] He decides to scare them into respect for the court and his efforts. So, he pulls a gun on the next one, not intending to use it. But the player grabs it and kills the old man. What the old man failed to understand was the change in rules that says that violence and individualism are more important than the game. Respect is gained through ruthless power, not skill or tradition.

"Genocide" concerns a Homewood player whose game seems to be perfect. His skills and style change the game, making the court smaller, leading other players to understand that he makes them better. The narrator imagines this to be the game as the Buddha would see it, since the Buddha only sees perfection. It is also perfection for the speaker, since it is the game as he always dreamed he would play it one day. But this leads to a strange desire: "I wanted to kill him."[73] The reason is that such quality cannot last; he does not want to see "the pop or slide of him going down slowly, coming apart."[74] To stop it now would be to preserve the perfection. Since it cannot get better, it can only decline. In making this point, Wideman is expressing a Romantic artistic idea, that beauty is connected to death,[75] whether that beauty is in art or nature or athletics. Once the ideal is achieved, there is no place to go. The story may reflect not only the author's own declining physical skills, but also his sense in writing these stories that, at his age, he can no longer take on major long works.

This point is reinforced when we turn to his pieces on storytelling. In "Haiku," he tells of the African American novelist Richard Wright spending the last days of his life writing poems in the traditional Japanese form of the haiku, which has strict rules about length and subject matter. Wideman describes the writing as a kind of prison, but one that is highly productive; Wright was able to produce thousands of the three-line poems.[76] It is easy to see how Wright's experience could be a way for Wideman to talk about his own work. At almost 70, with 10 novels behind him, he could find in very short fiction a way to revitalize himself, to take on a new challenge; while flash fiction is not as restrictive as haiku, it does require a disciplined way of thinking about how a story gets told. The fact that he could produce 100 of them for *Briefs* suggests that he took to this discipline like Wright took to haiku.

"Writing" and "Writing (2)" are about the process of creating stories and the relationship of stories to reality. In the first, we seem to be getting a lesson on technique: "A man on a bicycle passes down Essex Street in the rain. Gray. Green. Don't go back. You won't write it any better. More. You can write more or less. That's all."[77] We seem to be in a creative writing class, with a discussion about precision and conciseness. But it becomes almost philosophical when he insists that the world is not a place full of stories waiting to be written. They only exist when writers complete them:

> To hang people's hopes on, the hope that their story will be revealed one day, worth something, true, even if no one else can see it or touch it, a beautiful story like in that girl's sad eyes on the subway, her life story real as anyone's, as real as yours, her eyes say to me, a story no one has written, desperate to be written. Never will be.[78]

Stories are what storytellers create, not what people live, which means that the experiences of the vast majority of human beings will never find expression. Lives can be made into stories, as Wideman has demonstrated over his 45-year career, but most will not.

In the second piece, he tries to explain the effect of stories in the world. He compares two dreams that will not come true—being the best writer in the world and gaining the freedom of his son. His point is the question we would naturally ask—how are these things connected? They are not, even if he would like them to be. Becoming the best writer would not change the situation of his son. And if his son were free, it would not improve his writing. Part of what he describes as his sadness in the story is the impossibility of achieving either thing, though they are the two most important things in his life. Art cannot fix the world, though he has devoted much of his career to trying.

In "Wall," he nearly reaches the point of despair. In it, he returns to the garden in Brittany, where he likes to write. After he follows his routine, a voice says to him:

> No. No matter how many words you write or how carefully you choose them, no one's able to see the world through another person's eyes. Another's eyes negate yours, verify the fact a world you will never get to see is moving along quite well, thank you, whether you're present or absent The world commences just beyond the margin of your vision, with what you don't see, and the rest is simply you, what you do see, your separate gaze of no consequence, impermanent, arbitrary as what you don't see. no matter how closely you look or another looks at you.[79]

This is the ultimate fear of a writer, that what he or she says is totally irrelevant, that what they claim as important matters to no one else. Especially for someone like Wideman, who has tried to speak to reality as he knows it, to make others see Homewood, Philadelphia, and prison through his eyes for so many years, the possibility that no one listens or understands is devastating. But writing about that fear may well be the way to overcome it, since he can turn even that nightmare into a fiction.

Some of the pieces on writing are not so pessimistic. In "Ruins," he turns an argument with his wife into a game for the reader. The narrator, a writer over 60, remembers a line from a Latin American novelist, "the ruins of her backside." As a writer, he considers it a "striking phrase." His wife, however, wants to know why it is not an insult to the woman described. He tries to explain that it is part of a work of fiction, a symbol of human frailty. But the wife wants nothing to do with this; she wants to know why it cannot be the husband's backside if he has to expose somebody's body to the public. The narrator insists that if his wife only knew the actual couple, she would appreciate how much they loved each other. But then we get to the real point. He assumes that she has not "read Pepe's novels as far as I know and sometimes I wonder if she really reads mine, since her upset with Pepe is a replay of numerous upsets with me when she confuses my fiction with our lives. What do you think, Dear Reader. Does she have a case."[80] Here, Wideman is having fun with his own claim that he carefully disguises the connection between real life and his fiction in his own writing. In at least this case, he is called on it. The argument brings him back from the idea of writing as a separate world to the very practical perspective of a reader.

"Review" pretends to teach readers how to write book reviews of collections of short stories, but it, in fact, makes fun of the whole process of evaluation of writing. The narrator explains that these reviews do not take any intelligence. All you have to do is say that some of the stories are better than other stories, since readers will assume that such a statement is always true; moreover, the reviewer randomly picks which ones are better, because readers are unlikely to read much, if any, of the book. You also do not want to be too precise in your comments; that would suggest that you might be smarter than the audience, which believes that it does not take much intelligence to either review or write stories. The piece implies that Wideman has considerable experience with reviewers, which would be expected in his long career. And since many of those people work for newspapers and popular magazines, it would not be surprising to find them baffled by much of his work. This is his opportunity to get even.

In the end, he regains his sense of his role. "Shadow" consists of one sentence: "He notices a shadow dragged rippling behind him over the grass, one more silent, black presence for which he is responsible."[81] It has almost the effect of haiku in its brevity and precision. But more than an image, which is what haiku is, it also suggests a story. The shadow being dragged implies reluctance or resistance. If it is his shadow, why does he notice it in the present and not take it for granted? And why is it "one more" presence rather than the only one? And, of course, what makes him responsible? The story suggests the burden of being John Wideman, who feels obligated to carry the weight of many black presences in his work. The shadow can be seen as part of himself that he must try to understand, just as he tries to understand his brother, his son, the other members of his family, the history of Homewood, and the reality of the nation. His calling, to use a religious term that he would not necessarily choose, is to take responsibility for telling about all of it. He must do this because so many of those black presences have been "silent," not willing or more likely, not able to tell their own stories. In this one sentence, he adds himself to those whose tales must be told if we are ever to come close to the African proverb he often quotes—all stories are true. Despite his fears about lost stories and an inability to tell them right, it is his obligation to do as much of that work as possible.

CONCLUSION

The Achievement of John Edgar Wideman

The first lesson given to would-be authors is that they should write what they know. In some cases, this advice is followed directly. Laura Ingalls Wilder, Ernest Hemingway, and Willa Cather gained success by writing about their childhood experiences about Minnesota, upper Michigan, or Nebraska. The knowledge can be gained in a more voluntary way, such as William Shakespeare reading histories of Scotland or Denmark, Charles Dickens wandering the streets of London, or Stephen Crane becoming a war correspondent. Sometimes writers have to go away from what they know, at least temporarily, in order to turn it into literature. William Faulkner had to leave Mississippi to create Yoknapatawpha County; Zora Neale Hurston had to go to Columbia University to invent the tales of Eatonville, Florida; Carson McCullers moved to New York City so that she can recreate Columbus, Georgia. Even works of fantasy can be based on an author's knowledge; J.R.R. Tolkien used his studies of mythology, fairy tales, and Catholic theology in producing *Lord of the Rings*.

In the case of John Edgar Wideman, a combination of these approaches applies. From his first novel in 1967 to his 2010 collection of stories, Homewood is present as a key setting. He gives us the history of the family in that place and locates particular streets, parks, and buildings that can be found on real maps. He creates that place for his readers as completely as Faulkner gives us Oxford, Mississippi, or Sherwood Anderson gives us Winesburg, Ohio. He adds to this, his experience of Philadelphia, both as a place he lived and as a place with its own history available to both residents and tourists. To those memories, he adds research into the yellow fever epidemic, the MOVE organization, the American prison system, and the arts, such as painting, sculpture, and photography. But in order to make sense of this as stories, he had to go away, first to college, then to England, and then to Wyoming. Only by moving away could he come back. And sometimes, the past came to him, as when Robby, a fugitive, shows up at John's Laramie home, or when he returns to Homewood for his grandmother's funeral, only to have his aunt tell the stories of Sybela Owens and the founding of Homewood.

But for Wideman, these places and these people are more than just the factual basis for his work. They are also the emotional and spiritual truth of what he does and who he is. He can never escape their impact on his life and his career. Part of his story is, in fact, his effort to escape them, to go off to the university, to England, to Wyoming, in order become something and someone different. His great achievement is that he both tries to do this and ultimately fails. He could not become the writer of so much important work without studying the great tradition of literature and learning the methods of writing modern literature. Whatever he or others may say about his work, from beginning to end, he has been caught up in the techniques of modern and contemporary writing. His work is considered by many to be extremely difficult, in large part because he refuses to talk down to readers; he expects them to figure out his methods and his language.

At the same time, he would not have his distinctive voice as a writer without returning to Homewood and its people and stories. It gives him a solid base from which to work, with its deeply human problems and possibilities and characters. He could not invent anyone as rich as John French or his own mother. Here is a deep history and a set of social problems and ethical issues as rich as anything in any other culture. His complicated relationship to that community and history is itself a very modern problem that makes for rich stories. It is the same theme we find in the great work of James Joyce and William Faulkner—how can you write about a place that you both love and hate? The achievement of John Wideman has been his ability to give us a contemporary version of that problem, as he blends real life with his imagination to create a truly impressive body of writing.

Notes

INTRODUCTION

1. Vanden Heuvel, "Interview with Jean Stein Vanden Heuvel," *The Paris Review* (Spring 1956); James B. Meriwether and Michael Millgate, eds., *Lion in the Garden: Interviews with William Faulkner, 1926–1962* (Reprint, Lincoln: University of Nebraska Press, 1980), 255.

2. Bonnie TuSmith, ed., *Conversations with John Edgar Wideman* (Jackson: University Press of Mississippi, 1998), 95.

CHAPTER 1

1. Bonnie TuSmith, ed., *Conversations with John Edgar Wideman* (Jackson: University Press of Mississippi, 1998), 15.

2. Ibid., 48.

3. John Edgar Wideman, *Brothers and Keepers* (New York: Holt, Rinehart and Winston, 1984), 72.

4. Ibid., 73–74.

5. John Edgar Wideman, *Fatheralong* (New York: Pantheon, 1994), 122.

6. Wideman, *Brothers and Keepers*, 44.

7. Wideman, *Fatheralong*, 86–87.

8. Ibid., 117–120.

CHAPTER 2

1. Bonnie TuSmith, ed., *Conversations with John Edgar Wideman* (Jackson: University Press of Mississippi, 1998), 42, 86–88.

2. Ibid., 3.

3. Steven Beeber, "John Edgar Wideman: The Art of Fiction, No. 171," *Paris Review* (Spring 2002), http://www.theparisreview.org/interviews/422/the-art-of fiction-no-171-john-edgar-wideman.

4. John Edgar Wideman, *Brothers and Keepers* (New York: Holt, Rinehart and Winston, 1984), 29.

5. Ibid.

6. Darryl Dawson had his own frustration and anger issues, which emerged several years later, when he left a position at Howard University to become Col. Rafik Bilal-El of the Volunteer Army of Liberation, a group that fought drug trafficking in America's ghettos, but also advocated secession of black people from the United States. The group was investigated during the House Un-American Activities Committee hearings on the urban disturbances of the late 1960s.

7. Wideman, *Brothers and Keepers*, 29–31.

8. The John Edgar Wideman Papers are housed at the Houghton Library at Harvard University. They have not been catalogued, though they are open to researchers.

9. TuSmith, *Conversations*, 35–37.

10. Ibid., 36–37.

CHAPTER 3

1. Bonnie TuSmith, ed., *Conversations with John Edgar Wideman* (Jackson: University Press of Mississippi, 1998), 34.

2. See James W. Coleman, *Blackness and Modernism: The Literary Career of John Edgar Wideman* (Jackson: University Press of Mississippi, 1989) and Doreatha Drummond Mbalia, *John Edgar Wideman: Reclaiming the African Personality* (Selinsgrove, PA: Susquehanna University Press, 1995).

3. See Steven Beeber, "John Edgar Wideman: The Art of Fiction, No. 171," *Paris Review* (Spring 2002), http://www.theparisreview.org/interviews/422/the-art-of-fiction-no-171-john-edgar-wideman.

4. See Thomas Stearns Eliot, *The Waste Land and Other Writings* (New York: Modern Library, 2002).

5. TuSmith, *Conversations*, 9.

CHAPTER 4

1. See undated materials in Wideman Papers, Boxes 4 and 5.

2. "Children of Promise, Children of Pain," *Post-Gazette*, August 19, 1987.

3. See Box 40 of the Wideman Papers.

4. Leslie Bennetts, "Seeds of Violence," *Vanity Fair*, March 1989: 211.

5. Ibid., 212.

6. Ibid., 213.

7. Chip Brown, "Blood Circle," *Esquire*, August 1989: 127–128.

8. Bonnie TuSmith, ed., *Conversations with John Edgar Wideman* (Jackson: University Press of Mississippi, 1998), 29.

9. Undated letter from Roy E. Hampton, John Edgar Wideman Papers, Box 6.

CHAPTER 5

1. Gary Smith, "Out of the Shadows," *Sports Illustrated,* March 17, 1997.

2. This is a term often used in jazz to refer to working on new techniques or styles.

3. John Edgar Wideman, *Damballah* (New York: Avon, 1981), iii.

4. Ibid., 25

5. See Joseph Fontenrose, *Orion: The Myth of the Hunter and the Huntress* (Berkeley: University of California Press, 1981).

6. Herbert G. Gutman, *The Black Family in Slavery and Freedom, 1750–1925* (New York: Vintage, 1977), 185–201.

7. Wideman, *Damballah,* 47.

8. Ibid., 158.

9. Ibid., 178.

10. Ibid., 178.

11. Ibid., 181.

12. Ibid., 189.

13. "On His Blindness," http://www.sonnets.org/milton.htm.

14. Wideman, *Damballah,* 199.

15. Ibid., 203.

16. Ibid., 201.

17. Ibid., 204.

18. Ibid., 205.

19. John Edgar Wideman, *Homewood Trilogy* (New York: Avon, 1985), 189.

20. Ibid., 210.

21. In *A Glance Away,* the character who lost a son named Eugene in the war was Martha, who is a generation younger in the *Damballah* family tree. The woman who actually lost a son was Martha Wideman, John's paternal grandmother.

22. Wideman, *Homewood Trilogy,* 319.

23. Ibid., 344.

24. Ibid., 287.

25. Ibid., 335.

26. Wideman, *Sent for You Yesterday* (New York: Avon, 1983), 54.

27. In this desire for invisibility, Junebug is similar to Toni Morrison's character Pecola in *The Bluest Eye* (1970). She reacts to her parents' domestic fights by trying to make herself smaller and smaller until she disappears.

28. Wideman, *Sent,* 142.

29. Ibid., 144.

30. For example, in one version of his prison record, Jake is listed as "Caucasian."

31. Wideman, *Sent,* 150.

32. As another version of his play with family history, Wideman puts her death in the novel three years before it occurred in real life.

33. Wideman, *Sent,* 159.

34. See John Henrik Clarke, *Christopher Columbus and the Afrikan Holocaust* (Brooklyn: A&B Publishers, 1992); S.E. Anderson, *Black Holocaust* (New York: Writers and Readers, 1995); and Del Jones, *Black Holocaust: Global Genocide* (Philadelphia: Hikeka Press, 1992).

35. Wideman, *Sent*, 194–95.

36. Ibid., 207–08.

37. See online lyrics at cduniverse.com, http://www.cduniverse.com/jimmy-rushing-sent-for-you-yesterday-and-here-youcome-today-lyrics-6871604.htm.

38. Wideman, *Damballah*, 134.

39. John Edgar Wideman, "Backseat," *The Stories of John Edgar Wideman* (New York: Pantheon, 1992), 45.

40. John Edgar Wideman, *Reuben* (1987; reprint, New York: Penguin, 1988), 1–2.

41. Bonnie TuSmith, ed., *Conversations with John Edgar Wideman* (Jackson: University Press of Mississippi, 1998), 9.

42. Frederick Douglass, *Narrative of the Life of Frederick Douglass, An American Slave,* in *Frederick Douglass: Autobiographies* (1845; reprint, New York: Library of America, 1994), chapters 6–7.

43. Wideman, *Reuben*, 42.

44. Ibid., 42–43.

45. Ibid., 43–44.

46. Ibid., 44–45.

47. See "The Passing of the First-Born" in W.E.B. Du Bois, *The Souls of Black Folk* (1903; reprint, New York: Library of America, 2009).

CHAPTER 6

1. Matthew Carey, *A Short Account of the Malignant Fever,* Harvard University Library, http://pds.lib.harvard.edu/pds/view/7374219?n=22&printThumbnails=no,63.

2. Carey, *A Short Account,* 32.

3. Richard Allen, and Absalom Jones, *A Narrative of the Proceedings of the Black People.* Harvard University Library, http://pds.lib.harvard.edu/pds/view/6483355?n=3&printThumbnails=no, 5.

4. Ibid., 8.

5. Wideman, *Fever: Twelve Stories* (New York: Henry Holt, 1989), 136–37.

6. Ibid., 157–58.

7. Ibid., 128.

8. Ibid., 132–33.

9. Ibid., 151.

10. Ibid., 154.

11. See, for example, the work of John Henrick Clarke on this topic.

12. Wideman, *Fever,* 161.

13. Part of what led Allen to break with the white Methodists was that he was only allowed to preach in the early morning, when the congregation was almost entirely black.

14. This episode is patterned after several that Allen describes in his *Narrative,* though it is not identical to any of them.

15. For details of this tragedy, see J. B. Peires, *The Dead Will Arise: Nongqawuse and the Great Xhosa Cattle-Killing Movement of 1856–7* (Bloomington: Indiana University Press, 1989).

16. Wideman, *The Cattle Killing* (Boston: Houghton Mifflin, 1996), 7. Italics in the original.

17. Ibid., 7–8; italics in original.

18. Ibid., 8; italics in original.

19. See Sacvan Bercovitch, *The American Jeremiad* (Madison: University of Wisconsin Press, 1978) and Willie J. Harrell, Jr., *Origins of the African American Jeremiad* (Jefferson, NC: McFarland, 2010).

20. Wideman, *Cattle Killing,* 48.

21. See Paul E. Lovejoy and David Vincent Trotman, *Trans-Atlantic Dimensions of Ethnicity in the African Diaspora* (New York: Continuum International Publishing Group, 2003), 85–86.

22. Wideman, *Cattle Killing,* 137.

23. See Isaiah 5:24.

24. Glassey's role may partially explain Wideman's interest in the story of MOVE. Like Leslie Bennetts, the former student whom he felt betrayed his own family in telling her version of Jake's crime, Glassey, a white man, betrayed the MOVE family by going to the police with information that led to the devastation of that family.

25. For details on the bombing, see the following websites: http://www.philly.com/philly/photos/Philadelphia_The_1980s_MOVE.html. http://www.neufutur.com/Rants/operationmove.html.http://www.pierretristam.com/Bobst/07/wf040407.htm.

26. The role of basketball in Wideman's life and in American society is the subject of several of his essays and the book *Hoop Roots,* which will be discussed later.

27. Wideman, *Philadelphia Fire* (1990; reprint, New York: Vintage, 1991), 42.

28. Ibid., 49.

29. Ibid., 81.

30. See Box 1.

31. Wideman, *Philadelphia Fire,* 97.

32. Bonnie TuSmith, ed., *Conversations with John Edgar Wideman* (Jackson: University Press of Mississippi, 1998), 108.

33. Wideman, *Philadelphia Fire,* 98–99.

34. Ibid., 99.

35. Wideman here echoes W.E.B. Du Bois's famous statement from *The Souls of Black Folk* about what he called double-consciousness: "One ever feels his

two-ness,—an American, a Negro; two souls, two thoughts, two unreconciled strivings; two warring ideals in one dark body, whose dogged strength alone keeps it from being torn asunder." In making the connection, Wideman is subtly linking his son's situation to race.

36. Ibid., 110.

37. Ibid., 110.

38. Ibid., 116.

39. "Vernacular" here means the language of a particular community rather than the standard or literary form of it.

40. Wideman, *Philadelphia Fire,* 127–28.

41. TuSmith, *Conversations* 107.

42. Stephan Salisbury, "Memory Game from the Basketball Courts of West Philadelphia," *Philadelphia Inquirer,* October 20, 1998.

43. Wideman, *Two Cities* (Boston: Houghton Mifflin, 1998), 7.

44. Ibid., 80–81.

45. Ibid., 172.

46. Ibid., 218.

CHAPTER 7

1. John Edgar Wideman, "Reflections on America Transformed," *The New York Times,* September 8, 2002.

2. Ibid., 6.

3. John Edgar Wideman, "Whose War," *Harper's Magazine,* March 2002, 36.

4. Ibid., 36.

5. Ibid., 37.

6. Ibid., 38.

7. John Edgar Wideman, "What Black Boys Are Up Against," *Essence,* Nov. 2003, 186.

8. Ibid., 187.

9. Ibid., 187.

10. Ibid., 187.

11. Christopher Metress, ed. *The Lynching of Emmett Till: A Documentary Narrative* (Charlottesville: University of Virginia Press, 2002), 278.

12. John Edgar Wideman, "Looking at Emmett Till," *In Fact: The Best of Creative Nonfiction,* ed. Lee Gutkind (New York: Norton, 2004), 26.

13. Ibid., 28.

14. This fear further connects him with Wally of *Reuben,* who we are told did not want to touch or otherwise come into contact with anything dead.

15. Wideman's language here is very similar to that of Peggy McIntosh in her 1988 essay "White Privilege: Unpacking the Invisible Knapsack," http://www.nymbp.org/reference/WhitePrivilege.pdf.

16. Wideman, "Looking," 43–44.

17. Ibid., 47.

18. John Edgar Wideman, "The Seat Not Taken," *The New York Times,* October 7, 2010, A38.

19. Ibid., A38.

20. See "Of Our Spiritual Strivings," the first chapter in Du Bois's classic work.

21. See *The Awl,* October 8, 2010.

22. John Edgar Wideman, "Visiting Privileges," *The Washington Post,* July 11, 2004.

23. John Edgar Wideman, "Father Stories," *New Yorker,* August 1, 1994, 36–41.

24. See Timothy Williams, "Execution Case Dropped Against Abu-Jamal," *New York Times.* December 7, 2011.

25. "Doing Time, Marking Race." In *In Defense of Mumia,* ed. S.E. Anderson and Tony Medina (New York: Writers and Readers Publishing, 1996), 127.

26. Ibid., 127. This may be a reference to Sanford Kane's comments at Jake's hearing, though Wideman is not specific.

27. Mumia Abu-Jamal, *Live from Death Row* (New York: Harper, 1996), xxxii.

28. "Ascent by Balloon from the Yard of Walnut Street Jail." In *In Defense of Mumia,* ed. S.E. Anderson and Tony Medina, 252.

29. Ibid., 252.

30. See "Eastern State Penitentiary," Eastern State Penitentiary. org., http://www. easternstate.org/learn/timeline; and Chai Woodham, "Eastern State Penitentiary: A Prison with a Past," Smithsonian.org., http://www.smithsonianmag.com/history-archaeology/eastern-state-penitentiary.html.

31. Anderson and Medina, "Ascent," 252.

32. Ibid., 256.

33. See Susan M. Reverby, "Tuskegee Syphilis Experiment," Encyclopedia of Alabama.org., http://www.encyclopediaofalabama.org/face/Article.jsp?id=h-1116.

34. John Edgar Wideman, "My Daughter the Hoopster," *Essence,* November 1996, 79.

35. Ibid., 79.

36. John Edgar Wideman, "Playing Dennis Rodman," *New Yorker,* 29 April 1996, 94.

37. Ibid., 95.

38. John Edgar Wideman, "Michael Jordan Leaps the Great Divide," ed. Gena Dagel Caponi, *Signifyin(g), Sanctifyin', and Slam Dunking* (Amherst: University of Massachusetts Press, 1999), 389.

39. Ibid., 392.

40. Ibid., 403.

41. Ibid., 404.

42. Ibid., 405.

43. Ibid., 406.
44. John Edgar Wideman, *Hoop Roots* (Boston: Houghton Mifflin, 2001), 3–4.
45. While Ivy League schools do not give athletic scholarships, the fact that Wideman was a celebrated high-school athlete certainly helped his application.
46. In fact, she would live another 20 years, though with disabilities from the stroke. Her funeral in 1973 is the occasion when Wideman listens closely to the family stories that become the Homewood trilogy.
47. Wideman, *Hoop Roots,* 111.
48. Ibid., 52.
49. Ibid., 57.
50. Ibid., 57.
51. See Mihaly Csikszentmihalyi, *Creativity: Flow and the Psychology of Discovery and Invention* (New York: HarperCollins, 1996), 110–116, for a full discussion of "flow."
52. Wideman, *Hoop Roots,* 58.
53. Csikszentmihalyi, *Creativity,* 110–113.
54. Wideman, *Hoop Roots,* 158–159.
55. Ibid., 167.
56. Ibid., 178.
57. Ibid., 211.
58. Ibid., 220–221.
59. Ibid., 220.
60. Ibid., 222.
61. Ibid., 223.
62 Clare Green "Pok ta Pok: The Mayan Ball Game," http://www.discover chichenitza.com/chichen-itza-mexico/pok-ta-pok-the-mayanball-game-athletes-or-worshipers/.

CHAPTER 8

1. See Jim McKinnon, "Court Pulls Plug on Wideman Retrial," *Pittsburgh Post-Gazette,* May 23, 2000.
2. John Edgar Wideman, *God's Gym* (Boston: Houghton Mifflin, 2005), 1.
3. Ibid., 2.
4. Ibid., 3.
5. Ibid., 5.
6. Ibid., 5
7. Ibid., 7.
8. Ibid., 4.
9. Ibid., 15–16.
10. Ibid., 56.
11. Ibid., 65.
12. Ibid., 70.

13. Ibid., 93–94.

14. Ibid., 158.

15. Ibid., 168–69.

16. Ibid., 171–72.

17. For a summary of the project, see Dalia Sofer, "Directions for Armchair Travelers," *Poets&Writers,* July/August 2002, http://www.pw.org/content/directions_armchair_travelers?cmnt_all=1.

18. Wideman, *The Island: Martinique* (Washington, DC: National Geographic, 2003), xxv.

19. Ibid., 5.

20. Ibid., xx.

21. Ibid., 65.

22. Ibid., 65.

23. Ibid., 70.

24. Ibid., 110–11.

25. The movie is probably "Lumumba," a 2000 documentary by director Raoul Peck.

26. Wideman, *Island,* 119.

27. Ibid., 128.

28. John Edgar Wideman, *Fanon* (Boston: Houghton Mifflin, 2008), 4.

29. Ibid., 4.

30. Ibid., 17.

31. Ibid., 21–22. Romare Bearden was a famous African American painter and collage artist of the mid-20th century who graduated from the same high school as Wideman.

32. Ibid., 25.

33. Ibid., 62.

34. Ibid., 73.

35. Ibid., 132–33.

36. Wideman acknowledges drawing this and other biographical information from David Macey's *Frantz Fanon: A Life,* published in 2000. We can also date the writing of the novel, since Wideman notes that he is writing about Casablanca on March 30, 2005.

37. Wideman, *Fanon,* 154–57.

38. Ibid., 166.

39. Wideman is talking about a similar psychological power in his writings about incarceration when he discusses the new technology of prisons such as Pelican Bay. See Chapter 7, especially his essay "Doing Time, Marking Race."

40. Wideman, *Fanon,* 176.

41. See Thich Naht Hanh, *Interbeing: Fourteen Guidelines for Engaged Buddhism* (Berkeley, CA: Parallax Press, 1987).

42. "Flash Fiction," http://oxforddictionaries.com/definition/flash%2Bfiction.

43. For a discussion of length and other characteristics of flash fiction, see Thomas and Shapard, *Flash Fiction Forward* (New York: W.W. Norton, 2006).

44. There are rumors that Houghton Mifflin did not renew his contract, but these could not be confirmed.

45. "Why Wideman's Here," http://www.lulu.com/blog/2010/03/why-wideman's-here/.

46. "John Edgar Wideman's Blog—Posts Tagged "short stories," http://www.goodreads.com/author/show/20703.John_Edgar_Wideman/blog/tag/short-stories.

47. John Edgar Wideman, *Briefs* (Raleigh, NC: Lulu, 2010), 21.

48. Ibid., 139.

49. Ibid., 140.

50. Ibid., 23.

51. Ibid., 23–24.

52. Ibid., 137.

53. Wideman here may have had in mind Martin Luther King's campaign in Memphis for sanitation workers at the time of his assassination. An earlier story in the collection, "Ghetto," is about King's death.

54. Wideman, *Briefs,* 138.

55. Ibid., 135.

56. Ibid., 2.

57. Ibid., 46.

58. Ibid., 6.

59. Ibid., 32.

60. Ibid., 33.

61. Ibid., 61.

62. Ibid., 62. Berry's version can be heard on Youtube: http://www.youtube.com/watch?v=ggwqn6xBgas. Richard Berry is best known for writing "Louie, Louie," which was intended as the B-side for "You Are My Sunshine," but became a much bigger hit for him.

63. Wideman, *Briefs*, 114.

64. Ibid., 41.

65. Ibid., 41.

66. Ibid., 67.

67. Ibid., 38.

68. Ibid., 4.

69. Ibid., 15.

70. Ibid., 8.

71. Ibid., 47.

72. Ibid., 37.

73. Ibid., 134.

74. Ibid., 134.

75. See, for example, John Keats, "Ode on a Grecian Urn" and "On Melancholy," as well as A.E. Housman's *Shropshire Lad.*

76. A large sample of Wright's poems can be found in *Haiku: The Last Poems of an American Icon,* ed. Yoshinobu Hakutant and Robert L. Tener (New York: Arcade Publishing, 1998).

77. Wideman, *Briefs,* 26.
78. Ibid., 26.
79. Ibid., 40.
80. Ibid., 49.
81. Ibid., 155.

Selected Bibliography

WORKS BY JOHN EDGAR WIDEMAN

Books

A Glance Away. 1967. New York: Holt, Rnehart and Winston, 1985.
Hurry Home. 1970. New York: Henry Holt, 1986.
The Lynchers. 1973. New York: Henry Holt, 1986.
Damballah. New York: Avon, 1981.
Sent for You Yesterday. New York: Avon, 1983.
Brothers and Keepers. New York: Holt, Rnehart and Winston, 1984.
The Homewood Trilogy. New York: Avon, 1985.
Reuben. 1987. New York: Penguin, 1988.
Fever: Twelve Stories. New York: Henry Holt, 1989.
Philadelphia Fire. 1990. New York: Vintage, 1991.
The Stories of John Edgar Wideman. New York: Pantheon, 1992.
All Stories Are True. New York: Vintage, 1993.
Fatheralong. New York: Pantheon, 1994.
The Cattle Killing. Boston: Houghton Mifflin, 1996.
Two Cities. Boston: Houghton Mifflin, 1998.
Hoop Roots. Boston: Houghton Mifflin, 2001.
The Island: Martinique. Washington, DC: National Geographic, 2003.
God's Gym. Boston: Houghton Mifflin, 2005.
Fanon. Boston: Houghton Mifflin, 2008.
Briefs. Raleigh, NC: Lulu, 2010.

Short Stories

"Ascent by Balloon from the Yard of Walnut Street Jail." *In Defense of Mumia,* edited by S. E. Anderson and Tony Medina. New York: Writers and Readers, 1996: 252–256.
"Father Stories," *New Yorker,* August 1, 1994, 36–41.

Essays

"Playing Dennis Rodman." *New Yorker,* April 29, 1996: 94.

"Doing Time, Marking Race." *In Defense of Mumia,* edited by S.E. Anderson and Tony Medina. New York: Writers and Readers Publishing, 1996: 126–30.

"My Daughter the Hoopster." *Essence,* November 1996: 79.

"Michael Jordan Leaps the Great Divide." *Signifyin(g), Sanctifyin', and Slam Dunking,*edited by Gena Dagel Caponi. Amherst: University of Massachusetts Press, 1999: 388–406.

"Whose War." *Harper's Magazine,* March 2002: 33–38.

"We Won't Deny Our Consciences." *The Guardian,* June 14, 2002.

"Reflections on America Transformed." *The New York Times,* September 8, 2002.

"What Black Boys Are Up Against." *Essence,* Nov. 2003: 186–188.

"Looking at Emmett Till." *In Fact: The Best of Creative Nonfiction,* edited by Lee Gutkind. New York: Norton, 2004.

"Visiting Privileges." *The Washington Post,* July 11, 2004. http://www.washing tonpost.com/wp-dyn/articles/A32536–2004Jul6.html.

"The Seat Not Taken." *The New York Times,* October 7, 2010.

Secondary Works

Abu-Jamal, Mumia. *Live from Death Row.* New York: Harper, 1996.

Allen, Richard, and Absalom Jones. *A Narrative of the Proceedings of the Black People.* http://pds.lib.harvard.edu/pds/view/6483355?n=3&printThumb nails=no.

Anderson, S.E. *Black Holocaust.* New York: Writers and Readers, 1995.

Beeber, Steven. "John Edgar Wideman: The Art of Fiction, No. 171." *Paris Review,* Spring 2002. http://www.theparisreview.org/interviews/422/the-art-of fiction-no-171-john-edgar-wideman.

Bennetts, Leslie. "Seeds of Violence." *Vanity Fair,* March 1989: 156–161, 210–214.

Bercovitch, Sacvan. *The American Jeremiad.* Madison: University of Wisconsin Press, 1978.

"Biography." Romare Bearden Foundation. http://www.beardenfoundation.org/ artlife/biography/biography.shtml.

Brown, Chip. Blood Circle." *Esquire,* August 1989: 122–132.

Bry, David. *The Awl,* October 8, 2010. http://www.theawl.com/2010/10/ john-edgar-wideman-on-the-sadness-of-emptiness.

Byerman, Keith E. *John Edgar Wideman: A Study of the Short Fiction.* New York: Simon and Schuster, 1998.

Callaloo. Special issue on John Edgar Wideman: The European Response. 22.3: Summer 1999.

Carey, Matthew. *A Short Account of the Malignant Fever.* http://pds.lib.harvard. edu/pds/view/7374219?n=22&printThumbnails=no.

Clarke, John Henrik. *Christopher Columbus and the Afrikan Holocaust.* Brooklyn: A&B Publishers, 1992.

Coleman, James W. *Blackness and Modernism: The Literary Career of John Edgar Wideman.* Jackson: University Press of Mississippi, 1989.

Coleman, James W. *Writing Blackness: John Edgar Wideman's Art and Experimentation.* Baton Rouge: Louisiana State University Press, 2010.

Csikszentmihalyi, Mihaly. *Creativity: Flow and the Psychology of Discovery and Invention.* New York: HarperCollins, 1996.

Douglass, Frederick. *Autobiographies.* New York: Library of America, 1994.

Du Bois, W.E.B. *The Souls of Black Folk.* 1903. Introduction by John Edgar Wideman. New York: Library of America, 2009.

"Eastern State Penitentiary." Eastern State Penitentiary. org. http://www.eastern state.org/learn/timeline.

Eliot, Thomas Stearns. *The Waste Land and Other Writings.* New York: Modern Library, 2002.

Faulkner, William. "Interview with Jean Stein Vanden Heuvel." *The Paris Review* (Spring 1956). Reprinted in Meriwether, James B., and Michael Millgate, eds. *Lion in the Garden: Interviews with William Faulkner, 1926–1962.* Lincoln: University of Nebraska Press, 1980.

Fontenrose, Joseph. *Orion: The Myth of the Hunter and the Huntress.* Berkeley: University of California Press, 1981.

Green, Clare, "Pok ta Pok: The Mayan Ball Game." http://www.discoverchichen itza.com/chichen-itza-mexico/pok-ta-pok-the-mayan-ball-game-athletes-or-worshipers/.

Gutman, Herbert G. *The Black Family in Slavery and Freedom, 1750–1925.* New York: Vintage, 1977.

Guzzio, Tracie Church. *All Stories Are True: History, Myth, and Trauma in the Work of John Edgar Wideman.* Jackson: University Press of Mississippi, 2011.

Hanh, Thich Naht. *Interbeing: Fourteen Guidelines for Engaged Buddhism.* Berkeley, CA: Parallax Press, 1987.

Harrell, Willie J., Jr. *Origins of the African American Jeremiad: The Rhetorical Strategies of Social Protest and Activism, 1760–1861.* Jefferson, NC: McFarland, 2010.

Jones, Del. *Black Holocaust: Global Genocide.* Philadelphia: Hikeka Press, 1992.

Kalson, Sally. "Children of Promise, Children of Pain." *Post-Gazette,* August 19, 1987.

Lovejoy, Paul E., and David Vincent Trotman. *Trans-Atlantic Dimensions of Ethnicity in the African Diaspora.* New York: Continuum International Publishing Group, 2003.

Macey, David. *Frantz Fanon: A Life.* New York: Granta, 2000.

Mbalia, Doreatha Drummond. *John Edgar Wideman: Reclaiming the African Personality.* Selinsgrove, PA: Susquehanna University Press, 1995.

McIntosh, Peggy. "White Privilege: Unpacking the Invisible Knapsack." http://www.nymbp.org/reference/WhitePrivilege.pdf.

McKinnon, Jim. "Court Pulls Plug on Wideman Retrial." *Pittsburgh Post-Gazette,* May 23, 2000.

Metress, Christopher, ed. *The Lynching of Emmett Till: A Documentary Narrative.* Charlottesville: University of Virginia Press, 2002.

Mosley, Walter. "Love Among the Ruins." *New York Times* October 4, 1998.

Peires, J.B. *The Dead Will Arise: Nongqawuse and the Great Xhosa Cattle-Killing Movement of 1856–7.* Bloomington, IN: Indiana University Press, 1989.

Reverby, Susan M. "Tuskegee Syphilis Experiment." Encyclopedia of Alabama. org. http://www.encyclopediaofalabama.org/face/Article.jsp?id=h-1116.

Rosenbaum, Art. "McIntosh County Shouters." http://www.georgiaencyclopedia. org/nge/Article.jsp?id=h-520.

Salisbury, Stephan. "Memory Game from the Basketball Courts of West Philadelphia." *Philadelphia Inquirer,* October 20, 1998.

Smith, Gary. "Out of the Shadows," *Sports Illustrated,* March 17, 1997.

Sofer, Dalia. "Directions for Armchair Travelers." *Poets&Writers,* July/August 2002. http://www.pw.org/content/directions_armchair_travelers?cmnt_all=1.

Thomas, James, and Robert Shapard. *Flash Fiction Forward.* New York: W.W. Norton, 2006.

TuSmith, Bonnie, ed. *Conversations with John Edgar Wideman.* Jackson: University Press of Mississippi, 1998.

TuSmith, Bonnie, and Keith Byerman, eds. *Critical Essays on John Edgar Wideman.* Knoxville: University of Tennessee Press, 2006.

Williams, Timothy. "Execution Case Dropped Against Abu-Jamal." *New York Times.* December 7, 2011.

Woodham, Chai. "Eastern State Penitentiary: A Prison with a Past." Smithsonian. org. http://www.smithsonianmag.com/history-archaeology/eastern-state-penitentiary.html.

Index

Abu-Jamal, Mumia, 103, 106–10
  and MOVE, 106–7
Allen, Richard, 59–60, 73,
    179nn. 13, 14
  as character in "Fever," 61–67
  connection to Wideman,
    66–67

Basketball, 6–7, 93, 101,
    179n. 26
  in *Briefs*, 167–68
  Dennis Rodman and, 114–15
  essays on, 112–17
  in Homewood, 4
  in *Hoop Roots*, 117–27
  Jamila and, 25, 113–14
  Michael Jordan and, 115–17
  in *Philadelphia Fire*, 76
  in *Reuben*, 53
  in *Two Cities*, 88
Bennetts, Leslie, 20–22,
    179n. 24
Black Arts Movement, 15–16, 44,
    70, 147

Carey, Matthew, 61–68

Dawson, Darryl, 6, 7, 15, 176n. 6

Fanon, Frantz, 84, 141–42, 146–56
  in *The Island*, 144–46
Faulkner, William, 11, 69, 138,
    173–74
Fleming, Ed, 4, 119–20, 124
French, Freeda, 1, 2, 11, 25–26, 33,
    87, 158
  as character in "Lizabeth: The
    Caterpillar Story," 29–30,
    40
  as character in *Sent for You Yes-
    terday*, 40–42, 45, 47
  in *Hoop Roots*, 117–19, 124–27
French, John, 4, 55, 87, 107, 119,
    124, 126, 150, 163, 174
  as character in *A Glance Away*,
    11
  as character in "Lizabeth: The
    Caterpillar Story," 29–30,
    40
  character of, 2
  death of, 45, 50, 100, 118, 125

Gaines, Ernest, 15, 36, 137
Goldman, Morton, 8, 19, 105

Haley, Alex, 28, 106
Hollinger, May, 1–2, 26, 36, 158

Jet (magazine), 98–99, 101
Jordan, Michael, 112, 114–17, 152

Kane, Eric, 19, 21–22, 76, 82, 106, 162

Lamed-Vov, 66, 77

Morrison, Toni, 15, 26, 36, 138–39, 157
MOVE, ix, 59–60, 82, 85–86, 106–7, 156, 173, 179n. 24
  bombing of, 67, 75
  history of, 74–75
  in *Philadelphia Fire*, 75–78
  in *Two Cities*, 85, 89–90

Nedonchelle, Catherine, 122–23, 129, 134, 139, 144
The New Yorker, 93, 105, 114
The New York Times, 94, 97, 102, 103

Owens, Charles, 1, 35, 36
Owens, Sybela, 1, 3, 35, 36, 174

Prison system, 103–4, 106, 109, 136, 173
  in "Ascent by Balloon from the Yard of Walnut Street Jail," 110–12
  in *Brothers and Keepers*, viii
  in *Damballah*, 35
  in *Philadelphia Fire*, 82
  in *Two Cities*, 89

Rodman, Dennis, 112, 114–15
Rush, Benjamin, 62, 64, 68, 73, 111

Till, Emmett, 98–102, 115

University of Pennsylvania (UPenn), 5–6, 8–9, 20, 26, 60, 118, 137, 148
  in *Philadelphia Fire*, 76–78, 84
  in *Reuben*, 52–53, 56

Walker, Alice, 15, 36, 137
Wideman, Bette French, 2, 4, 11, 86, 99, 132, 154–55
  as character in *Fanon*, 149–51, 154–55
  as character in "Solitary," 31–33
  as character in "Weight," 130–33
  in *Hoop Roots*, 118
Wideman, Daniel, vii, 9, 16, 21, 117, 129, 157
Wideman, Edgar, 2, 3–4, 99, 107, 117, 119, 125, 159
  as character in "Are Dreams Faster Than the Speed of Light," 133–34
  as character in "Work," 159–60
Wideman, Harry (Hannibal), 3, 38, 49
Wideman, Jacob (Jake), vii, 9, 16, 49, 75–76, 91, 117, 130, 134, 177n. 30, 179n. 24, 181n. 26
  as character in *Briefs*, 162–63
  killing of Eric Kane, 19
  lawsuit by Eric Kane's family, 81–82
  press treatment of case, 19–23
  and prison system, 103–6
  related to character in *Philadelphia Fire*, 78, 80–82
Wideman, Jamila, vii, 16, 104, 113–14, 117, 130, 151, 155, 162
  basketball career of, 113–14
  difficult birth of, 25
  relationship to Robby, 25
Wideman, John Edgar
  "Across the Wide Missouri" (short story), 48–49
  "Ascent by Balloon from the Yard of Walnut Street Jail" (short story), 110–12
  "Backseat" (short story), 49–50
  "The Beginning of Homewood" (short story), 33–35

Briefs (short story collection), 24,
129
    discussed, 156–71
    theme of time in, 158
Brothers and Keepers (memoir),
    viii, 2, 16, 18, 23, 27, 40, 60,
    76, 106, 108
    discussed, 23–24
The Cattle Killing (novel), 60, 78,
    95, 111
    attack on Enlightenment in, 74
    discussed, 68–74
    Philadelphia as symbol in, 70
    self-destructiveness as theme in,
    68–69
childhood, 4–5
college, 5–7
"Damballah" (short story), 27–29,
    86, 154
    discussed, 27–29
Damballah (short story collec-
    tion), 22, 26–27, 36–37, 48
    discussed, 27–36
"Doing Time, Marking Race"
    (essay), 107, 181n. 25,
    183n. 39
Fanon (novel), 130, 157, 160
    discussed, 146–56
Fatheralong (memoir), 2, 4, 24,
    97, 105
"Fever" (short story), 60, 68, 70,
    77, 111
    discussed, 60–68
    Philadelphia as symbol in, 64
Fever (short story collection),
    60–70
first marriage, 8
A Glance Away, 8, 9, 42, 147,
    150
    discussed, 10–12
God's Gym (short story collec-
    tion), 130–39
Hiding Place, 22, 26
    discussed, 36–40

Hoop Roots (memoir), 24, 112,
    130, 137, 139, 167
    discussed, 117–27
Hurry Home, 9, 51, 147
    discussed, 12–13
The Island (travel narrative), 130,
    146–47, 155
    discussed, 139–46
    as ghost story, 140–41
"Lizabeth: The Caterpillar Story"
    (short story), 29–30, 40
"Looking at Emmett Till" (essay),
    98
The Lynchers (novel), 3, 9, 25,
    44
    discussed, 13–15
"Michael Jordan Leaps the Great
    Divide" (essay), 181n. 38
"My Daughter the Hoopster"
    (essay), 113, 181n. 34
Philadelphia Fire (novel), 60, 74,
    90, 107, 114
    criminal justice system in, 81–83
    discussed, 75–85
    MOVE as subject in, 74–75, 90,
    107
    use of *The Tempest* in, 83–84
"Playing Dennis Rodman" (essay),
    181n. 36
"Reflections on America Trans-
    formed" (essay), 180n. 1
Reuben (novel), 26, 75, 79
    discussed, 50–57
as Rhodes Scholar, 7–8
"The Seat Not Taken" (essay),
    102, 181n. 18
Sent for You Yesterday (novel),
    22, 26, 30, 50, 60, 70, 125,
    158
    discussed, 40–48
"Sightings," 136–39
"Solitary" (short story), 22, 30,
    35, 37, 105, 131
    discussed, 31–33

teaching at the University of Pennsylvania (UPenn), 9, 25–26, 148

"Tommy" (short story), 22, 30–32, 37, 150

Two Cities (novel), 60, 74, 107, 115, 167

    criminal justice system in, 89

    discussed, 85–91

    MOVE as subject in, 86, 89, 90

at University of Massachusetts, 19, 21, 60, 129, 137

at University of Wyoming, 9, 10, 16, 19–20, 25, 136

"Visiting Privileges" (essay), 181n. 22

"Weight" (short story), 130–33, 134

"What Black Boys Are Up Against" (essay), 96, 98, 180n. 7

"Whose War" (essay), 94, 180n. 3

Wideman, Judith Goldman, vii, 7–9, 16, 21, 25, 91, 92, 105, 106, 117, 130, 132, 162

Wideman, Martha Wright, 3, 11, 49, 177n. 21

Wideman, Omar, 86–87

Wideman, Robert (Robby), vii, 2, 4, 12, 16–19, 25, 27, 33–34, 36, 56–57, 70, 75, 86, 103, 104, 117, 124, 153, 174

    in *Brothers and Keepers*, 23–24, 60, 76

    compared to character in "Tommy" and *Hiding Place*, 22, 30–31, 37, 160

    effort for retrial, 129

    involvement in crime, 18

    Jake compared to, 20, 22

    in prison, 18–19, 149

    as teenager, 17–18

Yellow fever epidemic, ix, 59, 110–11, 156, 173

    African Americans and, 60–68

    in "Fever," 60–67

About the Author

KEITH E. BYERMAN, PhD, is professor of English, African American Studies, and Women's Studies at Indiana State University, Terre Haute, IN. His published works include *The Art and Life of Clarence Major*, *Remembering the Past in Contemporary African American Fiction*, and *The Short Fiction of John Edgar Wideman*. Byerman holds a doctorate in American Studies from Purdue University.

CPSIA information can be obtained at www.ICGtesting.com
Printed in the USA
BVOW04*0035090414

350109BV00007B/31/P